One Man's Odyssey

T0316139

First published in 1986 by
The C. W. Daniel Company Limited
1 Church Path, Saffron Walden
Essex CB10 1JP, England

ISBN 0 85207 179 5

Printed and bound in Great Britain by Clays Ltd, St Ives plc

IAN PEARCE

One Man's Odyssey

SAFFRON WALDEN
THE C. W. DANIEL COMPANY LIMITED

First published in 1986 by
The C. W. Daniel Company Limited
1 Church Path, Saffron Walden
Essex CB10 1JP, England

© Ian Pearce 1986

ISBN 0 85207 179 5

Printed by
Hillman Printers (Frome) Ltd.,
Frome, Somerset.

CONTENTS

PREFACE

If there is one single thing in this late twentieth-century period which distinguishes it more sharply than anything else from the ages which have gone before, it is the sense of mechanistic materialism which has overcome the thinking of the vast majority of ordinary people. The onward march of so-called science, combined with an ever-increasing understanding of the mechanical processes of life, has served to produce alike in individual persons, in communities, and in nations at large a conviction that all existence begins and ends with the experience of life in a material world. Perhaps at no time in the history of mankind has there been a greater need that Man should believe in the existence of a living force outside the confines of matter, and in the continuing nature of personal life, and at no time has he been further divided from such a belief.

The mystery of what happens – or even if anything at all does happen – after death has intrigued mankind from the very earliest times. The traditional view has always been that a non-physical part of man existed which was able to survive the disintegration of the physical body. It was this intuitive belief which gave rise to the funerary customs of the ancient Egyptians, with their emphasis upon proper provision for the soul on its journey to the next world. From it were derived the beliefs of the Greeks and Romans with the gloomy river Acheron, and the dreadful figure of Charon, ferryman across the Styx towards the Place of the Shades and the Elysian fields. We see also the Valhombrosa of Norse mythology, the happy hunting grounds of the Redskins, and the mediaeval Christian beliefs of Heaven and Hell, Heaven somewhat picturesquely envisaged as a state of eternal bliss in a sort of celestial Albert Hall on the last night of the Proms, with everyone rather high on the music, and Hell as a state of perpetual punishment in an eternal torture chamber. All these give evidence of man's intuitive belief that there is more to him than meets the eye.

Concepts of this sort were prevalent in the western world up until the dawn of the so-called Age of Reason. Here, for the first time, with the discovery that the earth was not the centre of the

7

universe, with the sun and the moon and the stars revolving ceaselessly around it, and the realisation that the waters were not confined beneath the earth, there came the first challenge to the authority of the Bible as the source of all Truth and as being the literal word of God. The continuing challenge of the Darwinian theories of evolution and natural selection, with the suggestion that man gradually evolved over many myriads of years from the primitive animalcules which swam in the primaeval oceans still further eroded traditional beliefs, to which the *coup-de-grace* was dealt, it seemed, by the discovery of the DNA and RNA molecules and their role in the transmission of heredity. All this has combined to bring about the present belief that every aspect of man is explicable upon a material basis, and that the phenomena of personality and memory recall rest upon a system of multiple and interconnected behaviour patterns implanted computer fashion upon the physical structure of the brain. The consequence of all this has been the system of mechanistic materialism which dominates so much of scientific and political thinking today. The crucial and all important question remains as ever: what is the whole man? Has man got a soul? Beside this all other considerations pale into insignificance, since without soul, all else is meaningless.

Probably at no time in the history of the world have the religions of the world had less influence over the beliefs and conduct of mankind. **At no time has the need ever been greater.** Throughout the world, both the western, mainly Christian world, and the eastern world, we are witnessing an emptying of the churches and the temples. No longer do the old faiths, with their emphasis upon morality, belief in God and in the teachings of his prophets, seem relevant to the age of atomic power and space travel. At every turn and on every side rolls on the mighty tide of sensuality and materialism.

No one looking at the world today can fail to recognise the depths of mankind's degradation. A series of constantly escalating crises have led to the polarisation of mankind. On every side life itself is threatened; from nuclear destruction and proliferation; from man-made pollution; from environmental interference leading to drought and famine; from the wasteful exploitation and eventual exhaustion of natural resources; from threat of global war and sectional strife. We see nation set against nation; race against race; class against class; family against family; individual against individual. All of these serve to demonstrate man's spiritual poverty. Moreover all of these dangers are man made. They are the patterns of man's own thought and behaviour. He has no one, other than himself to blame. Unless man is eventually to destroy himself in a holocaust, beside which that which overtook the cities of Sodom and Gomorrah would appear as no more than a garden bonfire, there has to be a radical change.

At the root of all this there lies, I believe, Man's failure to appreciate the true nature of life. A philosophy that persists in regarding the present life as all that matters, or even exists, cannot help but lead to materialism, greed and selfishness, and a denial of the very existence of God. If our beliefs are confined to accepting the brief span of earthly existence, with all its joys and sorrows, its pains and pleasures, its loves and hates, as being all there is – or ever will be – it is understandable that all should clamour for a larger and yet larger slice of the cake. Greed, envy, fear and selfishness inevitably rule in the hearts of those imprisoned in such beliefs.

Despite their instinctive belief in the existence and continuation of a non-physical 'anima', a large number of educated people today are sceptical of survival, or, at least, allow such a concept to have very little influence upon how they actually live out their lives. The concept of a creative, conscious intelligence, sustaining the cosmos, and expressing itself there through the interplay of energies as yet unrecognised by science, together with the recognition that Man, with all his faults, is an integral part of this cosmos, and, therefore of the expression of this divine, creative intelligence, seems to many to be the merest moonshine and wishful thinking. **The most fundamental need of the world today is a return to God-consciousness in everyday life.**

It has not been my purpose in this book to set forth in detail the evidence for the existence of this wider, non-material life and environment. This has been done many times before, and by others far better qualified than I to set it down. Saints and mystics down the ages have testified to and died for their knowledge of it. Great thinkers and scientists have stood up, facing contempt and ridicule at the hands of disbelieving colleagues, and proclaimed the evidence upon which they based their conclusions in its favour. At this very moment carefully checked and collated experiments to establish yet further data are being carried on in many of the world's seats of learning. The evidence is there for those who will seek with an open and impartial mind.

During the course of a long life I have been blessed with certain experiences which have helped me to understand a little more about Man and the nature of his life on earth. The effect of these has been to lead me away from the sterile philosophy of scientific reductionism back to the faith in which I was brought up and which I thought was gone beyond recall. My sole purpose in writing this book has been to share with others the experiences with which I have been entrusted, in the hope that they may bring comfort to some and inspiration to others. The conversations with my discarnate friends which I have related are direct transcripts of the recordings made at the time. Nothing has been added apart from punctuation. The unfamiliar order of words employed from time to time by the communicators took place exactly as written. To me it seems to confirm, as hinted in places, a certain lack of familiarity with the English language. Inevitably, since there were well over twenty hours of conversations, which took place over a period of two and a half years, much has had to be omitted. Such editing as has taken place has been confined to selection. Not a word has been altered or added.

I am greatly indebted to my friends Robert Findlay and Captain Hugh Corbett for much helpful advice and friendly criticism in the text, to Archdeacon The Venerable Michael Perry for correcting certain errors of fact with regard to Origen, to my publishers C. W. Daniel and their editorial staff for their help and expertise in preparing the final version, and above all to my wife, Ruth, for her never-failing help and support. The writing of the book has been a labour of love. If those who read will find within its pages a fraction of the insights and inspiration which we found as we travelled together along our Odyssey, its purpose, and that of our discarnate friends, will have been fulfilled and my living will not have been in vain.

DISS
February 1986

CHAPTER ONE

EARLY DAYS

'Tell me, Dr Pearce,' said the young interviewer, as we sat and talked together in a sunny first-floor room in down-town Montreal, 'how did you first become interested in looking at illness in this way? Did you always think as you do now, or has it been a gradual process?' The answer to the last part of the question is an emphatic and uncompromising 'No!' For at least two-thirds of my present professional life I was very firmly in the conventional groove. I was a perfectly normal, orthodox doctor. I made use of drugs and surgery, regarding so-called functional disease as 'hysterical' – a pejorative expression much used in my student days to explain disease for which no physical changes could be identified – and healing, spirit communication and witchcraft as being all very much part of the same thing, and an area into which it was forbidden to delve.

I was born into a conventional Anglo-Catholic Christian home in June 1914. My paternal grandfather had been a professor of mathematics at Gonville and Caius College, Cambridge, who had subsequently taken holy orders and been rector of the large mining parish of Bedlington in the north of England and a canon of Durham cathedral. My father was educated at Durham School and had sung as a boy chorister in the cathedral choir. He subsequently graduated in medicine from the University of Durham before finally settling in practice in the country market town of Diss on the borders of Norfolk and Suffolk. He was a sincere and devout Christian with a tremendously strong but simple faith, which he put into practice in devoted service to the community in every possible direction. My mother, a Scot, trained as a nurse with the eventual intention of going out to work in the mission field in China. She was a woman of immense strength of character and courage with considerable organising ability, which she put to good effect in running the

11

Mothers' Union, the Moral Welfare, and other offshoots of the parochial work of the day.

Attendance at the parish church for Sunday worship was part of our way of life and in my earliest days, I remember, there was a special shelf of books – lives of the saints and so on – which alone were considered fit reading for Sundays. After I went to school this strict, almost puritanical, Lord's Day observance was relaxed somewhat, and we used to play golf on those Sundays when father was not on duty, always provided, of course, that Sunday worship had first been attended.

My education was the conventional one for a boy in my position during the twenties and thirties. I attended a preparatory school run by a headmaster who was both an Oxford cricket blue and a cleric, and then a public school, to which I won a classical scholarship, from the age of fourteen to nineteen. In those days religious observance at a public school was *de rigeur*. Chapel was attended twice a day on weekdays and three times a day on Sundays, including attendance at Holy Communion at 8 am. Compulsory cold baths were a daily routine, as were cross country runs on the South Downs, cricket and football, and, in summer, early morning school before breakfast. We were given the perfectly conventional religious instruction of the church of the day. This included a vague understanding of a faint hope of bliss for those who tried to do their best in life, and kept free from the deadly sins of homosexuality and smoking at school, together with a firm underlining of the terrors of the Last Judgement, at which the sheep would be firmly and finally separated from the goats, and we should all disappear in our respective and opposite directions to the tortures of Hell or the unimaginable bliss of Heaven. If ever any questions were asked about this future state, one was referred variously to the words in the Bible about burning eternally in Hell Fire, or to the vivid word pictures descriptive of Heaven in the book of Revelations, which we were encouraged to believe was an inspired and literal description.

On leaving school I went up to Oxford University to study medicine. Here, for the first time in my life, I found myself out on my own. Religious instruction and observance were entirely at the discretion of the individual, though I have a fleeting recollection that one was expected to put in an appearance in the beautiful college chapel on three Sundays during each term. Occasionally, for want of something better to do, one might attend matins in the University Church of St Mary and listen to the University sermon, which was generally on a level of such intellectual and philosophical rarity as to be far above the head of the average undergraduate. On the whole, despite the gradually gathering storm clouds over the continent of Europe, the atmosphere was one of a cheerful, unthinking hedonism. It was the time, too, of the beginnings of the Oxford Group movement (now Moral Rearmament), headed by Frank Buchman, from whose meetings the average undergraduate shied away like a frightened horse, considering them to be communal exercises in hysterical exhibitionism.

I was, of course, during all this period, busy with my medical studies, and becoming disturbingly aware that patterns in behaviour were often the consequence of the conditioning influence of past experiences, and, more worrying still, that certain physical changes, such as from injury or disease, seemed to be followed by changes in the behaviour and personality of the individual sustaining them. One was being forced, willy nilly, into the belief, to which so many of my present-day colleagues subscribe, that mind and personality were no more than a physiological function of brain tissue. The further I progressed with my studies, the more convincing did this concept become. I still believed in the existence of a soul. I still clung, rather pathetically, to my belief in God. But these beliefs seemed remote, and irreconcilable with the knowledge gained from the dissecting room, the physiology laboratory, and the post mortem room. Like many others, I swept the problem underneath the carpet and tried to pretend that it did not exist. Besides, we were at war by this time, and there was more than sufficient professional work to do.

I emerged from the war with my beliefs unchanged. I clung defiantly to the belief that there had to be SOMETHING out there, way beyond the horizon. How else, I asked myself, could the Christian Church have existed for so many centuries, and, despite all its faults, gradually contrived to raise Man's thinking at least to an awareness of the essential wrongness of war, of cruelty, of misused power and selfishness, unless there was something of truth in its teachings? I took pride in the realisation

13

that mine was a profession that tried always to alleviate rather than create suffering, and that Jesus Christ, our Lord and Master, had been the greatest physician of them all. I believed then, literally, in the truths of the gospel story and of the Resurrection. But this, I also believed, was a very special and unique occasion. It happened because Jesus was the literal Son of God, and you cannot kill God, whatever else you do. The fact that it happened on that one occasion was no guarantee that this was possible for the rest of us. THAT would depend upon the sort of life we had lived here on earth, and in any case, there was an infinity of time to wait before we knew what would happen to us. I had a vague idea that when we died, we went to sleep – a long and dreamless sleep if we were lucky and had deserved it – until, at the Last Day, like a celestial alarm clock, the trumpet was sounded, and we all arose to appear before the Judgement Seat of God. We should then, I hoped, be reunited once more with those we had loved, who had gone before or followed after.

This philosophy of life, so I am told, is not altogether un-common amongst Christians, and is in some circles irreverently referred to as 'The Black Box State', or 'The Long Sleep'. Indeed, I recall a delightful story told in certain spiritualist circles of a new arrival on 'the other side' who was being taken round the summerlands by his guide. On their way he saw the beauties of the world to come, the mountains, the landscapes, the halls of music and learning – very much an idealised replica of the world which he had left. Amongst all this, so the story goes, he noticed a number of cemeteries, whose existence caused him to open his eyes very wide. But, being a very newly arrived soul, he did not like to ask questions. At length, however, on passing yet another burial ground, he could contain himself no longer. 'Sir,' he burst out, 'please tell me. As we have been going round I have seen quite a number of burial grounds. Here, in this world, there is no death. So why, oh why, is there a need for burial grounds, when there are no dead to be buried?' At this the guide stopped and looked rather embarrassed. 'Well,' he replied, 'we are really rather ashamed about this. You see, these are all the souls who come over with the fixed idea that they are going to sleep until St Peter blows the last trumpet – AND WE CAN'T WAKE THEM UP!'

This, of course, is a mediaeval philosophy, but I suspect that there may yet be many who subscribe to it. It is well exemplified in the traditional words of the lovely Iona boat song, to which I shall later return:

'Softly glide we along,
Softly sing we this song,
As a king to his resting is born,
O beloved and best,
Thou art bearing out west
To the dear isle, Iona, thy home.

Calmly there wilt thou lie,
With thy fathers gone by,
Their dust mingled deep with thine own:
Never more to awake,
Till the last morn shall break,
And the trump of the judgement is blown.'

Iona Boat Song

(Traditionally sung by the rowers of the royal funeral barge taking the corpse of the king to burial on the sacred isle.)

I have taken this lovely old Scottish song as the starting point for my Odyssey, that journey which took me from the conventional viewpoint of medical orthodoxy to the holistic philosophy which I now hold and which I have spent so much of my time and my strength expounding to those who are willing to hear. I have called it my Odyssey, because, like the journey homewards of the Greek king Odysseus from the Trojan War, my journey was also prolonged. It, too, led me into unknown and hitherto unimagined territory and into a number of strange experiences, some of which were so fantastic as almost to defy belief. At the end, like Odysseus, I came home to find a vision of what I believe to be the truth; a vision which has jerked me out of my previously comfortable rut, and overturned many of my cherished beliefs and previously conceived ideas, revolutionised my life, and sent me out in the autumn of life, on a completely new path of work and service. I must emphasise here at the outset, before anyone gets any misconceived ideas about it, that the initiative did not come from me. I can take no credit for this. The revela-

15

tions which came to me were completely unsought, but were brought to me. Indeed, I felt at times that I had been taken by the elbows on either side, and was being rapidly guided by benevolent hands along a path which was not of my choosing.

I was, at the start of this journey, still in country practice as a family doctor in the NHS, using all the conventional methods of treating disease. As a doctor, death was always the ultimate enemy; something to be cheated and fought against until the very last gasp; to be delayed until the last and final minute. I had a faint and pathetic belief that when my own time came, I would, in some dim and distant future, at last be awakened from the sleep of death to attend a court of judgement for the way in which I had lived my life on earth. Here, through the grace and sacrifice of Jesus, I might hope to be reunited with those whom I had loved on earth. I remembered with a shudder the story of Dives and Lazarus, together with a passage in the gospels which spoke of it being better to enter into life halt or maimed than to be cast whole into the eternal fires of Hell. Sometimes I would try to imagine what it must feel like to die, and would awaken from time to time in the small hours of the night in a sweat of fear, from which I would utter fervent prayers to be delivered. Today I know better. Those heartfelt prayers have indeed been answered. The revelations which I have been granted have left me without any doubt that the ancient saying, 'Mors janua vitae' (Death, the gateway to life) is literally true. I know, too, that having been granted a vision of this truth, it was not just for me alone, but only that I might share it with others.

CHAPTER TWO

VICKY

Our only daughter, Victoria, was born on 28th November 1955. The rest of the family consisted of my wife, Ruth, and three sons; Simon and Timothy, born 1943 and 1944 respectively, Andrew, born 1950, and a large, intensely amiable, but ferocious-looking boxer dog, named Bouncer. In view of the fact that my professional duties resulted in my being absent from the house for the greater part of each day, and not infrequently for considerable periods at night as well, added to which we lived on a busy through-road with a far from salubrious cafe a couple of hundred yards away. I was always profoundly glad of Bouncer's totally undeserved reputation for ferocity! No tramps or travelling door-to-door salesmen ever approached the door while Bouncer lived, and even normal callers were inclined to be a trifle discerning as to how they ventured within the castle grounds. Like most boxers he was simply wonderful with children, to whom he would permit any liberties and was devotedly attached. Vicky on her part grew up with him, which helped her to develop a natural understanding and ability to handle animals of all sorts.

Her early years were unremarkable except for a persistence of effort, and a kind of dogged perfectionism, which refused to be satisfied with the second-rate. She learned early and easily to read, and by the time she went to school fell naturally into the top bracket of her age group, which she usually managed to head. As we lived only a couple of hundred yards from our local open-air swimming pool, she was early introduced to the water, of which she was completely fearless. Indeed, my earliest and happiest memories of her are of halcyon summer afternoons on a Suffolk beach at play in the breaking surf. She went everywhere with us, including the long journey in 1960 down to the Costa Brava by road. Here we camped near Palamos, and she was able to enjoy the delights of the water and a beach on which she never felt cold. Even the three long days' drive in the baking heat of the August sun troubled her but little, and to this experience she was able to add that of flying home with my wife to leave room in the car for Simon, who had had to join the party later, as he only had a fortnight's holiday away from his firm. Another year we went to Austria, where we camped for a week on the edge of the Füschlsee in the Salzkammergut, before moving on into Tyrol for the second part of our holiday. Here for the first time she was able to be amongst high mountains, 'with snow on them, Daddy!' To give her and the other children a wider experience, we took them over the famed Gross Glockner Pass, where they could get out at the top and paddle in deep snow in the height of summer. They were able, too, to take the chair lift up to the cool freshness of the heights, hopefully seeking gentians and alpenrosen (though it was by far too late in the season for these), and to listen to the music of the cow bells floating up from the grassy slopes below. Indeed, when I look back on my life, little though I knew it at the time, and though it was not without complications, including the virtual destruction of our tents by a ferocious summer storm, drenching rains at times, and mechanical trouble with the car which delayed our return for over a week, this was the happiest period of my life. The next year, disaster struck, and the sun has never seemed so bright again.

It was now 1965. Vicky was nearly ten, and returned from the excitements of her Austrian holiday to the responsibilities of being head girl at the kindergarten, and to the challenge of winning a place at Norwich High School, a member of the Girls' Public Day School Trust, then under the headship of the renowned Miss Bartholomew, and reputedly requiring a very high standard of performance in their own entrance examination. Vicky took her responsibilities as head girl very seriously. It was the custom at her school for each class to perform a small play at the end of the Christmas term. The writing of the play was a joint affair, but the production, by common consent, seemed to devolve upon Vicky. Perfectionist that she was, this was a considerable challenge to her, and many times she would return from school and retire to her little den almost speechless with frustration at her inability to get the results which she

18

wanted from her cast. However, in the end she prevailed, the cast began to cooperate, and the eventual production was, we understood, a great success.

The school year ran its allotted course. The entrance examination to Norwich was sat successfully; the next grade of music exam was passed with flying colours; and the delights of summer and the swimming pool came along once more. Vicky was now an enthusiastic member of a small swimming club which assembled regularly on Monday nights, and, despite trembling knees, forced herself into learning to dive and to go in off the top board. (Ten feet can seem an awfully long way down when you are only ten years old.) There seemed to be a gradual change, or development rather, in her character during this year too. She had always been anxious to please, but this became combined with a thoughtfulness for others, and an understanding and maturity of outlook, which sat oddly on the brow of a little girl of ten. She seemed able to induce a state of harmony around her – though she competed violently and noisily with elder brother Andrew, whom she desperately sought to emulate – and nowhere was this more apparent than when she went to tea with my partner's children. Here the age group rivalries were apt to rage – literally! – loudly and violently between three girls close together in age and of very different tastes and attainments. The arrival of Vicky on the scene, however, was wont to bring almost immediate peace, and she was, in consequence, a frequent and welcome visitor.

At the end of term, there arrived in Diss a tented Bible Study school. Vicky was taken along by one of her chums from the swimming club, and at once became a fervent attender. Every evening there was a passage of scripture to be read, and texts to be learned by heart, and recited at the next attendance. I remember her becoming almost hysterical with frustration one night at finding that the school would clash with club night at the swimming pool. School won, of course, as one might have expected, given the knowledge which we now have; but it was an unusual decision for a child of her age. It was at this point, I remember, when I came in to find she was giving up her cherished evening at the swimming pool in favour of the Bible Tent, that the thought came to me: 'Vicky! You are becoming almost too good to be true. We shall have to take extra care of

19

you, lest something happens, and you are taken away from us.'
It was, I now think, an intimation in preparation for the way
which lay ahead.

Stimulated by my partner, who knew the country well, and
anxious to avoid quite so long and tiring a journey as we had
had to Austria the previous year, we had chosen this year to
camp in southern Brittany for our holiday. Vicky was in the
highest spirits, enjoying every moment of the crossing and of the
journey. Even the advent of a thunderstorm so violent as completely to obscure our view of the road, and to force us to a halt
at three in the morning, did nothing to abate her ardour. We
came to rest at last at Plouharnel, near Carnac, at the base of the
sandy spit of land with Quiberon at its southern end, and known
as the Quiberon Peninsula. Here we found a pleasant site and
spent the rest of the afternoon pitching our tents and setting up
camp. It was Thursday, 5th August, and the following day was
spent exploring the beaches in our immediate vicinity, the
enjoyment of which was to form the *raison d'être* of this particular holiday. The water was warm, the sun was hot, and the
beaches were on one side golden sand gently shelving into a sea
of idyllic calmness, and on the other reefs of sharp pointed rocks
running into the long, slow Atlantic surf. Vicky, who had just
won the championship of her swimming club, was in her
element. It was not until the Sunday afternoon that anything
happened to mar our happiness. It was cooler and less settled
that day, and after a morning bathe we had driven to explore the
attractive little town of Auray, as being more suited to the conditions than an afternoon on the beach. Vicky was quiet, and
seemed, unusually for her, a trifle irritable and difficult to please,
and complained of a headache. All the signs seemed to indicate
that she had gone down with a mild summer throat, an ailment
to which many children are prone in hot weather. On returning
to camp we found that she had a temperature of 100°F, a sore
throat, and enlarged tonsillar glands. She was promptly packed
off to bed with penicillin and aspirin, and, to her intense disgust,
bidden to stay there the following day, in the expectation that 24
hours of bed and penicillin would see her rapidly on the road to
recovery. And indeed, so it proved. By Wednesday she was
much better, though hardly ready yet for bathing. Tiresomely,
her throat remained inflamed and her glands refused to go

20

down, but her temperature was settling, and she was trotting about the camp site and begging to be allowed to come down to the beach again. By this time I had made up my mind that this was no ordinary summer throat, but most probably an attack of glandular fever, a harmless fever of an undulant nature, and common enough among young people. In this warm sea, provided that the temperature was not unduly raised, and she felt up to it, little harm would be done by allowing her a short swim. It would help, too, to compensate for what she was missing. And so it was. Whenever she felt well enough she would come with the others to the beach to bathe. Her only complaint was: 'Oh Daddy, I wish I didn't get so tired so quickly.' Gradually, almost imperceptibly, her condition worsened, until towards the end of the second week she was spending most of the time on her bed within the shade of the tent, emerging, only occasionally, like a gleam of sunshine on a cloudy day, to play a game of boule with Andrew, or go for a short walk under the shady pines. One afternoon especially stands out in my memory, when we drove to the little fishing port of Portivy, and then walked along the grassy slopes of the Beg Naud, high above the blue waters of the broad Atlantic. It was a brilliant Sunday afternoon of sun and wind, and my last and fondest memory is of her standing beside her mother upon the cliff top, her fair hair streaming in the wind behind her, watching the spume flying and the waves breaking on the rugged rocks two hundred feet below. It was her final fling. The next day found us striking camp two days before our time, to drive through the cool of the night for the channel ports, determined, reservations or no, to get home as quickly as we could. I still thought, rather defiantly, that she had glandular fever, though from time to time, like a recurring nightmare, the thought of leukaemia did just cross my mind. I thrust it quickly aside. It just could not be, not to Vicky. Things like that just did not happen in our family. One read about such tragedies, but they did not happen to people whom you knew, least of all to yourself. Not even in twenty years of general practice had such a case come my way.

I pass over the nightmare journey home. Never the best of car travellers, Vicky started to be sick, and continued to be so at intervals of twenty minutes throughout the night. We were fortunate to get a place on the early ferry, and a cabin in which she could lie down, and by early evening she was safely tucked up in her own little room. It was now Tuesday, 17th August. I was still not unduly worried, though distressed at her continued suffering. There were more glands to be felt, and I could feel an enlarged spleen, but, I thought, these things go with a severe attack of glandular fever, and Vicky had never done things by halves. I was not due into work until the Thursday, and on the Wednesday morning my friend and partner J. came across to see her and to take a blood specimen for a Paul-Bunnel test which would confirm whether or not she had indeed got glandular fever. While he was doing this, J. told me later, something, he did not know what, prompted him to take an additional sample of blood and to request a full blood count.

On the Thursday I went into work as usual. Vicky was more comfortable in her room, but she was still feverish, vomiting from time to time, and somnolent. It was not until the middle of evening surgery that the blow fell. Following a brief telephone call, which I had left to my receptionist to answer, as I was consulting at the moment, J. came through and gently put a piece of paper in front of me. I can see it to this day. It read: 'Paul-Bunnel –ve. White cell count 40,000. Mononuclears 90%, many primitive cells present.' I looked at him dumbly. 'But this,' I said, 'means leukaemia.' He nodded. I put my head in my hands as the full horror of it overcame me. Someone, I have no idea who, thrust a stiff brandy in front of me. The waiting room was emptied, as if by magic. This was the moment of truth. My darling Vicky, who had come so late into our family, who had brought such joy and gladness with her, whose life was so full of such rich promise, was going to die, and the awful irony of it was that I, who had spent my life in fighting death and disease on the part of others, could do NOTHING to save her. As if in a dream I heard J. telephone and arrange for her admission to the Children's Hospital in Great Ormond Street, and for our own ambulance driver, alongside whom I had worked so many times to convey the injured and the dying to hospital, to drive us up to the hospital that selfsame night.

Within the hospital all were kindness itself. We were able to see our darling settled in a lamp shrouded ward, and were found a bed and an armchair in one of the rooms set aside for occupation by nursing mothers, who had to be on hand to feed their

22

sick infants. Next morning we were able to be with her again in the ward. This was bright and brisk and rather noisy. Outside the sun shone with a brilliance and intensity that seemed to mock the heaviness in our hearts. I read to Vicky for a little while – an old and favourite tale – but she had difficulty in taking it in. Presently we were asked to leave for a little while as the doctors would be coming to examine her and make certain tests. Gently we explained to her that we would have to leave her, but that we would be back again after dinner. She smiled at us and said she understood. 'In any case,' she said, 'you don't want to stop inside on such a lovely day.' They were the last conscious words we heard her speak, and in the light of what we now know, it was perhaps characteristic of her that her last thought should be for those she loved.

I can remember little of the intervening hours. I remember asking our way down to the embankment and there falling asleep on one of the seats. I can remember going to the hospital chapel, and praying there with desperate intensity that if she had to leave us, at least that it might be swift, and that she might be spared the long drawn out suffering of remissions and inevitable relapses that so often characterise leukaemia. I remember meditating in the chapel that I had allowed my vision of God to become obscured by the material world, and that I was paying more attention to my pleasures and hobbies that I was to God. Perhaps, I wondered, this was God's way of recalling me to the path from which I had strayed, and that if I had not so strayed, Vicky might have been spared. By ten thirty that evening she had crossed the great divide, and we were left with the empty, empty shell which had once enshrined her spirit. From start to finish her illness had lasted just thirteen days. Even now, with all that I have learned I can scarcely bear to recall those poignant moments, which still have the power to bring a lump to my throat and tears to my eyes.

In a small community like the one in which I live, a doctor is a prominent figure, but even I was amazed by the number of people who turned out to say 'Goodbye' to Vicky. We have a large and magnificent parish church in Diss, and this was filled to overflowing. Many of those present I did not even know, but Vicky did. She seemed to have friends in every walk of life. We had been asked if we would like the burial service to be private, but somehow we all felt that that would be wrong. Little as I knew then about the facts of death and survival, I had realised instinctively as I stood looking down at her lifeless body that that at which I was looking was not Vicky. I was certain that she had gone on, where I did not know, but that she had gone on, probably for some very special reason. This service of farewell would be an opportunity to bear witness to this belief before my fellow townspeople, and to my absolute certainty of the infinite love of Jesus and the immortality of the human soul. I selected and read the lesson myself, and tried, as I followed her flower-laden coffin down the aisle, to hold my head high, and not bowed as if crushed by fate.

The following day I was interviewed by the local press – the unthinking exacerbation of trauma to which the media subject one in moments of severe stress. At the conclusion of the interview I found myself saying, and that I wanted this quoted literally, that I was certain my daughter lived on in a far fuller, freer and more glorious life than she had known on earth. Quite why I said that I had no idea. It came to me as I was speaking, and after I had said it, I knew that it was true. I know now that this early inkling was no more than a literal statement of fact.

After a loss such as ours, one inevitably receives many messages of attempted consolation. I remember our Rector coming to call on the Sunday after her death with words of intended comfort. Of all that he said just two things have stuck in my mind: one I believe to have been truly inspired, and which was of great comfort to me at many moments, the other less so and, indeed, oddly disturbing. Taking the first, 'You know,' he said, 'I think the veil is a great deal thinner when viewed from the other side'. This, of course, is literally true – at least at some points of the other side – as I was to discover in the course of my Odyssey. His second and more disturbing remark was this: 'I don't think that God means things like this to happen. These things are accidents.' Poor man! Wanting above all else not to disturb my faith in an all-powerful, all-loving God, he said the one thing most calculated to give support to an atheistic philosophy of life, by implying that somewhere or somehow things could happen that were not under the control of God; that God, in fact, was NOT all-powerful. Had I been in a state seriously to reason things out at this stage, which fortunately I was not, this well-meant but highly dubious remark could have led to terrible confusion.

Fortunately I was far too busy to have much opportunity for thought. J., who had delayed the start of his holiday in Ireland for a week so as to see us through the funeral period, had departed to join his wife and children, who had not been allowed even to wait and say goodbye to their erstwhile playmate. Professionally I had as much as I could carry. Probably this was as well. Hard work has ever been the traditional antidote to grief, and though I was aware intellectually that to the Christian grief was primarily a selfish emotion, in that one's thoughts are centred upon the loss that one has oneself sustained, such intellectual casuistry did little to numb an aching heart. My distress was greatly aggravated by the discovery, on his return from holiday, that I was to lose the close friend and partner with whom I had worked for a number of years. J. had accepted the offer of a partnership with an old friend of his wife's in the west country, so that in addition to bearing the pain of bereavement, I was to lose my colleague and friend, and have all the problems attendant upon finding a successor. However, even here, the way in which his successor was found has shown me once again that help is always at hand when we most need it. He proved to be a deeply committed and practising Christian, with enough wisdom to understand what I was about and to give me support, the support which I so badly required. He had had a wide experience of general practice and was also a man of sufficient substance to be able to take on the financial commitments associated with a change of practice. Despite wide advertisement for several months, he was the ONLY candidate even remotely suitable as a replacement. In the event, his wonderful qualities, both personal and spiritual, which helped to give me strength over this most difficult period, seem with hindsight to have been an act of succour from the unseen helpers who surround us all.

CHAPTER THREE

TANIA

It was probably about the end of October, some six weeks after Vicky's passing, that 'the other side' began to take a hand in things. It started with a chance remark from a patient of mine one evening surgery. Eric had only recently come to town, and this was my first encounter with him. He had come into the surgery, not knowing really quite why he was there or what he wanted, but asking for a 'check-up, please, Doctor'. At that time such a request was apt to send a cold shudder down the spine of most family doctors, since it usually indicated that the patient was a bit of a hypochondriac, and obsessed with his own health. Only very rarely on such occasions was anything of any major significance discovered. Eric was no exception. However, he himself had had just such an experience as I had recently undergone in that he had lost a son who died from nephritis at the age of eight, some five or six years earlier. Thus knowing and understanding so much of what was in my heart at this time, he suddenly asked me, just as he was leaving the surgery, if I was interested in ESP'.

'In ESP?', I replied. 'Whatever is that?'

'Extrasensory perception.'

'Oh!' I replied. 'I'm afraid it is not a subject of which I have any experience. I always try to keep an open mind, and I am quite sure that some people have gifts that are denied to others. Yes. I suppose I am.'

'Well, I'll talk to you another time about it. There's not time now.'

There certainly was not, for the waiting room was crowded. The next day I called at Eric's shop, and he told me the following remarkable story. Shortly after his arrival in Diss he and his wife had begun to make a few friends, and a small group of these had been spending the evening together. During the course of the evening the conversation drifted around to the question of survival. This led on to others saying that they had heard that it was possible to 'call up the spirits'. 'During the course of the conversation,' said Eric, 'I know that I asked the question "Have you done this?" of each in turn, and each one replied "No, but I know of somebody else who has".' The result of this was that after discussing it, somebody said 'Well, why not try it?' So they got round the table with some letters and a glass, and waited for something to happen. In fact, nothing did happen, and they tended to dismiss the idea.

Two weeks later, however, the same group met in somebody else's house, and the subject cropped up again. So they tried again. Once more nothing happened. Some weeks later the same group found themselves together for a third time, when somebody said: 'Well, third time lucky. Let's try again.' On this occasion the glass began to move, and it moved to various letters in turn. At first these made nonsense. Towards the finish, however, it appeared to spell out a message, and the message was this: 'For Eric. Look in the national newspaper, page 5 column 5.' Highly excited at this unexpected development, they at once grabbed all the available newspapers, only to be bitterly disappointed to find that page 5 column 5 seemed in each to be entirely occupied by advertisements. At this point they dismissed the whole thing with the feeling that perhaps the conventional view was right after all, and that the glass and the letters were best left alone.

Experienced workers in the psychic field will certainly agree with this, and that the lower forms of communication such as table turning, ouija boards and glass/letter work are highly dangerous for inexperienced people and can cause untold problems.

Following this, Eric, who at this point was still very much the rising young businessman, interested mainly in his family and business prospects, put the matter right out of his mind. However, some ten days or a fortnight later he had occasion to make a business telephone call to a woman whom he understood was a medium. 'By the way,' she said at the end of the conversation, 'I have a message for you. It comes from spirit.'

'Oh yes?' replied Eric. 'A message from spirit? I'm afraid I don't follow.'

'Yes,' she continued. 'The message is for you to look in the national newspaper, page 5 column 5.'

At this Eric burst out laughing, and explained what they had been doing. 'But,' he went on, 'it doesn't make sense, because all the national newspapers have there is advertisements.'

'Ah', rejoined his friend. 'You have been looking in the wrong papers. It should have been a Sunday paper. I have that paper here, and it is an article on spiritualism. On page 5 column 5 it says "Will you work with us?" '

At this point, Eric told me, he just could not go along with this at all. However, his friend went on to tell him that she had another message for him which came from 'his relatives in spirit'. He was instructed to sit quietly with a pencil and some paper, and that if he did this, writing would be done through him. This again, he told me, he took very lightly. He knew nothing about automatic writing, and in fact had never read anything on the subject.

'Well,' said his friend, 'I have done my part. Now it is up to you.'

After giving the matter considerable thought and discussing it with his wife, who shared his views, he eventually decided that no harm would be done if he attempted to try this new approach. Accordingly, two or three days later, he sat down with a pencil and paper. Nothing happened. He tried this again on three successive occasions. On the third occasion just as he had got to the point of giving up – he had been sitting each day for about ten minutes – he found himself idly writing down the message 'Will you work with us?' However, for some unexplained reason, instead of writing down 'Will you work with us?', on this occasion he wrote down 'Will you work with me?' At once, he said, he found his whole arm going rigid and, seeming to go under someone else's control, it began to write, slowly and laboriously, the letters Y–E–S. Intensely surprised at this unexpected development, Eric took his hand over to the other side of the paper to see what would happen. Now he found himself writing, or, as he put it to me, controlled in writing, and it went on to say, 'You are going to do healing. You must be patient.' At this point the power ran out, and the pencil ceased to move any more. Daily after this breakthrough, however, Eric sat with pencil and paper for ten to fifteen minutes at a stretch,

28

and began to get many messages through. Reference was made to the development of remarkable powers of healing and to a healing sanctuary in the country. (At that time he lived in a small maisonette above his shop on a busy main road, which was totally unsuitable for a healing sanctuary and could not by the wildest stretch of the imagination have been described as a beautiful place in the country.) All of this, especially the idea of healing, when he knew nothing about disease, he found extremely hard to believe. At times he was tempted to dismiss the whole idea, particularly when he began to get what looked like deliberate deception.

At some point in the course of the writings he had received a message which made reference to me and my daughter. Once again he had little faith in the writing and, in retrospect, Eric is astonished that he should ever have dared to mention the matter to me, since at that point the relationship was strictly on a doctor/patient basis, and doctors are inclined to take a long, hard look at patients who start talking about messages from the other side and wonder whether they may not be mentally unhinged. However, he did, and the upshot of it was that he told me that he had a message to say that if he sat at the same time the next night 'they' would bring Vicky with them, and would I like to come along? (The reader must recognise at this point I was not deliberately seeking Vicky – that came later. The last thing that had entered my mind following Vicky's death was to go out and seek communication with her. If I thought at all about the post-mortem state of a child, I probably thought of her in such conventional terms as 'safe in the arms of Jesus'. It is important to realise that *she was brought to me* without my going out to seek for her at this stage. Plainly help abounds at all times both for the bereaved and the newly dead.)

Naturally I jumped at this invitation, and the next night I sat and conversed with my dead daughter through the medium of Eric's pencil. I cannot say, in the light of my present knowledge and my present standards that it was a highly evidential sitting. Both medium, communicator and sitter were plainly complete novices. To my astonishment Vicky seemed to have forgotten the name both of her brother and her pet dog. (Knowing what I do now, I realise that the 'getting across' of names is probably one of the most difficult tasks for the novice communicator, and one must remember that she was only ten years old when she died, and had only been 'over' for less than six weeks.) However, she did seem to show an awareness of my movements at home, and there was sufficient in the conversation to support the hope that despite the seeming tragedy of death the individual mind lingered on, albeit in another dimension. It was the last crumb of comfort that I was to receive for many a weary month.

At this point I must diverge from my own search to that of Eric. Being of a sceptical turn of mind, Eric began to have serious doubts as to the truth of the remarkable messages that he had been given, and to start to look for confirmation. His first act was to approach the President of the local Spiritualist church, only to be told as she opened the door to him that he was a healer. He consulted other mediums locally, and was told the same story. Finally, feeling that he must have the best mediumship available, he decided to join the Spiritualist Association of Great Britain, at 33 Belgrave Square, for sittings with the mediums working for the Association. Here again he received the same confirmation from a number of separate mediums, together with just sufficient in the way of personal evidence to make him feel that there was something in it which was not arising from his own mind.

To any intelligent sitter, the constant stumbling block that arises in the interpretation of messages received is that much abused word 'telepathy'. Granted that mediums are abnormal, and that they have the ability to pick up and register the thoughts of others, how certain can one be that any references they make to personal factors have not simply been relayed by the medium from thoughts and memories present in the mind of the sitter, either at conscious or subconscious level? They do not constitute any evidence for the existence, or otherwise, of another, discarnate intelligence. Even when the information given to the sitter is completely unkown to them, but known only to a third party not present at the sitting, how certain can one be that this information has not been culled from the mind of that third party? Such thoughts were constantly churning round in Eric's mind throughout this period.

At length, still incredulous and doubting, he came to a medium named Mrs D. She was not one of the regular mediums working at 33 Belgrave Square, but came from the north of

England on an occasional visiting basis every couple of months or so. Talking to Eric some time later, he said: 'I know that to me it seemed at the time that this is the medium, because she comes from away somewhere, north, from right away. There could be no possible connection anywhere. She was visiting. So I said "Yes", would they please make an appointment. All this was done by phone. The sitting I had at that time with Mrs D was most revealing, and, of course, I was fortunate enough to have this recorded.'

I had fallen into the habit of lending Eric my small portable tape recorder, in order that he might have a full record of all that was said, and I was, in turn, allowed to listen to and discuss the content of the messages with him. This had worked admirably, but on this occasion, for some extraordinary reason (he must have failed to have the recorder input switched to microphone input, I suspect), he returned with only the ghost of a signal on tape, and one which it was quite impossible to amplify into anything intelligible. 'This first sitting', Eric continued, 'was most disappointing, because I sat through it and I really felt that here at last was evidence. I know that I was really excited when I handed you the tape and I thought you would be able to hear this for yourself. I remember that at the time I said little to you about what was on the tape, but it did actually make reference to the healing, and the pattern of things that would follow. I was rather surprised when you told me that there was nothing on the tape, but I always remember you saying to me that if there was truth in this, I would get it again. I must say that I thought at this point that this was highly improbable, because, as I have explained, Mrs D came from the north, and was just visiting at that particular time. I thought it would be more than a coincidence if I could arrange an appointment with her that would coincide with her visits.'

Nevertheless, the improbable came to pass, and in such a way that it now seems to me to have been deliberately arranged from 'the other side'. Four weeks later, on his very next visit, Eric had made an appointment with Mrs N, an extremely well-known London medium, who was a regular attender amongst the mediums at Belgrave Square. On arriving there on the Monday morning he was greeted with the news that they had a disappointment for him, since Mrs N had been taken ill at short notice. They had tried to contact him to say that his medium had been taken ill, but he had already left home for London. However, they had wired for a replacement medium to take the sittings booked, and this replacement medium came from the north. So to his astonishment, Eric found that my words had actually come true, and that he was again sitting with Mrs D. The message which was given and lost, was given and recorded again. Moreover, in this sitting, reference was actually made to the fact that they were aware that the recording of the first sitting had not been successful, and that therefore he was getting it a second time. To this message I had the privilege of listening, and a copy of it is in my tape files to this day.

Looking back on this series of events, two things stand out in my memory as helping to convince me that these were genuine communications. The first is the sheer quality of what was said on this, and a subsequent occasion. It was in fact initially responsible for breaking down my own resistance to communication, and for convincing me that there are higher and wiser powers in existence, and that, under certain circumstances, they make contact with us here on earth. The second was the strange sequence of apparently coincidental events surrounding the various messages. I shall return later to the contents of this spirit teaching which made so great an impression upon both Eric and myself.

I was naturally extremely interested to listen to Eric's sitting, and I was immediately struck by the very high spiritual quality of the message. I became convinced that he had made contact with a soul far progressed along the path of spiritual development. Outstanding perhaps above all else in this first communication was the voice of the communicator. Totally unlike the rather flat, broad Yorkshire accents of the medium, the voice was deep, unmistakably feminine, and rich with all the tones of tenderness and deep compassion, and an air, impossible to convey adequately in a written transcript, of wisdom and loving understanding, as from an old and very dear friend. The purpose of the message was to confirm to him the truth of what he had already been told from so many prior sources, namely that he was to be used to heal the sick on earth. Surprisingly to us at the time, though not now, in the light of later understanding, the communicator knew all about his conversations with myself, and approved. I quote an edited extract from the tape-recorded conversation which made such an impact upon us both. Although the communicator gave no name or identification at this sitting, we later came to know her as Tania, and so it is by that name that I will refer to her in the following passage. Tania greeted him warmly and went on to refer to the previous conversation which she had had with him, saying how sorry she was about the failure of the recording, but that it had not been possible to do anything about it. She went on to say:

It was to do with your healing. – excuse me! Sometimes I lose English! – Despite the fact that you did not particularly want to follow this pathway of service, you have been moved about like a pawn in a game, as it were. Right? These things are unfolding. There is a breakthrough from the other realms of experience – from the spirit world, if you like – and you are being moved about as the plan is unfolding. You understand?

Eric: Yes.

Tania: I am sure you are doing everything in your power to make sure that everything is in order, and we much appreciate the fact that you are experimenting also – that you are investigating, if I may use that word. I see that you have been holding conversations with someone who is much experienced in the ways of a man's physique. (Myself.) For this we are very grateful, for it is a good thing to bring someone into attunement with these things. You understand?

Eric: I understand.

Tania: Particularly if he has got a certain talent, which can be complemented through this knowledge, so that mankind receives the benefit of deeper knowledge from the world of spirit. You quite understand and agree with this?

Eric: Yes.

Tania: If a talent, which is one which one has in one's vocation can be used, it is a good thing; but (it is) much better if it is used in cooperation with the doctors in spirit life. Also, which is also perhaps much more surprising to the doctors in the body, is the fact that one can link with medicine without any knowledge of medicine. This, of course, is the proof of our world, the world of spirit, in that these things can be unfolded, and reveal themselves to people. As you well know, sometimes one is inclined to doubt these things, as you have perhaps doubted. Yet you see, you have been moved around. Time and again we have repeated things to you in order that you accept the truth about yourself and your mission in life. In order to make you sure of this, we have had of necessity to confirm it and get the point home to you.

*　　　*　　　*

Tania: I see that there are many things which have been in your mind in the relationship to certain diseases, which seem to be, according to the medical profession, incurable. But there are minds which have progressed beyond the minds which are incarnate here in your medical science, so it is only reasonable to suppose that they are going to seek out the channels that they can use in order to utilise the knowledge they have. You understand?

Eric: I understand. Yes.

Tania: Also, although people perhaps would doubt this very much, even after they accept the fact of survival and communication and activity from the world of spirit, there ARE master powers, who DO penetrate through to the earth conditions; whose past was used to take people who walked the earthplanes, with great desires to alleviate the suffering of the sick, both mentally, spiritually and physically. Is it reasonable to suppose, my brother, that they would now sit on some far distant heaven, when they love? When we love, we do not sit back and watch suffering. We try to do something about it, especially when we have the means to do it. So you are coupled with minds who have progressed through love, who have sought out knowledge, and they are using you according to their understanding of you yourself. And yet at first there was great opposition in yourself, you see, simply because to you it was so fantastic as to seem almost ridiculous. You see?

Eric: This is true.

Tania: But you see you cannot escape from reality, or from the truth, no matter how much you feel it is against all the laws which you know of. But you see, there is a law which does not change, and that is the law of survival, or of the eternity of life. There is another law which comes into operation and that is the law of the administration of love, which embraces all, whether discarnate or incarnate. From the higher sources, the higher intelligence, one finds a continual flow coming through to those who are physically handicapped, mentally handicapped and spiritually handicapped. This only happens because one has had experience through living here on the earth. For a long time there has been much thought and scepticism about these things, and simply because one has not wanted to accept the truth, maybe perhaps because of the responsibility, perhaps out of fear in one shape or another, if you follow me. But, at the same time this is a new era. Things are changing. There is a breakthrough, not on the psychic level, but in the *spiritual field, and this is working through to people like yourself*, who are part of this link. There are a group of souls who are working through in different parts of the world, *who have chosen their instruments for certain qualities which they possess*, and you belong to this group, if you like. We call it 'The Link'. Many have maybe been in this country and have been transferred to other countries because of the work which must be done. In and through it all there is the naturalness of living in the world. All these things are being brought in a masterly way, in one's material environment of life and in one's vocation. One could say that vocation raises a barrier, but not necessarily so. These can be overcome. There are a number of personalities who have been moved about to different places, still with their ordinary way of life, and yet with the consciousness of a mission which must be accomplished.

*　　*　　*

Tania: . . . (Such a mission is) not to accomplish anything (in) particular for yourself as for other people, and through this to bring people closer into the consciousness of the reality of God . . . For how otherwise can we find that consciousness of God, unless we see God in action in these things? And so, my brother, I do pray that you will accept the fact that everything that has happened to you has happened for that which is good.
Eric: Yes.

*　　*　　*

Tania: Can I tell you something which I feel would be important to you?

Eric: Whatever you wish.

Tania: There is one who comes and uses the medium whom I use now from the higher realms of spirit, and he too is working for people in this world, and he tells people about himself; not talking down to people or being critical of them; perhaps chiding a little sometimes. It is, he said, the most difficult thing to make people see what you want to make them see. To make them God conscious is very difficult. For they look at a man, and that which is done to them is done BY the man. It is the man who becomes the idol. (*cf* the experience of St Paul and St Barnabas at Ephesus.) And he said that to him it was the greatest sorrow of his life here on earth that, though he succeeded in many things, he failed in the greatest thing of all.

Eric: I follow. I understand.

Tania: And so therefore – and this is one of the great ones, who, although one would perhaps call him Saint, accepts none of that, except that he is about his Father's business –

Eric: Yes. I think the way that I understand it is this; I think what you wish to tell me is this: that when I undertake this healing, *I must make it perfectly clear to people that this is the work of God. They must understand; this is the work of God.*

Tania: That is true. They must be given to understand that this is not possible without the Father ... That alone I am nothing. Do not bow down and worship me. I am one tiny part of a wonderful whole. Do not worship me. Realise that for many years and many, many days people have thought of God in such a way that he becomes non-existent to them. The words of the Church do not suffice to make them realise that God is real. There is no real contact – no real conscious contact – with God. Therefore people have grown away, and there is great shadow in the world. Until one can really make men see God in Action, how can they believe there is a God?

Eric: Yes. This I follow very clearly.

Tania: So God comes into action, not to exhibit mankind, nor to make people feel that there is something supernormal, but that it is the natural law of love in operation. And naturally the greatest part of all love is the Father-power; and we are tiny parts of this. And sometimes we grow away a little and our light becomes dim. *But one has to know the goal for which one is striving.* How otherwise will one have the courage and the fortitude to go on? So one has to see the goal.

Eric: Yes.

Tania: This too is understood, and when it is asked 'Show me the Father', as it has been said before, then we can truly say, 'You have seen Him in action. That is God. God is in action in our compassion. That is God in action.' If we do not then just speak words, but we act, that brings God into action, and he is revealed in these things that are manifest through our surrender to him. You understand?

Eric: Yes. Yes I do.

Tania: Therefore it is important that we always remember. Otherwise, being perhaps as you are now – for me, I am discarnate. I borrow a body for a little while – but for you, who walk the earth plane, incarnate, it is the most easy thing for you, perhaps for a little while, to forget yourself. You understand?

Eric: Yes.

Tania: This we would not criticise you for, or condemn you, for you are human. Nevertheless, in all these things one is constantly reminded how far we can go without God.

Eric: This is true.

Tania: So today, when I have spoken to you, I know you will realise that I too am part of this Divine Plan.

I have quoted at length from this second communication to Eric because it was the high quality of this message and what I felt to be the intense spirituality which shone through every phrase, which first really encouraged me to start out to search for myself. Yes, I felt, there really ARE higher and wiser powers, and it IS possible to make contact with them under certain circumstances. We CAN learn of their wisdom and their love.

The speaker here, whose name as I have said we later learned to be Tania, was plainly one from these higher realms. She appeared a number of times in sittings with this medium, and we came to know her well and to love her dearly. No words can convey the warmth and compassion and understanding in her beautiful and tender voice. We shall return to her teachings further on in this account of my journey.

Brought up as I had been within the confines of the traditional Anglican church, I had viewed Eric's investigations with a lively interest, coupled with a good deal of awe. Though nothing had ever been directly said upon the subject by my parents or my teachers, it was an understood thing among those of my generation that attempts to penetrate beyond the veil were not approved by God. Not for nothing had our preparatory school scripture classes included the reading of the earlier books of the Old Testament, including the famous passage in the eighteenth chapter of Deuteronomy:

'There shall not be found among you any one that maketh his son or his daughter to pass through the fire, or that useth divination, or an observer of times, or an enchanter, or a witch, or a charmer, or *a consulter with familiar spirits*, or a wizard, or a necromancer. For all that do these things are an abomination unto the Lord.'

Deuteronomy 18. vv.10–12

In fact modern scholarship shows that the conventional understanding of this passage as being that communication and mediumship are forbidden is incorrect. The passage dates from the Deuteronomic reforms of King Josiah in the seventh century BC which sought to cleanse the worship of the Jews from superstitious beliefs and pagan practices assimilated during the exile. These would have included pagan methods of prognostication, including consultation with the dead through the practice of necromancy, and those forms of precognition which appear to involve 'randomness' (chance), as for instance belomancy (divination by arrows), or else involve a lower and amoral form of psychism whose advice would not match up to the higher and more spiritual message of the accredited prophet of Yahweh.

The passage is therefore part of a priestly revolt against the lower forms of primitive or atavistic psychism, perhaps not very far removed from those still found today in Haiti and parts of Africa – Juju, Voodoo, Obeah – and of a striving to establish a higher and more rational moral and spiritual form of communication. (Revd J. D. Bretherton: *Life, Death and Psychical Research*, p108, Rider 1973.)

Thus after hearing the message which I have just quoted, I could not feel that there was anything evil in communication, *per se*. It might even be, I felt, that we, poor, sinful, ailing

38

humanity could learn something with profit from the souls that had gone ahead. Could it be that the Church was mistaken in her attitude towards mediums? Perhaps the general idea of the sleep of death, the Judgement and the Last Trumpet was incorrect. For it certainly seemed that not all spirits slept, and that some were even actively trying to work for the good of mankind. I began to revise my views considerably. I looked a little wistfully at Eric, who, fettered by no such inhibitions, had joined the Spiritualist Association of Great Britain, and was actively pursuing his quest with monthly sittings with mediums at Belgrave Square. I insisted on him continuing to take my tape recorder, and would wait avidly to hear the recording of the next session.

Eric's third sitting with Mrs D was quite as illuminating as the first. Here are some extracts from it which helped us both to progress a little further along the way of understanding:

Tania: Is much light in the room . . . I mean spirit light . . . Can you hear me quite plainly?

Eric: Yes.

Tania: Sometimes one wonders, because the volume is very difficult for us to realise whether it is strong enough or not . . . It is like your wireless; sometimes if it is not turned up you do not get the sound very distinctly, and sometimes we wonder if there is a little distortion. So we are dependent on you to tell us whether it is all right or not.

Eric: It is all right at the moment.

*   *   *

Tania: . . . It is important to know whether one is to be of service in different ways or not . . . In your case there is no need to doubt it, because certainly your progression is assured . . . I think it is important for you to *want* to unfold; not only psychically but spiritually. One is spirit. Therefore I tell you that I have met you before. We are not strangers, you see. So therefore I say that I have met you before. I know you, but you have not been conscious of myself, you see, simply because you have gone out into the world, and like one forgets dreams, you have forgotten . . . It is imperative that you do not doubt your gift. If you do, you perhaps make yourself very unhappy, and certainly would feel that you are not developing.

39

But there is a difference between developing and unfolding, you know. With some it is a natural gift which unfolds; with others it is a talent which has to be developed, like all things which are talents. One finds that with an artist some are masters; others merely develop some talent they have in that direction. With yourself you are unfolding rather than developing, because it is a natural talent. There is a saying which goes something like this: 'Many are called, but few are chosen'. And, of course, this is true; that to many there are mediumistic qualities which can be on the psychic level. **But to have the spiritual level is important.** . . . So therefore what we are actually saying is that you are not merely an instrument for psychic phenomena, with clairvoyance as some people use it, but will know what it is necessary to feed.

Eric: Will know what is necessary to feed . . . ?

Tania: It is asked of us that we feed the people. It is always a good thing to be able to know what is necessary to feed them with. You understand?

Eric: Yes.

Tania: Various people, as you know, are in different stages of evolution; they are in different conditions of life in the world. Therefore you cannot say to someone who is in desperate need of help or reassurance, 'I have got someone here called such-and-such a name'. For to them it will mean nothing which will help them. Do you understand what I mean by this? In other words, to be conscious of the need of that person is terribly important, and you can only do this if you have compassion. Love is the key . . . If you were not conscious of this love, which is the Divine Love, then you would not make the effort. You would grow weary, and – like some people have a fascination for a thing for a time and then they get tired of it, you know? – this is what would happen to you, if you were not linked with the love vibration and had compassion for others. You see what I mean?

Eric: I do see.

Tania: There is a great deal of difference between the one who is seeking only to have a new experience, and the one who is really filled with the desire to serve others . . . Sometimes this makes demands upon you which are difficult for you, (so as) to take the steps which are required of you in order to serve.

As you go on, and as you aspire to higher and finer things, then **the pathway does NOT become easier. It becomes harder.** As you become more illumined within yourself, you know that in a way you are indeed your brother's keeper. You have responsibility to him. **You may see, as you will indeed, the weaknesses which lie within him, but despite this, you will not judge, but only will you try to show your great compassion, and certainly not unkindly criticise him. For this way you do not win any battle. But you will try to show that you have cultivated this love, which seeth all, and yet does not come to sit in judgement upon him.**

Eric: I understand.

Tania: It is important that you do not in any way set the rules yourself . . . You do not say to God, 'I will serve you IF . . .' Do you see what I mean?

Eric: No.

Tania: You do not say, 'All right, I am prepared to do what is your will, but make it MY way'.

Eric: I follow. Yes.

Tania: Now do you understand? If one once says, as one does many times without understanding what one is talking about – in your world you say The Lord's Prayer – you are not just to give lip service. You are to MEAN what you say. If you do not mean what you say, then you are being a hypocrite, and pretending to One who knows all things. Do you see?

Eric: Yes. I follow.

Tania: So therefore, when one comes to God in supplication, one surrenders to his supreme wisdom, knowing that wherever he wants us, there we will go – making no conditions, for we cannot bargain with God. If we really and truly grow into this love consciousness, we do not think about where we go. It is where the need is, there we go. You understand?

Eric: Yes. I understand.

Tania: Therefore, whatever is here that lies before us, we know then that the ways of God are wonderful, and they reveal to us the pattern as we can perceive it, a step at a time. Perhaps sometimes it is very difficult for us, maybe because we have to have what seems blind faith; unable to see what is going to unfold for us, and yet still having the confidence that

what is happening cannot be wrong. It MUST be right if we are not trying to do what *we* want to do, but what HE wants us to do. Do you see what I mean.
Eric: Yes.
Tania: **The only time when anything of this kind goes wrong is when we become conscious more of the 'I', the ego, than we are of God. It is then that the thing goes wrong. So it is important always to remember this, so that we do not in any way become puffed up, you know, to seek for the adoration of the people. So many, you see, are desirous of the acclaim of the people more than remembering, 'I am about my Father's business'.**

This, the third communication to Eric from Tania, coming as it did within a month of the previous communication, deepened still further the tremendous impact upon us both. While the content is of the highest importance (we shall refer later to the significance of some of the points raised), and can be read with profit and digested again and again, it was the personality of the speaker which made the strongest impression upon us. The mere transcription of the words in no way serves to convey the sense of tender compassion and loving wisdom which so characterised this spirit. At every sitting at which she appeared the personality remained the same, constant and distinct, and the voice consistent; deep, melodious and resonant, with just a hint of an accent suggesting a middle or southern European origin.

CHAPTER FOUR

I BEGIN MY SEARCH

It was at this point that Eric really started, as he would put it, to go along with things, and to accept that, however much he might want to deny and dispute, this must have been arranged by the higher powers. I, in my turn, recognising the quality and level of the teaching which we had been given, then began to study. I started, moreover, to read all the books I could lay my hands on. Eric was by this time accumulating quite a library, and the first book which I read was Mrs Jane Sherwood's famous book *Postmortem Journal*. This celebrated account of the passing of her communicator 'Scott', later to be identified, rather unwillingly, as the late T. E. Lawrence, and of his awakening and life on the next plane, made me aware for the first time of the reality of conditions in the world beyond. So far from being the misty, shadowy, unsubstantial 'place of the shades', which I had vaguely visualised, (it was not for nothing that I had had a classical education, and was familiar with the ideas of the Greeks and Romans on the subject!), it appeared to be a place every bit as substantial and, it seemed, a good deal more vivid, than that which we inhabited at the present moment. I followed this up by reading Anthony Borgia's equally famous book, *Life in the World Unseen*. Here again, from a completely different source, was the same picture; that of a world by no means dissimilar to our own, but lacking the flaws which man has introduced into God's creation; a world of light and harmony and beauty.

I was by now being strongly 'tempted', as I called it to myself at the time, though I now think the word 'impressed' would more accurately describe what was going on, to go up to Belgrave Square and have a sitting for myself. Only my lingering doubts about the propriety of such an action and the problem of reconciling this with my church upbringing restrained me. It was at this point, however, that I became aware of the existence of the Churches' Fellowship for Psychical and Spiritual Studies. This, I learned from the prospectus, was an organisation founded in 1954 by a group of clergy and laymen interested in psychical research and its relevance to the Christian faith. Looking down the list of patrons on the back of the prospectus I saw the names of no less than 19 bishops, and a further list of other clergy, who were household names – Dr Leslie Weatherhead, Dr W. R. Matthews, Lord Soper, Lord Macleod. Here, I felt, was a road that I could follow, beneath the umbrella of the Christian faith. I joined the Fellowship with a thankful heart, and determined to press ahead with my own investigations in the hope that some time and somewhere I might at least make contact with the little girl we had lost and loved so dearly. Eventually, believing that it would not be wrong for me to seek communication, I plucked up courage to go along with Eric for a sitting myself.

In the meantime, too, several curious things had been happening to one of my friends. For a number of years our receptionist/dispenser at the surgery had been a girl called Pat. She was a young woman who had been brought up in Australia, and had come to this country just after the war to get married. Sadly this had not materialised and, rather than return home unmarried, she had made up her mind to remain and seek work in the UK. She knew little about her father, but her mother had been of Hebridean origin, and undoubtedly was gifted with psychic powers. She had obviously been unhappy and, perhaps, a little ashamed about these powers as is not uncommon amongst the Hebridean islanders today, for she had strictly warned her daughter against 'dabbling'. Pat herself was a poet of considerable merit, and had had a number of psychic experiences, mostly associated with precognitive dreams, of which she was rather afraid. Most of these she had shared with me, generally seeking reassurance that she was not becoming mentally disturbed, and it was undoubtedly due to this that I was so readily able to accept Eric when he spoke to me about ESP.

After Vicky's death we had given Pat a pair of castanets which I had brought home for Vicky from one of my holidays in Spain, and which she used to keep hanging up in her room. Pat kept these hanging up in the hall of her little house on an old, swan-necked gas bracket. Repeatedly when she returned to her house from work, the house having been empty all day, she would find these castanets lying on the floor well away from the wall bracket upon which they had been hung. There was no possibility of their having got there of their own accord. On one occasion she woke from sleep to 'see' Vicky dressed in her blue uniform, lying face downwards on the bed beside her. On another occasion she was brought an apport, in the shape of a lock of golden hair. Not wishing to disturb me further, she told me nothing about these happenings at the time, but it is my firm belief that Vicky was trying everything she could to get in touch with me through the only person with psychic powers with whom I had contact.

My own first sitting was on 16th May 1968. This was with Marie Wheeler. I approached it with some trepidation, not knowing what to expect. Like many first sittings, this was entirely conventional. There was no dramatic trance, or obvious and conscious contact with another world; just a quiet conversation with a deeply sincere and understanding woman, who none the less seemed to be able to penetrate beyond the surface of superficial knowledge. It contained just enough of recognisable evidence to convince me of the genuineness of the medium, together with much that greatly surprised me then, but which time and the last few years have brought to fulfilment. I include here some quotes from this sitting.

MW: (speaking of my father) . . . 'I get with him that he was a spiritual man. He seems to have made progression in the spirit world, and he is linking with someone who was a priest or a vicar. I don't feel it was a Roman Catholic priest as we would know, but an Anglican or something of that sort.'

(*Comment:* True. My father's lifelong and best friend was a priest who subsequently became a bishop of the Anglican church and had died within a year of my father some ten years previously.)

Self: Yes, yes.
MW: This is a very lovely influence, I feel. Such a gentle person, and I always feel that whatever our gifts, or whatever we do, if we haven't got this gentleness and love, we might as well not do it. He's certainly got that and he comes round you very much, this vicar, and I feel here that you would feel his influence, because he gives you a lot of wisdom and things that you

could speak. *You really are a channel; this I feel you must know for yourself, because you are a channel for spirit.*

Self: Yes. That is why I have come to you.

MW: Yes: I do feel that it can be used by speaking, or by writing down on paper. They're rather keen on the writing on paper. So we have to watch for that.

At this time I was not doing any public speaking or writing on these subjects – nor had I any intention of becoming so involved. Mrs Wheeler then went on to speak of a link with Scotland and of a great sense of power emanating from Scotland towards me. This was certainly quite true. Throughout my life I had always had a great affinity for Scotland, to which we went every year for our summer holidays during one part of my childhood. Some years previously my parents had spent a summer holiday together on the island of Iona, and, though I had never had the opportunity to go there myself, I had always longed to do so, without ever really understanding why. Some years later, as will be seen further on in this book, I started to visit Iona on a regular basis, and it has played a very large part in my spiritual development.

Mrs Wheeler continued by informing me of an opportunity presenting itself from the spirit world, and of spiritual work which I had to do. This greatly surprised me, since I had never thought of myself in terms of carrying out spiritual tasks on the earth. My feet were still firmly planted on the ground! She spoke of difficulties which had to be overcome and of help that would be given. She asked whether I had spoken under 'control' from the world of spirit.

So far I had done no public speaking at all, and certainly was not contemplating a career of teaching or spiritual leadership. In fact I later had to learn, when speaking or lecturing, to do without a written text of my lecture, and to allow myself to speak under the inspiration of the moment. When I used a written text, it was never so effective. This was still some time in the future after this sitting. After delivering one of these scripted talks to the local branch of the Churches' Fellowship for Psychical and Spiritual Studies, one of my listeners, herself gifted with mediumistic powers, said to me: 'Ian, you really must stop using a written text when you speak. They are telling me that when you do this, they can't get through to you!' It took some time to gain the confidence to do this, and I still start out with a sheaf of notes in front of me. Usually, however, by the time that I have been going for five minutes I have wandered away from my notes and lost the place, and continue spontaneously. Listeners who know me well, such as my wife, invariably say that it is at this point that the lecture really 'takes off'. Interestingly enough, I have repeatedly been told of a presence seen behind me, often in radiant and glowing colours, when I am on the platform.

Given the fact that this was the first time I had ever sat with a medium, this sitting can be regarded as highly successful. I was disappointed at the time, because I felt it had not done anything to bring me closer to Vicky. However, the mere fact that this intense desire, which was uppermost in my mind at the time, was totally ignored, must, I think, suggest very strongly to all but the compulsive sceptic, that something other than telepathy was at work. Viewed in retrospect, it is remarkable how accurate the various predictions were over the ensuing fifteen years.

Mrs Wheeler went on to speak of my home conditions and of the presence of a power of healing beyond that normally exercised in the daily work of a doctor. Although I then lived in an early nineteenth-century, semi-detached house, situated on a busy main road, she described a large house in the country, surrounded by tall trees, well away from any main road, and with a great sense of peace. Eight months later I moved to my present home. This fits fairly well the description given. It stands well back from a quiet road leading out of the town opposite an open meadow. It is surrounded by some tall lime trees in the midst of a garden which has now become too big for us comfortably to manage! There is a large resident bird population, and a general air of peace, which strikes all who come here. I was born in the house just over the hedge next door, and I spent over ten years of my childhood in this very house. At the time at which this sitting was given we had no thought of moving, and this particular house, which, unknown to me, had always attracted my wife, did not even come on the market for a further two months. When we decided to make a bid for it, the transaction became dependent upon selling our previous house. Since this was semi-detached, had a semi-basement, nineteenth-century style, and three floors, plus two mezzanine floors, it was extremely difficult to sell. No building society would look at it for a mortgage! However, it so 'happened' that a local smallholder had just sold his smallholding with the intention of moving into the town, and his wife fell in love with the house, because it provided just the necessary amount of space for the very differing interests of her two teenage sons. The cash which we were able to realise from the sale together with the proceeds of a small legacy just received exactly matched the price of the new home plus the costs of removal! This was obviously a planned move from 'the other side', and something that was intended. We have been idyllically happy here, and there is a very lovely atmosphere about the place.

Mrs Wheeler then went on to talk of the feeling she had of my association with a Scottish doctor in the spirit world. She told me that I had a tremendous power of healing and wondered whether I had ever wanted to be a doctor. When I replied that in fact I was a doctor, she went on to say that this gift combined with my professional skills and she was sure that my patients must find that. I told her that I wanted to be able to develop this power so as to be able to help those whom conventional medicine could not reach. She replied that development was unnecessary for I had been born with this gift, and that right from childhood I had had a tremendous compassion for all living things. I would find that through quiet and meditation I would grow more fully to understand and to exercise the skill. This, she said, might be in some sort of clinic or sanctuary. This came true a number of years later, when I became involved with cancer help, both individually to patients and through our own cancer help group, of which more anon.

She herself, she told me, had done healing for two or three years, but she had been unable to continue because she found that it depleted her. (This certainly happens when healers seek to heal of their own energy, instead of learning to sink their own egos and become just channels for the transmission of energies arising from without.) This would not happen to me, she said, because, in my training as a doctor, I would have learned detachment. This side of my work would increase, because time would be made for it, and I would be able to realise my dream of helping those beyond present human aid.

This sitting was given in 1968. It was not until I retired from

48

the NHS eleven years later that these predictions finally came to pass. She forecast involvement with a small healing circle. 'It seems a small group to me, maybe five or six, and very much in harmony, and chosen people of your own standing, and as though you are on the same plane. . . . It seems just for healing, as though healing would be sent out and the power developed there. But I didn't feel it was connected with a church, or here, for instance. It seemed more in somebody's house. But it was very, very nice. I liked it.' This took shape in 1975, when I took over the running of the cancer meditation/healing group started by Gilbert Anderson. This initially met in my own house, and subsequently in a specially-built sanctuary at Eric's house. My 'dream', which did not exist in consciousness in any form at this particular time, eventually took shape as the Association for New Approaches to Cancer, of which I speak at some length later in this book. She also made reference to journeys to the United States and Canada. These, too, did not materialise until 1980 and onwards.

I have often found, both in my own experience, and in that of others, that predictions from 'the other side' tend to be extremely vague in terms of material earth-time. I think that this is probably because, *at the time the information is received by the medium* she has slipped out of the space/time dimension of the material world, and is forced to attempt to insert what she has experienced into a totally different realm of experience. As will be seen later on, one of my communicators, when questioned about this, said: 'All time is now'. Lawrence LeShan, writing of the time-phenomenon as perceived by the medium, likens it to holding up a strip of cinematograph film, on which is recorded everything, and having to look at it one frame at a time. The sequential aspect of time and events is, he suggests, an illusion. (LeShan. *The Clairvoyant Reality*. Ch3, p36. Thorsons. 1980.)

As I have said, when looked at in the light of the seventeen years which have elapsed since it was given, this must be regarded as a highly evidential sitting. However, at this stage, I was looking for Vicky – and I certainly had not found her here. I went on searching, and I had a succession of sittings with a number of well-known mediums throughout the summer and autumn months. All of these were inconclusive, apart from a certain amount of third-party evidence, which was almost certainly telepathic in origin. Amongst the sensitives with whom I sat was Mrs Ivy Northage, and early in January 1969 I went back for a second sitting with her in the hopes of being able to talk with her famous guide Chang and to being able to record the sitting. As usual I was accompanied on this visit to 33 Belgrave Square by Eric, who had his own appointment arranged with Mrs D.

My sitting went well, and I had a long and most interesting conversation with Chang. For the first time I started to realise that there were different stages and levels on 'the other side' and that there was a profound difference between the psychic and the spiritual levels. This difference between the merely psychic and the spiritual is an aspect which the novice tends not to appreciate at first. To him/her everything to do with 'spirits' necessarily appears to be spiritual. But this is not so. **Spiritual awareness, it seemed, was like a ladder leading up towards the heavens. Psychic phenomena, such as table turning, ouija boards, automatic writing, even communication with the newly passed over, were merely 'the lower rungs of the ladder'.** Souls progressed after 'passing over', in just the same way as do souls on earth. (The level we are able to reach in communication is influenced very considerably by the level we ourselves have attained, as well as by the level of the sensitive and, to a certain extent, the nature of the environment in which he/she is working.) *It was necessary that we began to move away from the purely psychic level, important though this was as a starting point, and proceeded to climb the spiritual rungs.* I went downstairs, well pleased with my sitting – until I started to play the tape back to see what I had got. To my consternation, I found that I had made exactly the same error as had Eric on his first sitting with Mrs D and had got no more than a ghost signal on the tape.

Disconsolately I told Eric about this over the lunch table in the basement at No 33. Eric's sitting had been extremely successful and he was very pleased at what he had received. He also told me that he had booked a couple of cancelled places in a group sitting with Mrs D if I would care to join him. Of course I agreed eagerly, after having heard the previous tapes. I had not yet had the chance to meet Mrs D but it was obvious that she was a medium quite out of the common run. However, I was not expecting anything very much. I had taken part in several group sittings previously, and had not been impressed. The usual practice was for the half dozen sitters to sit in a row and for the medium to go along the row with 'messages' received. It seemed to me that it was easy for lines to get crossed, and difficult for much in the way of a power link to be built up among a heterogeneous group of people meeting for the very first time. I had not been impressed with the results that I had experienced, and I had no great hopes of there being anything for me. I went more out of curiosity than anything else, and was actually seriously beginning to consider abandoning the quest as not being 'for me'.

Eric and I prepared by going into the sitting independently, and by sitting apart as if we were complete strangers. I was seated in the very middle of the line, and Eric on the extreme left-hand end. Mrs D walked into the room. She was a tall, slightly gaunt woman in her middle fifties, with a strong Yorkshire accent. 'Have any of you ever sat with a trance medium before?' she enquired. With the exception of Eric and myself none of us had. (The term 'trance medium' is generally given to a medium who goes into a deep trance and becomes completely under the control of a discarnate. Often there is a marked change in the voice, and this is very frequently accompanied by a change in the facial appearance. The medium usually has no memory of what has been said.) 'Well, don't be surprised at anything that happens', she told us. 'The things they do with me . . .!' And with that she went out like a light, and into deep trance. She was at once directed by her controlling spirit, a child spirit who called herself Snowdrop. I had listened to Snowdrop before on one of Eric's tapes, so I knew the form, as they say. What I was not prepared for was that she should start off by addressing me. Usually in a group sitting, as I have said, the medium starts at one end of the line and works slowly down to the other giving an equal degree of attention to each sitter. On **this** ocasion a start was made in the middle. Moreover it was very plain that Snowdrop knew an awful lot about me. She was talking to me for about half the sitting – and extremely embarrassing I found it in front of a group of total strangers. At length she said: 'Please be very still and relaxed. We are going to try an experiment. Never know whether it will work, but we are going to try. Please try to be very still.' As she finished saying this, the medium's face

51

began to change. Her eyes and her cheeks altered; her mouth took on a completely different shape. Before our very eyes her face was changing from that of a middle-aged woman into that of a small child! She took on an expression, which even then, before she opened her mouth, I could recognise as being that of my daughter. She came half forward out of her chair and put her mouth up, like a child coming forward to be kissed, and Eric whispered 'take her hands'. (This is sometimes done in developing circles in order to try and increase the level of power available, but it is most unusual, not to say dangerous to the medium, to touch a medium in trance.) Nonetheless, I did. Then, very slowly and hesitantly – obviously with the greatest of effort – Vicky spoke. 'Daddy', she said, 'I do love you.' 'Vicky', I said 'Is this your medium?' 'Yes', she replied. At that point the power ran out, and she faded away. But – she had got through. That was the all-important thing, and I knew that from then onwards this was the medium whom she and her friends would use. The medium then passed to the woman immediately on my left, and, just as it were to underline the genuineness of the whole affair, commenced to hold a conversation with her in rapid and fluent Italian! I knew just enough Italian to be able to appreciate this, though she was talking far too rapidly for me to be able to follow what was said. I was perfectly certain, however, that Mrs D, whatever else she was able to do, did not speak Italian. And so it proved, because later on, when I had got to know her, I asked her!

This, in fact, was the breakthrough for which I had been searching. My experience of listening to tapes had convinced me that communication **could** be real and genuine, and **thanks to the existence of the Churches' Fellowship I felt that this was no longer forbidden territory and that I was free to continue my search.** I lost no time in making an appointment for a private sitting with Mrs D. This was for the 10th March 1969. It was now two and a half years since Vicky's passing, and I felt that the stage had been fully set, and that at last I should make the longed-for contact with my daughter.

CHAPTER FIVE

ERIC AND ROGER

As I have said, following the group sitting with Mrs D and the all too brief contact with Vicky, I had lost no time in making a private appointment for a private sitting at the earliest possible opportunity. This was to take place some three months later, in early March, when Eric and I planned to go up together to Belgrave Square. The morning period was to be devoted to Eric, and I was to have my sitting during the afternoon. In the interval, however, Eric had had a further private sitting with Mrs D which is not without relevance to the story of my search, in that it still further confirmed for me that this was not the work of chance, but that there was planning and design behind the whole series of events.

This sitting took place on 20th January 1969, and on this occasion the main communicator was Snowdrop. She started off by talking about someone who was anxious to communicate with Eric but had been unable to do so because of excitement. She explained that excitement at 'getting through' on the part of the person in the spirit world was a very natural thing, but that they were defeating their own ends by getting over-excited. She said that the person about whom she was talking was Eric's son, Roger. They thought it would have been nice if he could have been the first person to speak, but that when people got too excited it was necessary to control things. She confirmed that it was she who had brought Vicky to make contact with me previously, and she said that Vicky had met Roger, and that she had been trying to say that he was there as well, but had been too excited to do so. She spoke of how happy Vicky had been, not just at getting through, but because she knew about the plan and wanted to encourage me in the part that I had to play. Sometimes it was very difficult to play a spiritual role when you had to walk blindly.

Discarnate souls are desperately anxious to communicate and to let their loved ones know that they are all right, that they are still alive, albeit in another dimension, and so they look around to try and find a channel that they can use. Unfortunately there are very few channels which they can use in this way that are open to them. Communication is not an easy thing. It is a skill that has to be learned, and it requires training and practice. Probably it is just as hard for the discarnate to acquire as is the capacity for mediumship amongst incarnate souls. But we need to know 'the facts of life' if we are to have a proper perspective on life. In this the Churches' Fellowship for Psychical and Spiritual Studies, whose motto is '**To Faith Add Knowledge**' has a major role to play in these materialistic times, for the love of our loved ones transcends the barrier of the veil between us and them.

'You see', Snowdrop went on, 'the thing is that everything is planned. It is just that you people are not quite so much aware of the plan. You know people are drawn together for a reason, and certain similarities of experience in physical life – people from different sources of life, different environments, and yet (having) the kind of similarity in experience they have passed through, loss, or something like that; in your case your son, and in his case his daughter. You see what I mean? In each case there had been a deep sense of loss. Also the girlie, she had an incurable thing, as you know. Naturally, he being what he is . . . he would have thought that there is a lack of knowledge to help people who have incurable sicknesses.'
Eric: Quite.
Snowdrop: So therefore you can quite understand that we do use these people. We don't mean this unkindly, but we think this is important.
Eric: I think they are glad to be used to help other people.
Snowdrop: But I do believe that many people, until they are faced with something that has really shattered them, don't begin to think about these things. I think the thing is that it is not reality to them.
Eric: Yes. One needs that experience.
Snowdrop: We think it is important to have experience, although at the time it seems so very shocking that one had to pass through these things. But it is this that quickens one from the dead, as it were, to begin the search for knowledge and

understanding of things. And behind it all is the long-term plan, which you have not been conscious of. In your case it is this: that what has to be done, will be done; and it is part of what you and the gentleman are both linked in.

Throughout this conversation Snowdrop appeared in a somewhat different guise to that in which which we had previously met her. Her voice was no longer the voice of a child – the shrill treble of a little girl – but deeper and more rounded, similar in timbre to that of Tania, but without the obvious middle European accent, and she was careful later to explain that although she frequently did appear as a child (she was seven years old when she died), she was now appearing as her adult self, the teacher of spiritual matters which both of us had to know. The idea that the early deaths of both Roger and Vicky had a profound reason behind them, even if we only faintly understood that reason at the moment, and that there was a plan which lay behind all things, was profoundly comforting. We began to see that our children had not died in vain or by accident. Certainly we were already proving the truth of Snowdrop's assertion that it was through our sense of loss that we had been brought to commence the search for knowledge. We were to hear more of this in the weeks and months to come, as we were brought to a deeper understanding of the plan. Gradually the knowledge that there was such a plan became as balm to our aching hearts. Our feelings have been well expressed by the poet Stevenson at the conclusion of *The Celestial Surgeon*:

'Or, Lord, if too obdurate I,
Choose thou, before that spirit die,
A piercing pain, a killing sin,
And to my dead heart run them in!'

We had certainly experienced that killing pain in full measure.

Snowdrop continued: . . . I am quite conscious of the plans that are unfolding. So being part of all these things, which I am too, I know that it must reach its fulfilment. It is very widely spread, although one is only a part of it. . . . If you want to ask any questions, you must never be afraid to ask them.

Eric: Well, I think I have only got one; you have covered some. But one thing that rather troubles me: I can do writing, and I have found deception in writing. (By 'deception' Eric was thinking of deliberate deception by mischevous discarnates.)

Snowdrop: You see the trouble is with these kind of things – here again it is not just deception – sometimes it is the mind. Your mind is creative; it is fertile; it produces; and therefore it can interfere. Of course there are occasions when it is deception, as you say, but there are times too when your fertile mind creates things, and then they become manifest (i.e. in the writing), and it is very disturbing to you. I would leave this alone for a little while. I think it is important to wait until you can become absolutely subject to the spirit, so that you are not controlled by anything of your own make-up. You understand what I mean?

Eric: Yes.

Snowdrop: Definitely it is important to come in subjection. Then there can be no mistake about that which comes from the discarnate and that which is incarnate. You see many people don't realise that they are creative. Or they might know that they are creative, and yet they might not understand to the fullest extent what being creative is all about. One can manifest from the incarnate that creative force just as much as one can when one is discarnate, if I make myself clear to you. Through the medium of writing you seek for knowledge, for information. But, being creative, you can produce evidence which comes from your own mind . . . The same thing applies to the utilising of the table etc. Very often the table can be moved, but not of necessity is it done by (the) discarnate. It can be produced from the incarnate. Do I make myself clear? Being creative, one has a power. Jesus said, 'Know thyself.'

Comment: To the best of my knowledge there is no record of Jesus having used these words to be found in the gospels, though he may well have done so when talking with his disciples. The remark as quoted here is commonly attributed to Socrates, and was to be found inscribed above the entrance to the schools of learning of ancient Greece. This could well be an example of the mind of the medium introducing something into the communication – in fact the very creativity of the incarnate of which she is speaking!

Snowdrop continuing: It is a very difficult thing to know yourself. But, if you seek to understand this, *you must realise that if you have power when you are discarnate, you must have it when you are incarnate. You don't suddenly acquire it when you pass out of the body.* You have always had it, and it can manifest, and it can produce phenomena.... It is always important, I think, to come in subjection to the discarnate. That way you can be sure that what you get is right. When I am talking to you, I am spirit, I am discarnate, and what I do is (to) subject the incarnate of the medium to my personality, which is not easy to do, but can, as you know, be done.... Of course, it is always wise to be balanced in these matters. It is a good thing, if you are in doubt, to ask. In that way you get the truth – well at least you do from us anyway! That way you cannot be misguided by something that may be a subconscious desire within yourself, or something. One naturally has ambition – I use the word because I do not know what other word to use. One has an ambition, and one produces evidence to support the ambition one has within oneself. In other words, you are fooling yourself because of the desire that you have.

Snowdrop's words need to be understood by all who are attempting to develop a quality of mediumship, as well as by all who may be tempted to 'dabble' out of a sense of curiosity. Not only is it easy to make contact with discarnates whose chief desire is self-gratification, but it is fatally easy to introduce elements of one's own personality into what comes through, and thus discredit not only that particular 'message' but the whole subject of communication. As readers will doubtless be aware, the classical 'explanation' for phenomena such as we are dealing with here is that we are communicating with secondary personalities, subsidiary to, but still a part of the personality of the medium. Snowdrop went on to reassure Eric that he had no need to worry about having become involved with any undesirable discarnate.

Snowdrop: Don't make too much of a worry over the writing. Don't worry about that at all. It is just a thing that has happened. There is no need to worry about it; it is perfectly in order. Certainly there is no unevolved soul attached to you, or anything like that. If there were, I should know immediately, and not only that; we have, as you know – mediums have doorkeepers, and had there been anything attached to you of that nature, then he would have come instead of me, and he would have dealt with the situation, which is not my work.

Snowdrop went on to talk about another of the discarnates involved in this great plan, who is known as Paul.

Snowdrop: You know of Paul, of course?

Eric: Well, I am not quite clear. Would you clarify?

Snowdrop: Paul is one of the higher evolved souls. He is one of the masterpowers, if you like, and he is one of what we call 'the breakthrough from the other side'. The proof of survival has been established to many people. This is an established fact in the minds of many people. But to some minds, unless they can touch, unless they can entirely eliminate anything which could possibly be attributed to a physical source, they will not accept this. Therefore it is the aim of the master-powers to eliminate this, and to bring to the minds of these people indisputable proof, not just of survival, but of the importance of the power which is around and can be used, if they will only use it. . . . It is important for humanity as a whole to accept this fact of there being a part outside of human agency; call it 'God', call it what you like according to how you think about it. The registration of this has not come to fruition as it should have done simply because of scientific minds, which will not accept it. . . . After all, science in the world discovers nothing which has not already been there all the time. They don't discover it themselves. It is merely uncovered when it is time to be uncovered. So no one can ever lay claim to that privilege of being the one to discover something, and take it upon themselves that they are all important in this. They are merely the one that has had the material that could further the plan through seeing this.

She went on from here to speak of physical mediumship as manifested in the past through the direct voice (i.e. speaking trumpet etc) and materialisation. This, she said, was now a phase of the past. Science in the world of spirit was advancing just as it is in the material world. Even these examples of physical mediumship had often been attributed to being a part of the medium. The all important thing was to eliminate entirely the possibility of the phenomena being attributed to the medium. It was not a matter of sensationalism, but of becoming aware that there was such a thing as spiritual power.

Snowdrop: This is of vital importance. It is not just for sensation. We are not seeking for any sensational thing or anything like that. But you must admit that if it is possible (and it is possible, given the right links) that not only can people become aware of the survival of many minds that they thought belonged to the past, but also eventually to bring through knowledge of disease, the answer to the disease, the way to combat the disease or the way to cure the disease, (then) all these things which you see are of vital importance. This is why your friend is so much a part of it. . . . We have the organisation in spirit. **What we need is to organise the people on the earth.** Paul speaks of the members of the body, and he says, 'If I am not then the hand, am I not then of the body?' **What he is saying is that if you are the hand, then you function according to the hand, which is part of the body, as being important in that particular function. So whatever you have, you will utilise that which you have. You must never try to be another part. It will never work.** So if all the members of the body work in perfect coordination, one with another, then the whole machinery will work in perfect harmony, and we can go ahead.

We all have our particular role to play, whether incarnate or discarnate, and we must be content to play that role and not seek for another. St Paul's eloquent words in 1 Corinthians xii are well known to Christians, but interestingly Mrs D was a Spiritualist and claimed to have no knowledge of the Bible. But these words of Snowdrop's come straight from St Paul, as can be seen from the following quotation, and to me they constitute powerful evidence that her 'Paul' was indeed whom he claimed to be.

> *'The body is not one member, but many.*
>
> *If the foot shall say "Because I am not the hand, I am not the body", is it therefore not of the body?*
>
> *And if the ear shall say "Because I am not the eye, I am not the body", is it therefore not of the body?*
>
> *If the whole body were an eye, where were the hearing? If the whole were hearing, where were the smelling?*

But hath not God set the members every one of them
in the body, as it hath pleased him,
And if they were all one member, where were the
body?
But now are there many members, yet but one body,
And the eye cannot say unto the hand, "I have no
need of thee": nor again the head to the feet "I have no
need of you."

1 Corinthians xii, vv 14–21.

Naturally, she went on, you will realise how difficult it is to
get every part of the body working in coordination. But this
has been going on for many, many years according to earth
time, and you will see how vitally important it is. It is NOT that
we want people to be aware of us. That doesn't matter. It is
that more knowledge can be passed through. After all, there
are so many limitations in material life which can be overcome. Given the cooperation of the people here, then we can
help with this. . . . You see one overcomes barriers. One overcomes inhibitions. It can be done. We have proven it. I was
seven when I passed to the spirit. I came from the day and age
of slaves, but I have overcome it. It doesn't matter. It has been
an experience that we have had to have. We have to accept
that and understand its value.

I think one attaches a great deal of importance, perhaps
naturally, to certain events in one's life and in one's experience. We perfectly understand these things. We know the
great sorrows . . . attached to people, but we still see that these
are pearls beyond price, once you understand them. (Without
them) you would never have accepted anything. If things go
right, and everything is going right, (if) there is nothing that
you want, nothing that you are really in need of, you think
you have everything, and that everything is all right. If then
you have everything, you never seek to understand yourself
or anyone else. . . . So one has to pass through certain experiences in order to quicken from the dead way of living in order
to become more alive and aware of things outside of oneself,
and within oneself too.

This passage contains two salient ideas. First the absolute
necessity of functioning within one's own sphere of activity, and

of not trying to appropriate to oneself the work of another. I often think of the importance of these words when I look out at the field of healing today, and see the jealousies and antagonisms that are apt to develop between exponents of different approaches, each of whom is inclined to say 'This is the way in which this condition should be treated. Any other is dangerous and harmful.' Each of us must function within our own permitted sphere and experience. The healer, the doctor, the acupuncturist, the homoeopath, the naturopath, the herbalist must all work together in harmony and cooperation, each, according to his own knowledge and training, making his contribution towards the whole, each laying upon the divine altar the gifts of his knowledge and unique experience. The relevance of this to us was that Eric was to accept his healing gift and use it, without worrying that he was not a doctor and had no medical knowledge, and that I, as the doctor, must learn to overcome the limitations of my training, and offer the gifts of my knowledge and expertise to help bring about true healing, even though my knowledge and experience of spiritual healing was non-existent at that time. I must be prepared to accept it as a fact when it occurred. She was also introducing us to the concept that given communication and spiritual power as facts, then it is possible that knowledge, previously unrecognised, about disease can be imparted from the spiritual world.

The second idea which Snowdrop is bringing forth, though new at that time to our way of thinking in relation to what we had each suffered, is an age-old truth; namely that suffering and pain, when properly understood, are opportunities for growth and spiritual progress. 'Out of my griefs Bethel I'll raise' sang the psalmist; or, as I was later taught to pray: 'I thank Thee, Father, for the blessings of my joys, but I thank Thee even more for the blessings of my sorrows, for out of them has come an illumination that has enriched my soul.' That we should ever come to see our bereavements as the greatest blessings in our lives seemed an extraordinary notion to us at this juncture, and one which rocked us back on our heels. Yet so it has proved, as the remainder of this book will show.

Snowdrop: Just a moment! I can see someone writing the letter R on you. It is someone's initial.
Eric: Yes.

Snowdrop: It is strange. Sometimes one is talking and they are also listening; they too are learning from us. This is wonderful, because you are learning together. It is important to feel this. He wasn't very old when he came over?
Eric: No.
Snowdrop: In fact he was a little bit disturbed. Many of them are, you know. But he is perfectly happy, and is looking forward to things so very much which can and must come. . . . Will you please excuse me for a moment? We wish to make an experiment, if you don't mind. . . . Be very patient, will you?

There was a brief silence at this point. Then gradually there came the sound of heavy breathing. We were later to become very familiar with this phenomenon of breathing, which we came to recognise as being characteristic of a first-time communicator endeavouring to gain control of the larynx of the medium. A childish voice calling 'Hallo!' – softly at first, as if a little uncertain – then more loudly, and with breathing becoming more and more rapid amid obvious and mounting excitement, the unseen spirit called 'Hallo Daddy! Roger! Roger!' 'Yes', replied Eric in tones of great satisfaction, 'This IS Roger! This is the way you used to get really excited, isn't it?'

They continued to talk, father and son, who had not spoken together for over eight years. Eric gave Roger his mother's love, and Roger told Eric he had heard her talking to him. He liked the flowers and the 'photograph'. This was a crayon drawing of Roger made by a psychic artist. Eric said that it was an excellent likeness of Roger shortly before his death. He had tried to come before, he said, when Vicky came, because he was with Vicky, and had been disappointed not to do so. But Snowdrop had explained to him that they had to take care of the medium, and that this was not possible. It was news to us that Roger had also been present at that memorable group sitting when Vicky had made her first, and to date only, appearance. (The reference to taking care of the medium must surely mean that inexpert and first-time communicators take more out of the medium in psychic terms.) Eric told Roger that he was recording his voice so that he would be able to speak to his mother. Roger said to his mother that she must not cry because he was all right and went on to speak of the number of flowers at his funeral. 'You didn't know I was there,' he said. 'You thought I was gone.'

Comment: The idea that the newly dead are actually – or can be – present but unseen at the funeral service was a novel one to us. We shall learn, as the story unfolds further, that our loved ones are much nearer to us than we realise, did we but know it, and very much aware of what goes on around us.

They spoke again of Vicky, and Roger said that he and Vicky were together in the spirit world. Vicky had been a sick little girl, but she was all right now. Eric asked if he knew what had been the matter, and Roger replied that she had had something wrong with her blood and that it had been incurable.

Comment: Eric, of course, was searching here for evidence. The passage is suggestive of evidence, since the fact that Vicky died of acute leukaemia was certainly not known to the medium at this stage. Equally certainly, however, it WAS known to Eric, and a sceptic would say that this was an example of the medium reading the mind of the sitter, although at a level below that of the conscious reason. We shall discuss possible ways in which mediums obtain information later in this book.

Eric and Roger then went on to speak of the great plans which had been made for his healing mission, and Roger said that he had been told that it had been necessary for him to die. This was in order that Eric would begin to understand and so that they could use him in this work. It was the same, he said with Vicky, because Eric and I were going to work together.

When I look at the content of this message today, with all the benefits of hindsight, I can see that already the element of design in our lives was beginning to take shape. At this time, however, I must, if I am to be honest, say that I could see very little of this. 'Now we see through a glass darkly' seems to express my attitude at this particular moment to what was happening. My feet were firmly planted on the ground and I still had a very long way to go before I was capable of appreciating the grand design. My own thoughts were concentrated upon my personal search for my daughter, whom I now knew was within reach, and I could see very little beyond this. I was, however, greatly encouraged to hear that Eric had actually succeeded in making contact with Roger, because it seemed that what he had succeeded in doing, she might well be able to repeat. I had already made an appointment with Mrs D and was greatly looking forward to this visit.

CHAPTER SIX

ERIC AND HIS FATHER

However, when the day for the visit drew near, it transpired that there were other forces at work besides my own wants and desires. The winter of 1969 had been hard and long, and the pressures on family doctors had been very heavy. Three days before our projected visit, Pat, our psychic dispenser/ receptionist announced that she felt so worn down by the winter rush of work that she was not coming in on the Monday and would have to take a few days off. So, feeling that I could not leave my long-suffering partner on his own on a Monday morning, I decided that I would have to forgo my cherished appointment. (When I look back on this period now, I am astonished that I even considered absenting myself on a Monday, receptionist or no receptionist. We certainly could not do such a thing in today's conditions. That it was possible, and that my partner never for one moment uttered a word of protest against this inconsiderate behaviour throughout all the time that I was visiting London for sittings, must, I think, have been due to the influence of the unseen in promoting this series of meetings.) It was too late to cancel the sitting, so Eric's wife, Cath, went in my place. The results of this switch were surprising.

Eric's morning sitting turned out to be very far from what he was expecting. He started off by discussing with Mrs D the two chief communicators with whom he had spoken so far, Tania and Snowdrop. Eric was wondering if these were different aspects of the same spirit, or whether they were actually two separate individuals. Their voices, certainly, were as different as their personalities; Tania, rich and tender, with just a hint of a foreign accent, and Snowdrop, high pitched, vivacious and quick-fire in speech, with quite a degree of a northern accent. 'No', said Mrs D, 'they are definitely two individuals. Tell me,' she went on, 'have you someone in spirit that had some kind of a seizure before they passed over?' 'Yes', replied Eric. 'Well I don't know whether it was a seizure – thrombosis – heart attack.' 'I could feel them near me,' Mrs D went on. 'I could feel this. I had to mention it, because they are apparently around here. I started to register them, you see; the condition. Some kind of heart trouble. Something like that.' At this point she went into a trance, and there was a prolonged pause, broken at last by the sound of heavy breathing.

Then faintly at first, and with obvious difficulty a voice came through. It was only a whisper at first, but gradually it became stronger and was able to identify itself as that of Eric's father. He was excited to make contact with his son and anxious to tell him that he was alive and well in the spiritual world. He enquired after Eric's health, and said that though he had been with Eric he had never imagined that they would be able to meet in this way. Eric, who took nothing for granted and was always looking for evidence, asked him whether he could give him some sort of recognition. Requests of this sort are always disconcerting to inexperienced communicators, and this was no exception. After a considerable pause, which was marked by prolonged and heavy breathing he seemed to collect himself. 'You've got the watch on,' he said, and Eric confirmed that his mother had passed it on to him, and said that he would tell her that his father had been and would give her his love.

Eric then enquired about his healing. His father replied that there was a wonderful plan in the spiritual realms, and spoke of how Eric was being linked with a doctor on the earth (myself) who was also a part of the plan. With my knowledge of medicine together with what was being imparted to Eric I would be able to understand what was being imparted. However, before this could happen, he said, I would first have to overcome the barriers of my own training, because that which was logic to me was not logic to spirit.

Eric's father went on to talk about the difficulties of communication, and how hard it is for spirits to get through. 'You know', he said, 'I didn't think I was going to make it; and when you started asking me questions, I sort of . . . I just couldn't think, you know . . . and then, all of sudden I just knew what you wanted.'

The conversation between father and son spoke next of the manner of the older man's death. He had had to come over so quickly into spirit life that it had been very difficult, as well as being a great shock to his wife. Often, he said, as she was looking at his photograph, he was standing beside her and tapping her on the shoulder and saying 'Don't you know I am here?', and she took no notice. 'I do everything to make her feel me' he said. 'We've been together, when she's been asleep, and I try to influence her mind so that she'll remember.' Eric reassured him that when he did this, she did, indeed, remember. He said how happy he was at having been able to get through, and that Eric was to tell her that he had not changed a bit. He was not going anywhere without her. He never had done, and he was not going anywhere now. He would remain in spirit waiting for her. He then went on to speak of his own father, and of the family feelings of love. But, he said, it was more important to get on with the work which they had to do. The experience was almost like being two people. 'You have your memories and your love of your family', but yet you had a 'wider love for those who do not belong to you personally.' Sometimes one dominated the other. (Tania laid great emphasis on the importance of this wider, universal love when she spoke to me later on.) Just before Eric's father took his leave Eric enquired whether anyone else whom he knew was going to come through. 'I am not permitted to say', came the reply. 'There are some things which we just do not divulge. I hope I know my place. If I did not, I would not be permitted to come!'

It is important for us here on earth to understand that there are some things which are kept hidden for the best of reasons. Our unseen friends are subject to the rule of law, just as we are, and can only work within the framework of that law. Had Eric's father revealed the identity of the next communicators and they had failed to get through, it could have endangered the whole harmonious working of the plan.

In the context of the whole series of communications, this was an important sitting, but to assess its value it is really necessary to have listened to the tapes to appreciate it. Firstly, the voice of this particular communicator was quite unmistakably a masculine voice. Although at the commencement he was having considerable difficulty in manipulating the medium's larynx, this very soon settled down. Plainly this was due at least in part of his own emotional excitement at being able to speak for the very

67

first time to one whom he loved. But, as we shall see later, this problem exists for most first time communicators. Heavy over-breathing in the case of an experienced deep trance medium such as Mrs D is almost always an indication of a first time communicator. Communication, it would seem, is both rare and difficult, and requires training and practice on the part of the communicator, the medium and the seeker.

A further point which came over very clearly in this sitting is the profound desire of the spirit to say to the loved ones: 'Hey! Look! I'm ALL RIGHT! I'm still alive!' Moreover, spirits try to get this information through in all sorts of ways, and become increasingly frustrated when we, being imprisoned for the most part within the cage of our senses, are unable to appreciate their presence and ignore them. Very often they do get through, giving us a sort of mental nudge, but all too frequently we only ignore this and label it is fantasy or wishful thinking. When I was in practice, it was by no means unusual to hear a bereaved person telling how they had 'seen' their 'dead' parent or loved one about the house in their customary places. Many doctors have had this experience. Most – and I was no exception, until the conclusion of this series of revelations – would explain this away as a 'compensatory hallucination'. *However, there is a profound difference between a hallucination and a true vision, or extrasensory experience.* To the hallucination there is a dreamlike quality. It swiftly fades, and it is difficult to recall it with any vividness or sense in detail in after years. The vision, however, is totally different. Like a colour transparency it retains in the mind all its vivid brightness and all its detail as crisp and clear as when it was first experienced. Our failure to appreciate the presence of the loved one causes deep distress, comparable only to our own distress of bereavement.

Another point brought out in this conversation is that the mere fact of passing through the veil into the world beyond does not immediately confer great knowledge or wisdom upon the passing spirit. They remain unchanged, with all their hang-ups, all their loves and all their hates. They are still essentially the same as they were during their earth life. That great soul, Frances Banks, who used to visit many of the prisoners in the condemned cell, used to say to the prisoners awaiting execution. 'The same a moment after as a moment before,' and it is reported to her that on at least one occasion a soul to whom she had given this advice returned after death to thank her for the help given, and to say that this was true. The only difference lies in the inability of the spirit passed over to manipulate a body. (*cf* Tania's remark in a preceding chapter, 'For me, I am discarnate. I borrow a body for a little while.')

Perhaps one of the most chilling aspects of life after death is contained within this fact. The discarnate spirit still retains all its earthly appetites and urges; greed, lust, sensuality, drunkenness, cruelty – if they were part of the earthly nature of the discarnate soul before its passing, they are still present. But the soul lacks a body with which they can be indulged. Still close to earth (or earthbound) and able to relate to conditions on earth, they frequent their former haunts, with fleshly appetites ever frustrated and unsatisfied. This is their private hell, which they have built for themselves. It is difficult to imagine anything more terrible – or more just and appropriate.

One is left to contemplate the question of whether it is possible for such spirits to impress an incarnate soul, perhaps weakened and made susceptible through indulgence in drugs or alcohol, through debilitating disease or deep depression or emotional disturbance, and thus seek a vicarious satisfaction of frustrated cravings through the temporary control of the body of another. If so, this could be the explanation for some of the unspeakable things that go on in the world today. It would certainly fit the story of the unexplained suicide of the daughter of a friend of mine, who with a young child, and everything to live for, committed suicide shortly after moving to a new house built on the site of a former suicide. It also gives point to the traditional warning. 'Don't dabble. If your motive for investigating is merely the satisfaction of curiosity, you may well have your curiosity satisfied. But, always remember, curiosity killed the cat! Your motives for investigation must be pure. That is your only protection against potential disaster. Dabbling can open the door to the earthbound and mischievous discarnate.' The last point that emerges from the discussion is that our friends on the other side **have work to do!** Life beyond the grave is no eternal bed of roses. Throughout my search this was constantly being made clear to me. This work is the most important thing of all for them.

Speaking personally about this sitting, the one outstanding

thing that stuck in my mind was a phrase used in connection with myself, 'overcome the barriers of his training'. I had never for a moment considered my professional training to be a barrier to the work that I would have to do. I thought that it was the fact that I had had a professional training which fitted me for this work. I was proud of my skills and expertise, my knowledge of material medicine. I now realise fully, especially when I approach my medical colleagues, endeavouring to find cooperation and understanding in true healing and in wholeness, that most of their minds are so cast in the orthodox mould, that their professional training does indeed constitute a barrier which only they themselves can remove.

At the end of this conversation with his father, Eric was hoping, if not actually expecting, that he would have a further talk with his son Roger. It would be difficult to say which of us two was the more surprised, he being present at the sitting, or I when listening to the recording which he brought back. First there came the voice of a child, high-pitched and treble, with just the faintest undertones of a local accent, the voice in fact which we associated with Roger. 'Hello, Daddy!' it said. 'Hello, Daddy!' Almost immediately this was followed by another voice, and it is noticeable that on this occasion there was no preliminary period of heavy overbreathing, a very 'pukka' English public-school type of voice, which said:

Daddy should have been here, and he isn't here!

Eric wonderingly: Daddy should have been here. Oh! Yes! Who's this then?

Same voice: Tell Daddy, will you? Will you tell Daddy?

Eric: Yes.

Same voice: Will you tell Daddy it doesn't matter?

Eric: Doesn't matter?

Same voice: Yes. Will you tell him?

Eric: Yes.

Same voice: You know who I am?

Eric: You're his little girl.

Vicky: Yes.

Eric: And what's your name?

Vicky, slightly indignantly: You know who I am. I don't have to tell you. I've been before. I came to my Daddy. My Daddy should have been here, and he hasn't come.

Eric: Never mind. He couldn't come.

Vicky: I know. But I wanted to come to you. I wanted to come . . .

Eric: You wanted to come to me?

Vicky: Yes.

Eric: Well, I'm pleased about that.

Vicky: . . . because Roger is here! And Roger and I came together.

Eric: That's right. You did.

Vicky: And I wanted to come to you because I knew that Daddy was busy, and that he couldn't come.

Comment: The ready acceptance of broken family engagements because 'Daddy is too busy to come' is part of the day-to-day routine of a doctor's family life. Such an experience had been commonplace for Vicky during her lifetime.

Eric: Well, he sends his love, and so does Mummy.

Vicky: Well, I send my love to Daddy and Mummy.

Eric: I shall play this back to them, so that they will hear that.

Vicky: Daddy will know that I would try to come if I could. And you must tell Daddy that we are very happy – will you tell Daddy? – We are very happy because he has had his . . . (here she took a deep breath, and seemed to hesitate for a moment before coming out triumphantly with an unfamiliar word) . . . evidence.

Comment: This plainly referred to her previous appearance at the group sitting, which was the first, and indeed only, piece of direct evidence that I had received.

Eric: Evidence? Yes. Yes.

Vicky: Will you? Because he had been so sad, and I wanted him to know I was alive. You will tell Daddy?

Eric: I will. But he knows that now.

Vicky: Yes. But he didn't before. He hoped it was true, but he had nothing to prove it was true.

Eric: Well, we were drawn together, so we helped each other.

Vicky: Roger and I had something to do with that.

Eric: You did?

Vicky: Can you hear me? Is my voice all right?

Eric: Yes. Very clear. . . . I was with your Mummy and Daddy, yesterday.

71

Vicky: Yes? And they are well?

Eric: They are well, yes.

Vicky: Will you tell Mummy something? Will you tell Mummy that I know about the flowers?

Eric: The flowers, yes.

Vicky: She should know what you mean. You will tell her?

Eric: I will. Yes.

Vicky: Oh! But I forgot. You've got it on that tape, haven't you? . . . Well, Mummy, if you can hear me, I know about the flowers. Thank you, Mummy. They helped me so much.

Eric: They did?

Vicky: Yes.

Eric: Well, she'll be pleased to hear this.

Vicky: I know. I love you very much, and I hope you will begin to understand more.

This passage about the flowers is extremely powerful evidence for the genuineness of this sitting, and one more example of the care taken by our friends, and especially by Vicky herself, to provide evidence which should eliminate such explanations as coincidence and telepathy. Ever since Vicky's death Ruth and I had 'adopted' a particular window on the south side of the chancel in our local church, and had made a point of decorating it with flowers both at the great church festivals and the anniversaries which were special to Vicky herself. The flowers were always regarded as a special gift for her. No one else, apart from my wife and myself was aware of this practice, nor of the significance of the flowers. Eric was not even a member of our church, and knew nothing of what we had been doing. So often evidence given at sittings, and purporting to come from the communicator, is explained away by the theory that the medium is reading the mind of the sitter. This could not possibly apply on this occasion, since there was no one present who knew this. It constitutes evidence as hard as any that I know.

Vicky: Were you very sad, like Mummy and Daddy, when Roger came over?

Eric: Yes, I was.

Vicky: But you are not quite so sad now?

Eric: No. Because we believe there was a purpose in it all.

Vicky: There is. God moves in a mysterious way his wonders to perform. And His people don't understand, do they?

Eric: No. They don't.

Vicky: They think that it is cruel and unnecessary. But it isn't so, because it is part of a wonderful plan. And we are so happy to be in spirit life, you know. And I – you know, Daddy is so funny.

Eric: Daddy is? Why?

Vicky: I hope you don't mind me saying this, Daddy, when you listen; but you know you thought 'I help sick people, and I can't help my own little girl.'

Eric: M'mm? This is what Daddy thought?

Vicky: This is what Daddy thought. He didn't understand then, but he does now.

Eric: And that makes you happy?

Vicky: You are not angry because I came instead of Roger?

Eric: No. I am pleased to see you as well as I should with Roger, or anybody; because I know that this will help Daddy and Mummy.

Vicky: We are part of a family, aren't we.

Eric: Yes we are, and therefore we must help each other.

Vicky: Yes. Do you know that flowers are not just something pretty and bright and that have a nice perfume? Did you know?

Eric: No. I didn't.

Vicky: Oh, they are something more than that.

Eric: And what is that?

Vicky: They give out an energy. . . . When people are loving and kind, and they give someone flowers – because – in kindness – Well the flower gives something out to the person that receives it; not just because they are beautiful, or because they smell nice, but because they give out something.

Eric: Yes I follow.

Comment: This concept of flowers as being a source of energy when given in love, was something which was totally new to both of us. It is, of course, the reason why we give or send flowers to the sick, or on special occasions. The flowers become charged with the energies of love, which they convey to the recipient. They can therefore play a significant role in the healing process.

Vicky: Do you believe in fairies?

Eric: Yes. I think I do now. At one time I wasn't sure but now I believe in a lot of things.

Vicky: I heard someone say 'They are little elementals'.

Eric: They are little . . . elementals?

Vicky: Yes. . . . You see, Daddy, I am learning. You see I was so limited while I was in the body. . . . But I am learning so much now. And . . . uh . . . there are fairies. Yes. Strange that people who are grown-ups don't believe, and children do believe. Do you know what Tania said? Tania said – it is strange to say this – 'but who are the ones who are adult, and who are the children?' You know? But she is very wise and she is . . . very, very beautiful.

Eric: Yes. I like talking to Tania. She has told me quite a lot.

Vicky: Your Daddy has been, hasn't he?

Eric: Yes.

Vicky: I know. Things are planned, you see, and no one on the earth can alter it, you know. Because it isn't like that, and you can't make bargains with God; not ever . . . Aren't I having a long conversation? Do you think that Daddy will be disappointed?

Eric: I should say that to get this conversation on the tape he will be thrilled.

Vicky: Oh. Well, I knew he wouldn't be here really, but I thought – I knew you would . . . and would not mind if I came.

Eric: I don't mind in the least, Vicky.

Vicky: Was I an awful nuisance when I came before?

Eric: I wouldn't have thought you were a nuisance. You were quiet, but you did very well.

Vicky: Daddy was very surprised.

Eric: He was surprised, yes, but very, very pleased.

Vicky: Do you know. I thought 'I bet he wouldn't know I am here? And won't he be surprised? Because this would be the evidence he has wanted.'

Eric: I have got Roger's voice on tape, and now I have got yours.

Vicky: Yes. And did Roger do very well, too?

Eric: You have both done very well.

Vicky: Sometimes we stand and watch each other, and we are willing each other to do well.

Eric: Well, I would say you have willed very well, because you have both done very well.

Vicky: And your Daddy, too. . . . You mustn't leave him out, because he was so anxious to come and give you the proof that you wanted.

Eric: Yes. I am glad of this.

*　　　*　　　*

Vicky: . . . Tell Mummy that I love her just as much as Daddy, but that Daddy has got something which will help her so much. I hope you don't mind Mummy. I don't mean it to be unkind. Goodbye.

Eric: 'Bye.

Vicky: Mummy! Mummy. When you listen, I have tried so hard. Please . . . Vicky sends you a big kiss, and . . . (her voice was becoming perceptibly weaker and she spoke more slowly and with evidently a tremendous effort) . . . I will try to do something so that you can hear me in the room . . . and . . . I will try to bring you flowers as you gave them to me, I will try to give them to you.

*　　　*　　　*

Tania: Quala sotonino nahania; sotonino nahanya. Quala sotonino nahanya. Is a very good day to you.

Comment: This strange greeting was constantly spoken by Tania throughout the series of sittings at the commencement of each sitting. No one who has heard it has been able to tell me the language which she is using. Tania went on to have a conversation with Eric. She said that it had been 'an afternoon for the loved ones' and asked if he had been impressed by his father. She emphasised the difficulties of communication and commented on how well they had all done. She then gave Eric a special message of love and thanks for me, saying that everything was all right and under control. It was the most wonderful thing for them, she said, to help with the loved ones and to bring this reunion about, although this was sometimes extremely difficult. Then she said her farewells. They would speak again, she promised.

The whole of this sitting is remarkable for a number of things, and constitutes the most perfect and hard piece of evidence that I have ever come across. It must be remembered that the explanation most frequently advanced for communication is that the evidence given is drawn from the mind of the sitter through the telepathic powers of the medium. In this case, such a facile explanation seems to be an impossibility. To begin with, my only previous contact with Mrs D had been at the group sitting held over two months previously, and at this Eric and I had taken care to dissociate ourselves from one another. Nor is it the practice at the SAGB for the medium to know in advance who the sitter is going to be. Eric's knowledge of Vicky was minimal. He had only met her once, two or three weeks before she died, when he sold her a pair of shoes. At that time he certainly did not know who she was, or associate her with me. Nor was she particularly in his mind on this occasion. On his previous visit he had at last made contact with his son, Roger, and if he was thinking about anything, it was about whether he would make this contact again, and about the further development of his healing mission. This was the perfect and classical 'proxy' sitting, long recognised by psychic researchers as being the most powerful form of evidence available. It underlines the care taken all through the series to provide firm evidence, and powerfully suggests the existence of a planning mind behind the sequence of events.

Some considerable time later we had confirmation both from Snowdrop and from Tania that this particular way of presenting herself in a proxy sitting had been Vicky's very own idea, because she wanted the evidence to be perfect. Right at the very end Tania referred to Vicky as 'a poppet'. This in fact was my own particular and very private pet name for her. It was quite unknown to Eric.

Another important point was made to Eric by Tania. The initiative for all this sort of thing remains firmly in the hands of 'the other side'. 'We are the ones who will make the arrangements', he is told. 'We stretch out our hands to you. All we ask is that you will take our hands.' It is no good running madly around looking for communication, for 'without a communicator there can be no communication' as Mrs D used to say. Intuitively we receive guidance when to talk to our friends. For the most part they are only too anxious to come and talk to us, and to reassure us of their continuing existence, their love and their wellbeing. In this we at first need help through a third party, but if we discipline ourselves and learn to still the restless probing mind, we shall eventually be able to dispense with such help.

Vicky talks about the energies of flowers – something quite unknown to us at that time – but which is gradually being confirmed by modern research into the energy fields of matter and living organisms. She also makes the point that all things are planned, and that these plans cannot be overthrown by people on earth. The plan may not be the way that Man would choose – indeed, it probably will not be – for God's ways are different from the ways of Man. 'God moves in a mysterious way His wonders to perform' she later quoted from one of her favourite hymns. We have to learn to accept those ways, even if they seem harsh and cruel by our human standards. Of this and its implications for our lives we shall have more to say further on.

After lunch, in the sitting which should have been mine, Cath, Eric's wife, took my place. This was the first time that she had sat with a medium, and she was plainly a little apprehensive to begin with. The whole of this sitting was remarkable and strongly evidential. The first speaker to come in was the medium's control, Snowdrop, who appeared on this occasion as a child with a lively and vivacious manner, just as she had appeared to me on that memorable group sitting. As with Tania, she became a frequent visitor to our sittings and we got to know her very well.

Snowdrop commenced by introducing herself and making certain that she was coming over strongly and that her voice was loud enough for Cath to hear. She said that sometimes it was a little difficult for them to judge the volume. She commented that Cath seemed to be going through a period of uncertainty, and told her that it was important for her to become very still in herself and to ignore her fears, for they were groundless.

Comment: This is important. Fear is no good when seeking contact with the discarnate. It gets in the way and clogs the channel just as effectively as does unbelief.

Snowdrop seemed to be putting Cath at her ease saying that

'people don't realise how natural spirit really is', and they agreed that many people were frightened by it and behaved as if it didn't exist. Such behaviour was pointless, because this was something which everybody had to face sometime. It created great problems, Snowdrop said, if when people died and went into the spirit world they were too dogmatic about the whole thing. It made things very difficult for them.

She then told Cath that she felt she had had a lot of sadness in her life, which she had bottled up and kept to herself. This gave her the outward appearance of being hard and unfeeling, which was not the real case. Cath agreed that she found it difficult to express herself in such matters.

Snowdrop then said that the purpose of their conversation was to introduce to Cath a gentleman in the spirit world who had been close to her, but who found communication difficult despite much encouragement. He was trying to project his thoughts, but though he seemed sure of Cath he was not at all sure about Snowdrop. He kept coming forward a little and then withdrawing, and, said Snowdrop, 'we have to be so gentle'. This man, she said, belong to Cath and his transition into the spirit world had been sudden and in a state of shock. He kept on mentioning a car which had something to do with his last moments on earth. 'And' said Snowdrop, 'we have got to get him out of it'. There was a prolonged pause, followed by the now familiar sound of heavy breathing and then:

New voice, in heavy whisper: Crash! Crash!. (Breathing recommences, becoming heavier with every other breath, and working up to a crescendo . . .)

Voice Oooh! Oooh! (intermingled with heavy breathing, becoming more rapid and more excited . . .) Oooh! Oooh! . . . Ooh! . . . Ooh! . . . Hallo! Hallo! Oh! Oh!

Cath, in gentle soothing voice: Hallo! Who is that?

Voice again, in obvious distress: Oh, Oh, Oh, Oh! . . . The car! The car! The car! . . . Oh, Oh, Oh! (Prolonged sobs.)

Cath gently: It's all over now. It is finished.

Sobbing continues, while Cath is speaking: It is finished. It is finished, you are all right now.

Sobbing begins to subside, while Cath continues: It is all right now! Do you love Dad? It is all right now. Can you tell me who you are? . . . Mmm? . . . Who? . . . It is all right now. Don't cry

any more. It is all finished. Brenda's(?) all right. (?)'s all right.
. . . Can you talk to me? Can you tell me your name?

No other reply other than a series of groans and sobs, gradually becoming quieter and less distressed. Spirit finally withdraws with a deep sigh.

Mrs D: Sorry dear.

Cath: It's all right.

Mrs D: I don't feel it was very successful. There's disappointment here (sighs deeply, as if they hadn't been successful in some way). Can you understand?

The heavy overbreathing of the second communicator was characteristic of a spirit attempting to communicate for the very first time, and grapple with the problems of producing sound vibrations through the larynx of the medium. The fact that so many spirits ask about the volume of sound which they have achieved, makes me think that this attempt at physical speech by a non-physical entity must be in some way rather like attempting to speak in a vacuum, in which there is no air to carry the sound vibrations. In this case, and those of my readers who have heard the lecture/talk, which I give on this subject, will know what I mean, the sound was considerably exaggerated by the fact that the medium was wearing a neck microphone, which picks up breath sounds very easily.

There can be little doubt, I think, that Cath was hoping for, and in a way expecting, to talk to Roger. After all, Roger had made the great breakthrough on the occasion of Eric's last visit, and he had said then how greatly he was looking forward to meeting his mother again. Moreover, Roger had not spoken during the morning sitting, so it was to be expected that he would come during the afternoon. Instead, Snowdrop brought with her Cath's brother, who had died some ten years previously in a motor accident. Shortly before his death he had greatly distressed his whole family by declaring quite categorically that he had no belief in God, that there was no survival of the spirit, and that death was the end of everything. It was plainly to this that Snowdrop was referring when she spoke of some people being very dogmatic, and consequently being unable to recognise what had happened to them when they suddenly found themselves across 'on the other side'. After all, a moment's reflection will convince the reader that if a person is firmly of the belief that consciousness resides in the body, and that death of the body is like snuffing out a candle, then they **cannot** accept that they are dead, because self-consciousness still exists. *'Cogito. Ergo sum.'* said Descartes ('I think. Therefore I am.') They can still think, therefore they still **are**. They cannot be 'dead'. Add to this the fact that, initially at least, the consciousness still seems to be clothed in a facsimile of the body which it has just left, but a body which is composed of a diaphanous, weightless material substance, though a substance which is fully real to the owner, and one can readily appreciate that the stage is set for confusion. How confused, one saw from the efforts of Eric's father in his attempts to attract the notice of his wife. ('She looks at my photograph, you know, and I've stood there, and I'm tapping her on the shoulder and saying, "Don't you know I am here?" and she doesn't hear.')

This particular spirit is further described as still living in the circumstances in which he died. He is still caught up in the motor crash, and in all the distress which succeeded that incident. From this he had to be rescued. In common with most earthbound souls – and this death had taken place over ten years previously – he was still very close to the earth vibratory rate, and thus it was necessary, if rescue was to take place, for him to be able to communicate with someone whom he could recognise as being alive on earth at the present time. Only in this way could he be brought to recognise the fact of his own passing into another dimension of being, and thus be released from his entanglement.

Finally, it must never be forgotten that this sitting had been arranged for **me**, and that I had been quite suddenly prevented from attending. Thus it would seem that we have here clear evidence of the power and ability of the spiritual world to manipulate and control events on earth to serve a greater and a wider purpose – in this case the rescue of an earthbound spirit. *It also underlines most powerfully the supreme importance of the realisation 'by souls on earth' of the facts of spiritual life.* I consider that these two sittings, taken together, are of the very highest evidential value. In each case the communicators were totally unexpected by the sitter. The final result, however, was that everyone, including my absent and hitherto disappointed self, was given clear evidence of the reality and the power of the spiritual world. It was not until 12th May, over six weeks later, that I was finally able to have my own first sitting with Mrs D.

The whole of the story of the earthbound soul, trapped in the circumstances of his death, because he never understood properly that consciousness was not dependent upon physical functioning, underlines very powerfully how necessary it is for everyone to understand what I call here 'the facts of spiritual life'. (The chilling possibility exists that some of the horrors of the present day may arise from earthbound souls who do not realise the essential fact that though they still exist they no longer have a physical body, and so fail to accept the reality of their own death. The victims of violence, too, may still be trapped within the circumstances in which they died.) To understand Cath's role in this it is necessary to realise that in some ways it seems to be required, if a rescue of such a soul is to take place, that contact be made with an *incarnate* soul before the discarnate can sense the reality of its own discarnate world. Such 'rescue' work is not to be lightly undertaken by souls on earth, and requires a very high degree of spirituality on the part of those who attempt it. It is easy to see that if preconceptions of death mean that a person believes that conscious perception can only take place by means of a functioning physical body, then the stage is set for confusion when the soul finds itself discarnate and still conscious of its individuality and its surroundings. The reader is referred to the rescue work undertaken during the war by Air Chief Marshal Lord Dowding described in *God's Magic* (p. SAGB). It is still worth remembering that the Churches' Fellowship for Psychical and Spiritual Studies owes its inception to the meeting between its founder, Colonel Reg Lester, and Lord Dowding after the death of Colonel Lester's first wife.

CHAPTER SEVEN

VICKY RETURNS

The happenings related in the previous chapter took place on 10th March 1969. It was not as I said until two months later that I was finally able to get up to London for my own sitting with Mrs D. I had been well prepared for this through listening to the previous tapes, but I was still slightly apprehensive about how things might turn out. After all, apart from the group sitting five months earlier, at which I had been one of six sitters and had had the moral support of Eric, by then a seasoned sitter, this was to be the first time that I had made a contact of this nature with a discarnate personality. Moreover it was so intensely important for me, the summit, as it seemed then, of two and a half years of searching. It is perhaps not surprising that I started off with what might have been a disastrous blunder.

Mrs D went quickly into trance, and the now familiar voice of Tania started to speak to me. She had been talking for some ten minutes, when all of a sudden the tape recorder started to make an odd squeaking sound! It was a good reel-to-reel Uher machine, of a type used by BBC professionals, and I was completely familiar with its workings. Never before had I heard it make a noise like that when I was recording. I looked hastily down at it and saw to my horror that on this of all occasions I had threaded the tape incorrectly; that the tape was stationary, and that consequently nothing was being recorded. Hastily, and with fumbling fingers, I started to rethread the machine, panic-stricken lest the sitting should suddenly abort and I should be left with nothing. On my ears fell, like distant music, the calm and reassuring voice of my communicator. '**Do not panic,' she said, 'I can hold. If you panic, that is when the connection is cut. Do not panic. I can hold.**' As if by a miracle the tape slotted into place at last, and the recording commenced.

Tania's words bear repetition. 'The surest way to cut us off is for you to panic'. **Fear is the great enemy** – a further reminder that the thoughts and emotions of the sitter have a most important influence upon the results obtained in any sitting with a sensitive. In any paranormal experiment the attitude and expectation of the experimenter become a crucial part of the conditions of the experiment. This has become recognised as the 'observer factor'. It exercises a crucial influence upon the results obtained, and is probably one of the main reasons why sceptics tend to obtain negative results from experiments in parapsychology. (It is also well recognised that schoolchildren tend to perform in accordance with the expectations of the teacher.)

Tania: It's all right. What I was afraid of was your panic. **You know the surest way to cut us off is for you to panic. So don't ever panic.** I can hold as long as you do not panic. So I was trying to keep you from panicking.

Self: You did.

Tania: All right? Ee–eeh, it is as good a proof, anyway, eh? Eeh – I think – ee–eh, in a little while we will be able to reveal things to you; things which it is necessary for you to understand, so that you may be able to do a little more to help.

Self: That is my wish.

Tania: One can administer to the needs of other people, but unless one passes through an experience one cannot have the understanding heart. One can, perhaps, with what talent one has, alleviate a little the sufferings of other people, but unless one has experience, one cannot fully comprehend just what it feels like. You do not know my medium personally, I believe?

Self: No. Once before we sat in a group . . .

Tania, interrupting: Yes, I know. I know all about that. You heard Snowdrop speak. We were very happy for you at that time. But you do not know my medium personally? Well, I tell you something. **We have passed her through various experiences in order that she can have this deep compassion for other people; so that, in having this compassion through experience, she gives with great love of her life, so that people's loved ones who come – the key of course is love.** It takes great understanding to be able to give yourself completely, unreservedly, without fear for self . . . If you would ask what makes this tick? How can it happen? It can only happen through love. You see all things that come with great joy to people, perhaps to lift them out of depression or make them feel that indeed life is not finished, can only come through the service of those who have great love; **(love) which is universal love; not just your united family love, you know.** Personal families naturally love one another – on the whole! – but to have the wider, universal love is a different thing. Is very difficult to love universal family. So, you see, many of us in spirit have come, who have never been known to the mediums. Yet it is through love, loving someone who is a stranger, and desiring to help, and it is only through this that it is possible.

Comment: As I write these words, the words of the Master, Jesus, come into my mind: 'I was naked, and ye clothed me; sick and in prison, and ye visited me.' Surely and indeed this love for a stranger, loving the stranger only because of his/her need at the moment, this wider love of which Tania speaks, is the epitome of what the Master is saying here. **It applies equally, perhaps with even greater force in the field of healing. Universal love is the key which unlocks the Kingdom of Heaven, which, we are told, lies within.** I am reminded at this moment of the story of the Good Samaritan. We have to learn to love the stranger for no better reason than that he is there and in need. It is love – loving and being loved – which is the greatest need, and lack of love which is the cancer which affects the modern world. One learns this lesson through one's own experiences in life, many of which are painful.

You know, *Tania continued*, I think many people, they exist; they do not live. When you speak of heaven, they think, perhaps, of going up into some sky, some heaven above. What they don't realise is that you can touch heaven here and now. Heaven is inside you, *I replied* and you can find it.
Tania: Yes, that's right, and you can find it; you can find that kingdom, particularly if you come together in love. You know when we feel, 'Oh this is good. We haven't seen each other for so long and we are so happy.' You know? And this is wonderful.

I tell you something, *she went on.* A long time ago, many, many years ago now, when I was on earth, I too had a mission on the earth. I had what you (would) call in this day a talent – a gift, a gift to heal, to help people who are sick. I had no

84

knowledge of medicine or anything like that, but only this gift, which was the creative power – you know? – and, well, my people they gave me the name of saint. You see? Men call people saints. It means nothing very much really. But, you see, I too knew what it was to have people who would crucify. So it is through all these experiences that we have an understanding of one another.

Comment: We had no knowledge of who Tania might have been in her earthly life. We had a shrewd suspicion that Tania was not her real name, but that it was, as it were, an alias, a spirit name, chosen to conceal her true identity, lest the knowledge of that identity should get in the way, and distract us from the teaching which she was imparting. Considerably later, as we shall see, Vicky told us her real name, which led me to identify her with a particular saint, whose present-day shrine is certainly a place of pilgrimage for healing. We shall come back to this in a later chapter.

Tania: For a long time there has been a plan in the realms of spiritual consciousness that those who are passing through the valley of shadows would come to us, and they would, in coming, lend themselves to us. And you are one of these. So you see it is a great joy to me.
Self: Yes. Yes.
Tania: As many people would say, 'It is you we thank.' But it is never 'I', it is always 'We' anyway. Alone, I am nothing. If I had not had the gift which I had, I would not have that great desire to help people, to reach them, to seek out the inner self – you know? – to heal, in a different way perhaps to what I used to do, but to heal by an understanding, to seek out something which is making someone sick. You may call me a psychologist if you like. I don't mind. But this is something which is essential.

It is asked of us that we feed the people. With what shall we feed them, if we ourselves are not fed? If I were to come and say to someone 'I have got Mary here, and Elizabeth here', of what value would it be in helping them if their present need is that they are in confusion, in darkness? How could I be feeding them? Instead of giving them bread, I would be giving them a stone.

Now, please, I must not waste too much time to talk to you! I am always watching all the time. We have what you call a 'doorkeeper'. His name is Chung-ling, and he is ver', ver' wonderful, ver' good. If he say, 'Now, we cannot let anyone in', then they can't come in. He watches the medium all the time, all the time watching the psycho-energy. Another thing is that unless you give of your energy – well – nothing is possible anyway. So that is why, when he says either 'You can't come in' or 'Now you must leave', then we have to obey. Otherwise we are not working together in perfect harmony. Gracias! May God be with you.

Self: I shall look forward to speaking with you again.

Tania: I shall look forward to speaking to you. All right. Now, whatever happens, please, when I leave do not grow tense in anyway. Please help as much as possible. We will try an experiment. Never know what is going to be successful, but we will try. All right?

After a short pause there came the now familiar sound of breathing, gradually becoming heavier and heavier, and more and more excited. I listened expectantly to hear what was going to happen. Gradually the breathing resolved into a high-pitched, childish treble, calling insistently, as if from a great distance.

Voice: Mmmm! Mmmm! Daddy–y–y–y–y–y!

Self: Hallo! Hallo, darling!

Vicky: Mmmm! Mmmm! Mmmm–mmm!

Self: Now don't get too excited. Calm down, otherwise we shall lose . . . How are you? . . . Mummy sends her love . . . Lovely to see you.

Vicky: Mmmmm! Mmmmm! Ha . . . ha . . . Ha . . . ha . . . Hallo Daddy.

Self: Hallo, darling!

Voice, in tones of satisfaction and great fondness: Daddy! Aaaaah! Vicky!.

Comment: Notice that on this occasion she unhesitatingly announces herself by name, as distinct from her previous appearance to Eric, when she would only say 'I don't have to give a name! I've been before!' The joy of meeting has overcome the desire to give evidence!

Self: Vicky! After all this time! This is lovely, isn't it?

Vicky: With Roger! Aaa–aa–ah. Aaa–aa–aah!

Self: And Roger too? Yes, I mustn't forget Roger!

Vicky: Daddy . . . Aaa–ah! I . . . am . . . so . . . happy! So happy!

Self: So happy? I'm sure you are. I'm happy too, darling.

Vicky: And Mummy? Is Mummy happy?

Self: Mummy is happy. She got your last message. She was so happy to get your message.

Vicky: Aaa–aah! Daddy! It is so–oo–oo wo–o–onderful! Can you hear me?

Self: Yes. I can hear you beautifully.

Vicky: Have I got through well?

Self: Yes. You have got through. Your voice is fine!

Vicky: Daddy! I'm not sick any more!

Self: No, darling. I know that.

Vicky: I have got a pretty dress!

Self: Have you? Can you tell me the colour?

Vicky: Pink. Rose pink. Rose pink means . . .

Self, interrupting: Is it a long one?

Vicky, in terms of satisfaction: Ye–es.

Self: I expect you have grown a lot since I saw you! Are you getting a big girl.

(My mind is plainly still running very much in the earthly groove at this moment! Obviously I have still everything to learn!)

Vicky: I–in learning.

Self: There are many things to learn, aren't there?

Vicky, in firm but reproachful tones: Daddy! Listen! (slowly and very firmly) Listen! Rose . . . pink . . . means . . . love. I am a spirit of love.

Self: You are a spirit of love? Well, you brought great love to us, Vicky, and you have had a great love from us. You know that. Otherwise I couldn't be here.

Vicky: Oh, Daddy! Dad! It isn't enough, Daddy.

Self, in tones of surprise: It isn't enough?

Vicky: No! You have to learn to love everyone.

Self: Yes, darling.

Vicky: Oh Daddy! It is so maa–aa–arvellous!.

Self: Yes, it is marvellous, darling!

Vicky: Daddy! Do you believe that Jesus knows your need?

Self: I believe so, dear. Yes, I am sure he does.

Vicky: Well, Daddy, I have learned a little.

Self: Yes, dear. Tell me some other things you have learned.

Vicky: Well . . . I . . . have . . . learned . . . that . . . love . . . accepts no barriers . . . but . . . seeks . . . to . . . overcome . . . all . . . obstacles. If you really love, then you will want to do something. Daddy! I am going to tee–each you!

Self: You are going to teach me? Yes, I need much teaching. Here, in the body, we see things imperfectly.

Vicky: Daddy! Were you very surprised when I came?

Self: Not really. I was hoping you might.

Vicky: The first time?

Self: Oh! The first time! Yes, I was **very** surprised!.

Vicky, chuckling: I wanted it to be a surprise!

Self: You always liked giving people surprises, Vicky you haven't changed.

Vicky: No . . . except that I know more why Daddy couldn't make me well.

Self: Do you, darling? You understand a reason for that? What was the reason?

Vicky: The reason was that I had to learn something, and you had to learn something; how limited people are . . . I had to go away for a little while, and then, when it was time, to come back . . . to be . . . to teach you. Daddy! . . . Daddy! You are a good doctor! But, please forgive me, men of the profession are very limited . . . because they won't listen. They are like the disciple, Thomas, you know, who wouldn't believe unless he could touch. You see, I had to learn, Daddy . . . I am very grown up really.

Self: I expect you are – very grown up now.

Vicky: I have met some wonderful people.

Self: Have you? Can you tell me about them?

Vicky: Well – Tania is really a saint. She's beautiful.

Self: Yes, I think she must be. I can't see her, but her beauty comes through in her voice and in her words.

Vicky: Yes. And, Daddy, I have seen HIM!

Self: Seen HIM? Who?

Vicky, very simply: JESUS.

Self, in awestruck tones: You've seen JESUS? How wonderful!

Vicky: Daddy! It's true! People don't believe you, do they?

Self: No. They don't, darling. They think it is all a wonderful story.

Vicky: But it isn't a story! It's true! You know, Daddy, if you want to help someone, then he knows. He really does know.

Self: Even one little person like me?

Vicky: **Everyone. No one is too little. No one. Then HE comes.** You know, Daddy, it is all so wonderful! I always hoped we would be able to talk together again, and you would see how I had grown. I have so many things to talk about – so many wonderful things to talk about.

Comment: As we were subsequently to learn, and as this story will show as it gradually unfolds, Vicky was, indeed, a highly evolved soul. What she meant here was plainly that she would presently be able to reveal herself in her true stature. For the meantime she had to go slowly. One must not attempt to feed meat to babes and sucklings.

Vicky: We meet people who have learned so much more than the people on earth; who have not stopped progressing because they have lost a body; who still want to be doctors and things; and they have so much to give, if only people will listen. If they will only listen! Why don't they listen?

Self: I don't know. They are blind; they are blind. I try to tell people, you know, and sometimes they listen.

Vicky: You know, I thought it was very funny, because – well you were giving up, and then I came in . . . You didn't know what we have planned. We got you here, because we could get to you – you know?

Self: Yes. I understand. You can get to me here. But I think sometimes you get through to me at home, don't you?

Vicky: Oh, I do, but . . .

Self, continuing: You get through to me, not in words that I can hear, but in thoughts in my mind?

Vicky, sadly: But I can't use a body, can I?

Self: But, if you get through like that, I think I am becoming more sensitive, and more able to know when you are with me, and too, what you are trying to say. I am trying too.

Vicky: Daddy, do you think – are you – are you proud of me? All this time, you know, I (have been thinking) 'When I can talk to him again, will he think I have grown – I have – grown in wisdom? This is what I have wanted so much.'

Self: Yes, darling. You have. You have grown in wisdom, and now it is you who will be teaching me!

Vicky: I am so pleased. If I cry, it is because I am so happy . . . I am so happy. At first I didn't think I would be able to come. There are so many difficulties.

Self: I know there are many difficulties, even more your side than there are for us.

Vicky: You know the photograph?

Self: Which one? The wedding one?

Vicky: Yes.

Self: The coloured one? Do you like it?

Vicky: Very much.

Comment: I had recently been spending much time in my photographic darkroom endeavouring to make a satisfactory colour print from a transparency taken at a family wedding just before Vicky became ill. I had just succeeded in getting a result that satisfied me. Vicky seems to have been aware of this, since it was she who introduced the subject.

Self: You know, there's one in the drawing-room, and you know that I have a black and white copy almost wherever I am, up in my loft and in my bedroom, so I feel you are always beside me.

Vicky: Oh Daddy, you don't need a photograph for me to be there!

Self: I don't, darling. But I like to look at you.

Vicky: Well, if it makes you feel good, well then, you have it! . . . Daddy, do you think now I am all right?.

Self: Yes. I think you are all right, darling.

Vicky: At first it was so difficult, and now I feel I am really me . . . At first I was so disappointed because I didn't . . . Perfect communication is so difficult.

Self: Well, I think you are quite perfect now, darling. It is just Vicky; really Vicky.

Vicky: Oh! How do I know unless you tell me?

Self: We can understand that by the way you can vary your voice and your expression. It is not just saying words, it is how you say them, isn't it? And you are saying them just as if you were really here in the body.

Vicky: I am – very pleased, Daddy. I know how difficult it was for you all that time. If you can't see, there seems to be nothing, just a void.

Self: But it must have been difficult for you too? To see me, and to know – to know that I couldn't see you?

Vicky: Oh Daddy! It is funny now really, when you think about it! **Because I used to reach out, and my hand wouldn't grasp you. And it was so frustrating.** Now, it is funny when I think about it, that now I can come so easily to you.

*   *   *

Vicky: Oh Daddy! What has the grave got? Nothing. Nothing at all. *Do you know, Daddy, it is so distressing to see people going to the cemetery. You want to say to them, 'Oh, please don't. You are burying us!'* You know, I think it is the same that people worship a crucified Christ. And that is wrong, too. **It is thinking of things as being past, when they are present, and it is so wrong. 'Lo! I am with you always, even unto the end of the world.'** You see, I have learned so much.

Self: You have learned so much, darling.

Vicky: Daddy, I must go now. I won't be far away . . . We have so much work to do, so much work to do.

Self: And you are helping me in my work? You are helping me in my work?

Vicky: I am helping you now, but there is so much to do. And . . . you won't be afraid, Daddy? . . . *Don't be afraid of people, Daddy. It is because they are not in the same state of evolution, that is all.*

Self: I am only afraid lest in some way they should put a brake on the work I am trying to do, and stop it.

Vicky: Oh Daddy, they can't do that. No, they can't.

Self: Because sometimes one tries to awaken people who are not ready to be awoken.

Vicky: Daddy, **there are none so blind as those who do not want to see.** You know that. I have questioned these things, and I know and understand. Perhaps because they are maybe afraid. Perhaps the thought of someone knowing about them and the weaknesses that they have; and they don't want to know. But it cannot change anything. They are foolish.

Self: And it cannot be hidden either.

Vicky: They should know that. And yet they try to hide. But they are foolish, so foolish. Nothing is hidden, nothing.

Vicky's point that not all people are in the same stage of evolution is fundamental to our understanding of human nature. We have to learn to accept people for what they are, and not expect more of them than they are capable of doing or understanding. In our enthusiasm and zeal at our newly acquired insights we must beware of pouring these out before those who are incapable of understanding. Jesus warned his disciples against casting their pearls before swine, and this was what he meant. There is a beautiful Mexican poem telling how we may find ouself walking alongside someone in life with whom we feel urged to share our experience. When this happens we should 'drop a petal from the flower of that experience' and see whether it is picked up. If it is, then we know that we can open our treasury of knowledge, and share the riches of our experience. But if it is not, then we should quietly and unobtrusively pick up the petal and put it in our pocket, before going our way.

Vicky: Bless you, Daddy! And bless Mummy!

Self: Bless you, my darling.

Vicky: Bless you, Mummy!

Self: I'll speak for Mummy. Mummy will come to see you.

Vicky: Vicky will always be with you, Mummy . . . Goodbye, Daddy.

Self: Goodbye, Vicky. Au revoir.

Vicky: Au revoir.

Self: It is better, isn't it.

Vicky: It is never goodbye, is it? . . . There is no goodbye.

Self: There's no goodbye. I like the French . . .

Vicky, interrupting: We used to think 'Auf wiedersehen'!

Self: Auf wiedersehen! Do you remember how we used to say . . .

Vicky: I do . . . Auf wiedersehen . . . Yes, I do! Auf wiedersehen, Daddy!

Self: Auf wiedersehen, Vicky!

Vicky: God be in your thinking – always.

Self: And in my understanding.

Vicky: And in your understanding. And Tania is a saint, whom I love very much, Daddy. Very much.

Self: I love her too, Darling.

Vicky: Her name is not Tania. It is Zara. Now, I have told you, haven't I?

Self: You have told me now. We wondered.

Vicky: I am so strong, so very strong . . . There is no disease. Nothing but music . . .

Self: How lovely!

Vicky, her voice gradually growing fainter and commencing to fade away: Music . . . and laughter . . . and light . . . and the radiance of love!

Tania, after a pause: It's all right. You can move! (I had been kneeling on the floor, holding the microphone. I did not possess a neck microphone at this stage.) I think perhaps it makes you a little uncomfortable, hein?.

Self: No, I was comfortable.

Tania: Now, please. I must leave. I am so pleased it was successful. One can never promise anything, you know.

Self: I thank you for that wonderful message, and I thank you for your help and your friendship.

Tania: Oh, it is great joy, always. The little one, she do very well, hein?

Self: Yes. She does very well.

Tania: Ee–eh, you know she is a good student . . . a very good student, very clever; so willing to learn.

Self: She always was! Always wants to be top, whatever she did!.

Tania: Always so much the perfectionist, you know? Oh, she makes the effort, and so she succeed. That is good. We–ell (rather archly), shall I say to you – au revoir?

Self: Au revoir! Auf wiedersehen!

Tania: Auf wiedersehen! I and my father are one, always.

I must leave to the imagination of the reader the joy which this sitting brought to my wife and myself. In any case this book does not set out to be an autobiography. It is, firstly, an account of a number of experiences through which we passed, told in the

93

hope that others may learn as we did and profit from those experiences; secondly, that it may bring comfort to the recently bereaved, together with the assurance that their loved ones are not lost, but closer than they could ever have realised (I remember an old friend, Vicky's much loved godmother, said to me shortly after the funeral: 'Well, no one can ever take her from you now!'; and she was right, more right than she could ever have known at the time); and, finally, that it may give some faint inkling that there is a plan that governs our existence on the earth. So let us pick out from this message some salient points for consideration.

Firstly, and, in one way, perhaps, the most trivial of all, is Vicky's farewell at the end, 'Auf wiedersehen'. She had learned this phrase during the course of our holiday in Austria, the year before she died, and it had since become a favourite with her and almost a catch-phrase with the family. It will be noticed that it was she who introduced the phrase, not I. I wasn't thinking of it at the time. I suppose the medium could have picked it up out of my subconscious, but it was certainly fairly deeply overlaid at that particular moment. To my mind, it ranks with Tania's use of the word 'Poppet' to Eric on the previous occasion as a piece of strong evidence that this communication was genuine and not contrived.

But perhaps the most important thing that we hear about is that there is a great design for humanity in the spiritual realms. It is **planned** that some of us here on earth should lend ourselves to be used in the service of spirit. It was no accident that there were two cancelled places at the first group sitting. (*cf* 'We got you here, so that we could join you.') This was **deliberately** arranged by the spiritual powers to serve the plan. They **do** have the power to influence events on earth. (This does not mean, of course, that we are puppets dancing on the end of a string. The choice is always ours as to whether we respond to the invitations laid before us. Free will is always ours. We can always refuse to cooperate. But the opportunities are made for us by the spiritual powers. Whether we take them is our concern. 'We stretch out our hands to you. All we ask is that you take them', said Tania on a previous occasion.)

Next, we are reminded that it is asked of us that we feed the people, but in the next breath we are told that we cannot do this unless we have first been fed. Therefore we have to seek and to understand; to receive the teaching offered by the spiritual powers. Nor is this feeding to take place through the mere exercise of psychic powers for the sake of display alone. ('If I were to say that I have Mary here or Elizabeth, of what use is that in helping them, if their present need is that they are in confusion, in darkness? How could I be feeding them? Instead of giving them bread, I would be giving them a stone.') We need to know and understand the real need of the other person, before we can start to feed them. So we have to cultivate loving compassion for all whom we meet upon the way, loving them for what they are, and for the needs which they have. Jesus said very much the same thing when he spoke of the man who, when asked for a loaf of bread by his neighbour in the middle of the night, would respond not to the neighbourliness of the man, but to his importunity – that is to say, his need.

We learn, too, that God's purpose lies behind all things, even an event so apparently traumatic as the death of a much loved child, could we only have the faith to perceive it. When my rector came to comfort us the morning after we had returned from the hospital following Vicky's death, all that he could say was that he did not think that God intended these things. Poor man! He meant it kindly. Had he understood more about the continuing life of those we love in the spiritual realms which await us all; had he known how close are those realms and their inhabitants; had he been able to perceive one jot or tittle of God's great plan, he would have sung a very different tune. **For God's ways are not as man's ways. They are higher and wiser. The grand design is conceived against a spiritual back-drop beyond the apprehension of our time-bound earthly life.**

We learn, too, from this communication that the strongest force of all is love, against which no barriers can prevail. The veil between this world and that which lies beyond, and 'death' itself, are transparent before the power of love. But, and this is constantly being reiterated by all who spoke, that love must be the wider, universal love, which is not confined to our own personal families. It is in the spirit of that love that we are called to serve.

We learn, also, of the continued presence with us of our dear ones in the spiritual world, and that, as Vicky put it in one of her subsequent communications, they are only a single thought away. 'Death', as we call it, has not changed them. They remain the same as we have always known them, but yet with the power to grow in wisdom and understanding. We learn of the way in which they are distressed by demonstrations of grief on our part, (for grief and negative emotions such as anger and hatred, can penetrate the veil just as surely as can love). We learn of the pain caused by our constant mournful pilgrimages to their graves, inspired by our own sense of loss, and the feeling that the loved one **is** that body in the ground. Such behaviour, and such thoughts, are tantamount to burying them within those graves, when, in fact, they are so free.

We hear, too, of the way in which tangible expressions of love on our part, such as the love-given gift of flowers, mentioned in the previous chapter, can help the newly arrived spirit. They too, difficult as it is, want to make contact with us, to convince us of the reality of their continuing life, albeit in another dimension, if only – if only – we would open our hearts and minds to their presence. To them, we too are unsubstantial and shadowy, and as lacking in material substance as is the popular conception of a ghost to us. Their arms reach out to enfold us – only to find that there is nothing there, and that we are not even aware of their presence.

We learn, finally of the continuing evolution of each one of us, and that stages of evolution vary between us, even though we are simultaneously incarnate here on the earth. *This, perhaps, is the most fundamental point of all, because once this is accepted, we can understand the existence of both saints and sinners here on the earth, and can begin to accept without bitterness the different circumstances of our varying walks of life.* From this it is but a short step to the mysteries of reincarnation, which in the minds of many, may well enshrine the secrets of our destiny. About this, as we shall see, Vicky and her associates had a good deal to say in subsequent communications.

CHAPTER EIGHT

FURTHER TEACHING

Following this dramatic visit to Mrs D I started to make regular visits to 33 Belgrave Square at intervals of every two months. At each of these visits I was able to speak with Vicky, with Snowdrop and with Tania. At my second visit, on 9th July 1969, Snowdrop confirmed that my attendance at that momentous group sitting had been no accident, but had been deliberately contrived by the spiritual powers. They had known, she said, of my disappointment over the recording of the sitting with Mrs Northage, and that I was on the point of giving up the search, so they made a place for me. 'You just walked in – and there she was! It was as simple as that.'

Actually, it is not at all simple! Communication needs special practice and training on the part of the spirit communicator, as Snowdrop and Tania made plain on subsequent occasions. Moreover, special conditions are required on the earth plane. Not all places are suitable for communication, especially when the more highly evolved spirits are concerned. Special arrangements had to be made for one of the communicators to be able to 'come'. Vicky referred to this even at this early stage, which was long before even the medium knew anything about it.

Vicky: Daddy! I think we are going to find another place to talk to you.

Self: Are you? I wondered whether you might. I am content to leave that to you. Just tell me in thought when the time comes.

Vicky: Do you know, the lady medium that I'm using? Well, I think we will be using her quite often. Not only me, Daddy, because there are others who are preferred before me, but in a different place.

Later, Mrs D moved from Hull to a house in a quiet part of north London, through the auspices of one of her sitters, who wished her to be nearer at hand. It was characteristic of her complete obedience to the spiritual powers that she had no reservations about undertaking the move but immediately accepted the idea. The problem of finding a sufficiently quiet environment, however, was another matter, and took some time to resolve. Certainly the conditions at the SAGB at this time were not very satisfactory, with almost paper thin partitions between the seance rooms, through which it was often possible to distinguish what was being said next door, and always possible to hear that a conversation was going on. Under such conditions communication lines can easily become crossed. It became apparent that our communicators needed a quieter environment.

I had many talks with Vicky during the succeeding months. For the most part the subject matter is of interest to none but ourselves. Intimate conversations between members of a family are apt to be of concern only to the family. But every now and then she would come out with some jewel of understanding, or a profound spiritual truth. As in the following:

Vicky: You know Daddy, I think that Jesus is a wonderful person. He's not dead, you know. He's very much alive – and – you know – he comes; to people who want to be healed.

And again, speaking of that last holiday together in Brittany, and of her passing from among us:

Vicky: Daddy! I really did enjoy the sunshine! . . . I knew that I was going to leave you, and leave the earth . . . but I knew that it would be all right, because Jesus said that he would prepare a place for us. I didn't know what it meant. But I know now.

Self: But now you know. You said last time, you remember, that you had to go away for a little while, because you had something to learn, and I had something to learn. Did you mean that you had to go away from the world of spirit for a little while? Or did you mean that you had to go away from me for a little while?

Vicky: I meant from you for a little while . . . Because I had to learn something.

Self: Yes, and I have too.

Vicky: I know. I know you have. God is very wise, you know; all wisdom . . . **Jesus said: 'Except ye become as a little child,** ye cannot enter the Kingdom', and I think that perhaps grown-ups are rather complicated . . . They seek for God in a very complicated way, and it raises a barrier between themselves and their seeing Him.

Self: And really it is all so simple, isn't it? So beautifully simple.

Vicky: So simple: I in the Father; the Father in me, and me in you. It is so simple when you know. Why do people complicate things so much? . . . They make things much more difficult for themselves nowadays.

*   *   *

Vicky continues: May I say a little prayer?.

Vicky prays: Dear God, we have given to you all our love, which is so little for what you have done for us. We wish to do Thy will. Help us in our union, that we may be about Thy business, and whatever our hands find to do, that to do with all our heart and all our soul. Give us the wisdom not to ask for that which we want, but to surrender to Thee in Thy wisdom and understanding in the things which we need. God bless Mummy and Daddy. And we know that you have blessed them, because you have helped us to talk together. Dear God, I am so happy! Help me to make other people happy too. Amen. Bye-bye, Daddy.

After Vicky left, she was followed by Tania, who praised her skill in communication. She said that, as we must know, Vicky was already an evolved soul, and that this was much easier for highly progressed souls. She asked God to bless our communication and the work which I was doing, and promised that we could speak together when the season was due. I said that sometimes I felt a little muddled at what I ought to be doing. Tania replied that it was important not to get myself all worried, because as yet I could do nothing. She said that when people on earth start to realise that they have a mission to fulfil they are apt to get impatient with thoughts about age and the passage of time. She reminded me of the mission of Jesus, which, after thirty years of preparation, lasted for only three years and yet accomplished so much.

When Tania was talking she spoke with a faint accent, suggestive of southern Europe, possibly France. Sometimes her con-

structions and the order of her words differed from that which
we would use. Here, for instance, what she actually said was 'It
is not important to get yourself all worried'. This lapse from
English – which my proof reader mistook for a printer's error –
seems to me to reinforce her identity as an independent personality. Later on I came to wonder whether she might not have
been Sara, the black servant of Mary Magdalene who, according
to tradition, was washed up with 'the three Maries' at Les
Saintes Maries in the Camargue, in southern France after they
had been turned adrift at Alexandria in an open boat without
oars or sails. Sara later became the patron saint of the gypsies of
the Camargue. She is certainly a healing saint, and in the crypt
of the 4th-century Romanesque church at Les Saintes Maries
there stands an incredibly old, black image of the saint, which,
when I visited it in 1980, was surrounded by votive offerings
commemorating miracles of healing.

You already have been preparing, *Tania continued*. All the
sorrows of the heart and the anguish of the mind have been
part of that preparation. Everything that happens, with
people like my medium – the sorrows, the difficulties of life –
they are the preparation. Without that foundation none of
this could be. So do not underestimate your being prepared at
all. You are prepared all right, and when the time comes, you
will be able to do what we want you do to. We know you will
have to be extremely strong spiritually. Therefore we know
that it will only be this which has happened to you, this
experience through which you have passed, that will be your
strength to take you through. . . . *Nothing happens until it is time
anyway.* I think that perhaps one has the thoughts because
one is limited in the body, and one thinks 'Perhaps I should
have done that sooner'. *But you do it when you have to do it.* The
seed, you know, is sown in the ground. We cannot see its state
of growth, and one would be foolish to open up the ground,
because one would damage the growth of the seed. But, in its
due season, then it comes in all its beauty. And so it shall be.
In the meantime, God be in your thinking, and rest in His
understanding. Farewell. From us all – '*Auf wiedersehen!*'

So, very gently, Tania dropped into my mind one of the greatest
of spiritual truths, and one which I had been all too loath

to recognise: that **all things in due season come.** How hard it is to understand this and put it into practice! But God's time scale is a different one from ours. I am reminded at this point of *A Tudor Story* (C. W. Daniel) which took thirty years to unfold. If something for which you have worked and striven does not come to pass and when you expect, it should not be a subject for self blame or for bitterness with others. Throughout the gospels there are constant references to Jesus' time as not having arrived, and therefore something not taking place which might have been expected. It is especially hard, as Tania pointed out, when one becomes obsessed by the sense of urgency inseparable from a mission. But, as I have had to learn – and I think that at long last I **have** learned it! – things happen when they are meant to happen. If a thing, however right it seems to be (and this applies with equal force in the ordinary matters of daily life and business!) does not happen at the moment when we wish it or expect it, then the reason is either that it is not meant to happen, or that the season for it to happen is not yet come. *We have to learn to work in God's time, not ours, and to realise that He uses a different time scale to that of human life.*

'The Lord is my Pace setter – I shall not rush.
　　He makes me stop for quiet intervals,
　He provides me with images of stillness which restore my
　　　serenity,
　He leads me in ways of efficiency through calmness of mind,
　　　And His guidance is peace.

　Even though I have a great many things to accomplish each
　　　day, I will not fret,
　　　　For His Presence is here,
　His timelessness, His all importance, will keep me in balance.
　He prepares refreshment and renewal in the midst of my
　　　activity,
　By anointing my mind with His oils of tranquillity,
　　　My cup of joyous energy overflows.
　Truly harmony and effectiveness shall be the fruits of my
　　　hours,
　For I shall walk in the Pace of my Lord
　　　　And dwell in His House for ever.'
　　　　　　A Japanese Paraphrase of Psalm 23. Tokio Megashio

A month later I was back in Belgrave Square for another sitting. Compared with the two previous sittings, this was quiet and uneventful. Vicky spoke mainly of domestic affairs, with, every now and then, telling little asides about her life in the world of spirit. She spoke also about the continuing arrangements being made for easier communication with those more highly evolved discarnates who were unable to 'come in' in the highly charged emotional atmosphere of Belgrave Square. It was coming up to the anniversary of her passing, which was why I had sought this particular sitting (I usually allowed a somewhat longer interval to elapse between one visit and the next), and she was becoming increasingly excited over this and over the commemorative flowers which it was our custom to place on 'her' special window in the church. She was growing up too, moving gradually but inexorably towards her full spiritual stature, which had not yet been revealed to us.

Vicky: Are you pleased, Daddy, that I come to talk to you.

Self: Very pleased, darling.

Vicky: Vicky is happy too. At first it was . . . so difficult. I kept touching you, and you couldn't feel me, and I was so sad.

Self: What? Today? Or before?

Vicky: Before. And I was so sad, Daddy, because I would say 'Vicky's here! Why don't you talk to Vicky?' and you couldn't hear me, and you couldn't feel me.

Self: But I often talk to you now in my . . . can you hear my thoughts?

Vicky: Yes. Yes, I do. . . . And the flowers – in the vase, Daddy. Place the flowers in the vase for Vicky! Place the flowers in the vase for Vicky!

Self: Yes, sweetheart, in the church.

Vicky: Yes, in the church. You place them in the church for Vicky – in the church for Vicky! (getting increasingly excited).

Self: Yes. I will put them there myself. For its nearly your day, isn't it?

Vicky: Yes. You'll put them there for my day?

Self: Yes. We will put them there for your day.

Vicky: You will? that's good, Daddy! That's good, Daddy! . . . Daddy! There's a lot of animals in the spirit world!

Self: Are there? All the animals who have been loved and who wait for us?

Vicky: And they come back, like Vicky. But it's sad, because they can't talk like Vicky, and people don't know. . . . I ask about things, and I am learning so quickly that I think I am growing old!

Self: I don't think that Vicky is ever going to grow old!

Vicky: But I seem to be growing.

Self: Growing in wisdom.

Vicky: Well, I seem to think different.

Self: You think like an older person.

Vicky: Yes.

Self: Growing up.

Vicky: And asking questions. It is wrong, Daddy, for people to tell children untruths, isn't it?

Self: Yes, it is darling. But sometimes grown-ups are afraid that children will not understand.

Vicky: Well, Daddy, if they believed in God, then they would know that God would tell them the way to answer children. But they haven't got time to listen to God, have they?

Self: No, a lot of them haven't. I think a lot of them, even if they had, would be rather frightened.

Vicky: Why, Daddy? What is there to be afraid of?

Self: Nothing. But I think a lot of people think there is.

Vicky: But there is nothing to be afraid of God for. God is love. Like I love you, and you love me. There is nothing to be afraid of in that, is there?

Self: No, of course not.

Vicky: Well, I have been asking questions, and I was told that when people just try to get out of answering questions, they are not very responsible.

*   *   *

Vicky: Daddy! I have to go now. . . . Are you happy, Daddy? More happy than you were before? Because if you weren't, then Vicky would think that she had not done everything she should have done.

Self: Yes, darling. Much more happy than I was before.

Vicky: You can't. Daddy, you can't – do you know what I want to say, Daddy?

Self: No, darling. What were you going to say?

Vicky: People have – some people have great compassion in their hearts for the sick. Jesus had great compassion for all people who were sick. But, Daddy, he was not God; he was about his Father's business, Daddy. And even he, with all his great compassion, could not heal everyone.

Self: There were some he could not reach.

Vicky: Yes, Daddy.

Self: I think it is true, and we have to be ready to be healed, do we not? And that is why sometimes we fail?

Vicky: Yes, Daddy. But sometimes you may think you have failed, but it isn't you that has failed, Daddy. Because it has to be that if you had not come to me, then I could not have come to you. **And it is the same with healing.** So you must never be unhappy if you can't heal everyone.

Self: No. But it is difficult.

Vicky: Bless you, Daddy!

Self: Bless, you, my darling!

                        *   *   *

Vicky: Can I sing?

Self: Yes. I love to hear you sing.

Vicky (sings in a clear, childish treble):
>There is a light that shines from above,
>>It brings us together through all His love.
>
>It helps us see the way so clear
>>That we may reach the ones so dear.
>
>It helps us see the shining ray,
>>It brings us closer day by day
>>>To His eternal love.

Self: You are getting on, sweetheart. That was lovely.

Vicky: Snowdrop taught me how to do that. She doesn't make songs up. She taught me how to make songs up. Bye-bye, Mummy! Bye-bye, Daddy! . . . I am strong now, very strong now. I can dance and skip about among all the flowers . . . and among all the birds . . . and . . . among the fairies . . . and . . . and I can walk with Jesus, and he will teach me to teach you.

Tania: *(introduces herself with her usual foreign greeting)* Is a very good day to you!

Self: A very good day to you!

Tania: I think the little one she do very well, hein?

Self: She does wonderfully. She is an apt pupil.

Tania: She is really very good. You know she enquires so much, because in her great love she wants to help people. But she wants to teach you so much too. And she is teaching you, and this is good. You know, she is so happy, so very happy; and I want you to know this. It has been a great joy to have been able to be of service to you. No one can ever take this away from you. This is **your** experience, and no one will ever appreciate as you have that experience. They had great fun at first, these little ones – Snowdrop and this little one, who is so bright and gay now but at one time so sad and forlorn. But Snowdrop take her in hand, you know, and she said 'Come on!', and she make her laugh, and she said: 'We will bring your Daddy to you, so you must try to learn how to talk to him.' And they do very well. It is good to see you.

Self: It is good to see you.

Tania: I am very happy as always to have been able to make a little contribution. I think sometimes it is very difficult for people to appreciate the difficulties of communication. They think it is all so easy, when really it is extremely difficult. The medium's condition, everything, you see . . . We are very grateful that we have a good instrument to use. But sometimes it can be a little difficult. All right?

Self: And you will teach me? I have so much to learn.

Tania: Oh, my dear friend, have we not all so much to learn?

Self: The knowledge of that lack of learning is a little over-powering.

Tania: Ah – well – of course one has come so far away from the sun – God, you know – that one has perhaps become a little cold. But one can slowly grow back into the warmth of his embrace . . . You know we can only hold out our hand to people. We can't make them take it. You understand?

Self: Of course, that applies to me in my work, doesn't it?

Tania: That is true. But we are always very happy when someone turns, and in recognising their own limitations, they will say, 'Someone is here who knows better than I how to do this thing.'

Self: You know how often I turn to you in my thought.

Tania: I do. Indeed I do. You know I have been in spirit quite a while, but I too knew how difficult it was to make people understand. Paul tells us in his ministry the greatest sadness he had was that people did not realise that the things which were done, were not done by him: that they just did not get the message. He talks about these things and he says: 'Well unfortunately they bowed down and worshipped the gift rather than the giver.' And so they missed the point of the whole thing.

Self: Yes. I understand very well.

Tania: The thing is that you and I, Vicky, Roger, all of us, we are all part of this. Not one of us is greater than the other one. Each one of us is interdependent upon the other. So, alone I am nothing. I need you just as much as you need me. So therefore I can say to you that you are giving your help to us, just as much as we are giving our help to you. I pray that you will remain in constancy at all times, realising that it was not just to meet your girlie. It was to stimulate you. You see God's ways are not man's ways. They are higher, they are wiser than man's ways. May I leave you with these words, which the little Vicky knows too:

> Deep in unfathomable mines
> Of never failing skill
> He treasures up his bright designs
> And works his sovereign will.

So he has brought us together. It is that we must accomplish our mission, and, if we accomplish it, we accomplish it together, and not alone. We can accomplish nothing as individuals, whether we be discarnate or not. So therefore I say to you in all sincerity 'Thank you for coming'. To all of your beloved ones I say: 'From me, who call myself Tania now, may God bless you with the revelation of His love, that you may accomplish your mission, as we are hoping to accomplish ours.'

Self: Amen.

Tania: Amen.

Six weeks later, on 29th September, I found myself again talking to Vicky at Belgrave Square. At every visit more was revealed of the truths about our lives on earth and of our relation to the 'other world'. Vicky started off by talking about the energies of flowers and their influence on healing.

Vicky: Do you know, Daddy? I've been learning something about the flowers. . . . I've been waiting to tell you. They give the life force. But you have to learn to obey the rules of God, and to obey the commandment 'Thou shalt not kill'. And when you take a tiny flower, it will give you some energy and strength, and that is why it is important to have the flowers, not just because they are pretty. But you must learn not to be selfish and take too much from them, or you will kill the flowers. Do you understand, Daddy? I want to tell you so many things, but it is difficult to talk and tell you what I mean.

Self: I understand.

Vicky: You see, it is so beautiful when you know. And when we are taught about God and Jesus, we don't really see them, do we Daddy? Not when we are on the earth. We are only told about them, so we don't really know; and when people grow to be big, they start to wonder because they can't see God, and they can't see Jesus. They don't know whether it is true or not, do they?

Self: No, but if we look, we can see God in action all around us.

Vicky: Oh, but Daddy, I **do** understand. Now then you know; but a lot of people don't understand. And this is God in action, now. And – Jesus visits with us, because, you know, he is not just of the past. HE IS OF THE 'NOW'. NOW. HERE.

Self: Of the 'Now', when it is always 'now'.

Comment: So many people turn their backs upon Jesus and deny the existence of God because they cannot 'see' God. They are locked into accepting the evidence of their five senses (not even six senses for most of them!) as telling them all that they need to know about 'reality'. But our senses are not senses of information, letting in the light from outside. They are *filters* to sift out the essential from the non-essential. Only information which is relevant to the business of physical existence is permitted to pass through to consciousness. The rest is filtered out lest it should swamp the conscious part of the mind with a mass of information too great for it to handle. But God and Jesus are transcendent, and exist in the transcendent reality, which is not

107

accessible to the senses, but has to be experienced as God in action – now.

Vicky: You know, Daddy, there are a lot of clever people in spirit; such a lot of people. Some are very clever people, with very good minds – and they learn how to use the energies. There are scientists and medical science in spirit, and they know more than the people here on earth, because if you love something, you don't give it up, do you? You keep on, don't you?

Self: Even when your state is changed, you still keep on.

Vicky: Even when your state is changed, you keep on and on. And it is wonderful to know that you can improve yourself – not to be ambitious, but to want to know more so that you can help more, do more.

Self: I wish there were an easier way for that knowledge to be imparted to us here on earth.

Vicky: I know. It is very difficult, sometimes, isn't it? But Daddy, Jesus loved people so much. But even he could not do everything he wanted to do. He loved people, everyone, and yet he could not heal everyone, Daddy, because he was not a law unto himself. Do you see.

Self: Yes. He was under the laws of the Father.

Vicky: And, of course, he wanted to help everyone because he loved everyone. And he still does. But **He** cannot do everything, and I can't do everything, and you can't. You can only do your little bit. Do you know what Snowdrop said? She said:

'Jesus bids us shine with a clear pure light,
   Like a little candle burning in the night.
 In this world of darkness so we must shine.
   You in your small corner, and I in mine.'

Comment: This, of course, is a very well-known childrens' hymn dating back to Victorian times. It is not one which was ever used in our home, and I am as certain as I can be that Vicky was not familiar with it. The medium probably was, though I didn't ask her. It **could** be interpreted as a bit of the mind of the medium showing through, though personally I doubt it.

Vicky, continuing: That is what she said, Daddy. And it is true that you cannot do everything, but you can only do such a little bit. But if you do it well, and someone else does their little bit well, then it becomes the perfect whole. I'm growing up, aren't I?'

Self: You are, darling.

Vicky: I am not leaving you behind. I'm taking you with me.

*   *   *

Vicky: Do you know, Daddy, everything is going to be so wonderful, because you are clever, and you can understand things of medicine, and know whether things are right or wrong.

Self: But our medicine is limited, darling. So many people I can't help.

Vicky: I know. But you have the foundation. This is what they tell me. You have the foundation; and you can't build a house without a foundation.

Self: No. I expect I am like everyone else. I am impatient.

Vicky: But, Daddy, **no one can make things without God places them there.** God gave what you have, and He will add to it because you so desire it. God only places the seed there, and if there is no seed there, there is nothing to grow. But, when He places the seed and you want it to grow, **sometimes it grows through tears.** And it is the tears which water the seed, and then there is this wonderful blossom which comes, and it is perfect. Oh Daddy, I do love you so much because I know that your heart is filled with love for people, and you want to help them, especially when they are confused and unhappy because they can't understand. You know, Daddy, there are some people who are – I had to find out, because I wanted to help in the plan – some people just don't understand themselves, and they are very confused and unhappy. That is because there is no one to teach them to understand, no one to illumine their darkness.

Self: And sometimes they come to me.

Vicky: Yes. And, Daddy, Vicky will illumine you so that you can illumine them. You know what Jesus said? He said: 'Feed my sheep.' But how do you know what they need to feed with unless you have someone to tell you? Because sometimes they don't know either what they need; and it is not what you want, which is good for you. It is what you need.

Vicky's remarks about Jesus not being God will antagonise

most conventional Christians, for whom the absolute Divinity of Jesus is **the** cardinal point of the Christian faith. This same argument created absolute mayhem in the early days of the Christian Church and was responsible for most of the schisms and arguments which split the Church and which were only finally resolved by the exercise of authoritarian repression. Without wishing to enter into the argument in this book, I think that what Vicky is saying here is that Jesus, **during his life on earth, accepted the limitations on His powers which were inseparable from being a man.** Throughout His life on earth he remained under the laws which govern the material realm and nothing that he did was incompatible with his true humanity. The suggestion that Jesus was unable to heal all the sick people who thronged about him for healing is also not one which will commend itself to conventional and traditional followers of the Christian faith. However, nowhere in the gospels are we told that everyone who came was healed. This is a tacit assumption made because of the belief in his divinity, to which all things were possible. However, we **are** specifically told that in his home town of Nazareth he was unable to perform any mighty works because of their unbelief. The atmosphere of disbelief resulting from familiarity with his home and his background specifically inhibited the display of paranormal powers. We shall discuss the laws which apparently govern healing in more detail later in this book. In the meantime I think it sufficient to realise the truth of Vicky's remark that he was subject to the laws of the Father.

At the conclusion of the previous chapter I referred briefly to continuing existence and suggested that the mysteries of reincarnation might well enshrine the secret of our destiny. Vicky and her associates had a good deal to say about this and some startling revelations to make. It was in this, her fourth communication, that she first hinted at existence prior to incarnation, and the influences of past experiences upon lives experienced on earth, and started me out upon a pathway of thought to which I was profoundly hostile from the start. We shall examine these experiences in the following chapter.

CHAPTER NINE

'BEFORE I CAME?'

It is not proposed to discuss all the arguments surrounding the vexed question of reincarnation at this juncture. We shall return to it in the second part of this book. There are, however, one or two points of which we should remind ourselves before we come to the messages received from my various communicators. It seems likely from a number of references made in the Bible, and from what we know about the general climate of thought at that time, which was strongly influenced by Greek thinking, that a general belief in reincarnation was accepted by the early Christian church. It was not until the extremely dubiously constituted 5th ecumenical council, which was held under the auspices of the emperor Justinian of Constantinople in AD 553, and at which the Pope was not even present, that such beliefs were anathematised by the Christian church. It is only since that day that the Church has come down squarely on the side of the 'once-for-all' hypothesis. Indeed, Origen, who was one of the ablest thinkers among the early Christian fathers, wrote in his book, *De Principiis*: **'Every soul comes into this world strengthened by the victories or weakened by the defeats of its previous life. Its place in this world as a vessel appointed to honour or dishonour is determined by its previous merits or demerits. Its work in this world determines its place in the world which is to follow this.'**

Of course, this need not necessarily be construed in terms of a previous incarnation in **this world**. (Our growing cosmic knowledge suggests that there may well be other worlds compatible with life, though probably not within our solar system.) What it does suggest very strongly is that it is incorrect to think of each soul coming into the world as a fresh and new creation of God. Vicky's first reference to these matters came towards the end of the sitting outlined in the previous chapter. We had been talking about the causes of sickness, when she pointed out that some-

111

times sicknesses had been created by things in the past. Some mental and physical illnesses are manifestations of past lives which can leave impressions on the soul which influence them towards particular forms of behaviour and experiences in future lives. Some of the things that we think are unjust and unfair are the results of things that we have done in our past. There were some people, Vicky said, who as a result of their experiences in a former life were unable to understand the sort of body they were in. 'If I am a little girl now' she said, 'then was I a little boy before and I don't remember? Sometimes', she went on, 'people do remember a little, and then they are confused'. She was deeply upset because such people are often wrongly treated because the cause of their unusual behaviour is not recognised.

Vicky was quite plainly referring to sexual problems, especially to such conditions as homosexuality, change of sex and transvestism. I had never given very much thought to this before, but it is blindingly obvious that if a spirit comes into incarnation after having had a succession of strongly sexed lives of the opposite sex, it may well retain vestigial memories of those previous lives. Unless the draught of forgetfulness has been sufficiently strongly mixed, the appetites and habits formed during those lives may persist in sufficient degree to influence behaviour in the present life. Thus it may fail to recognise and accept the body which it now inhabits; it may, for instance, while feeling like a woman, with all the attributes and tastes of femininity developed or acquired during previous lives, inhabit a masculine body, or vice versa, and thus, feeling strange in that body, either behave like a member of the opposite sex or even seek for a change of sex through surgery. (It must be remembered, in considering this, that in the embryo both sets of sexual organs are present during intra-uterine life, and that the final differentiation between the sexes only takes place in the concluding phase of embryonic life.) This, I believe, may well lie behind some of the sex change operations carried out. It is important, also, when considering such matters, not to forget that true spirit is sexless. Sexual differentiation is a phenomenon developed solely for the convenience of maintaining the species in the material world. Even so, each person retains within themselves the quintessential essence of the qualities of both the sexes. The Chinese refer to the ebb and flow of the Yin and the

112

Yang, each of which are integral parts of the whole, in which they exist in a state of perfect harmony and balance. This is paralleled in modern thought by the recognition of the essential differences between right and left brain activity. Just as we recognise that there needs to be a balance between right and left, between Yin and Yang, between the active and the receptive sides of the personality, so it seems to be necessary that the evolving spirit has had both masculine and feminine experiences on its journey.

Vicky continued: You know, Daddy, before I came to be your little girl, when I was in what Snowdrop calls suspension, waiting – because I chose to come to you to have my experience with you – but it was only to be a short experience, you know; and you were very sad. I am sorry if I caused you unhappiness.'

Self: But you brought us great happiness my darling, *I replied*, through going and coming back to us.

Vicky: Daddy! Will you please ask the medium to forgive me for having disturbed her? I shouldn't do that really. But it isn't just me. I am not sad for you, Daddy. I am sad for other souls, because I can see so clearly to them, and they can't see. And it is terrible to be blind and not be able to see.

Self: Well, we can only help them by shining out like a light, darling; a light that comes from our own spirits.

Vicky: Daddy, I am your lamp, and I will shine my lamp before your feet.

Self: And I will watch your light, darling, to walk there.

Vicky: Have you enjoyed talking to me, Daddy?

Self: Yes, darling, enormously. You know I have.

Vicky: **I chose you and Mummy, and I have known that what I chose at that time was the right choice. Because, in coming to you, I knew what you were, what you did, your talents and everything, and I knew that you believed in God. But I knew that you had to be able to understand other things as well. So, if I brought you tears, it was only that you might see more clearly.**

Comment: It is plain from these remarks of Vicky's that rebirth is not the haphazard affair it is sometimes thought to be – at least at Vicky's level of evolution, and I suspect not for any of us. Pre-

113

existence seems to involve planning, and we make deliberate choices of the life circumstances which will provide the opportunities which we need in order to evolve and grow, and also in the light of the needs of others. Past links and associations with others also come into consideration in accordance with the law of sowing and reaping. We do not need to worry about this. The east has a saying, 'When the pupil is ready, the Teacher arrives'. We each have, I believe, a blueprint for our lives (which may involve the needs of others as well as of ourselves), of what we hope to do and to achieve, though it is hidden from our earthly memory. (In the opinion of some a review of the life just lived against that blueprint constitutes the first phase of judgement.)

So the pattern of the events of our lives and the work which lay before us began gradually to unfold. We had a mission to carry out on earth. Before we could do this, it was necessary for us to be able to understand certain spiritual truths. We had to be taught certain things not generally known or understood on the earthly plane. She who had been our daughter was, in fact, our spiritual teacher and fellow worker in the task we had undertaken. She was a highly evolved spirit, with other lives in her experience. There was purpose and understanding both in her own short life, and in the manner of her return. On our next visit to Mrs D she spoke briefly about one of those former experiences of life.

By the time this visit was made Mrs D had moved to her new home in north London. This was a great improvement from several points of view. For us personally, it meant that we were able to drive up in the car and park outside in the quiet cul-de-sac in which her little house was situated, without having the hassle of trains and tubes to get to Belgrave Square. It also meant that sittings were given in complete privacy, free from the ever-present awareness of conversations going on in the rooms on either side. The result was that there was an immediate heightening of the level of teaching given, and the communicators seemed to reach us on a higher and more spiritually evolved level. At last, also, my wife felt emboldened sufficiently to come with me, and the conversations were addressed impartially to us both.

And so it was that Snowdrop came to say to Ruth that she was 'strong in the power of the Cross' which, she explained, meant that she was always trying to do what was right in the eyes of God and further explained by saying:

114

I want to say that you are a true servant of God; which should answer that within you which at times creates an anxiety in your mind and in your heart. Because this is something which we in spirit do understand. We know, and we know your problems, and sometimes you can become very confused, but it is only because you want to do what is right, and you don't just want it to be wishful thinking. . . .

Snowdrop, continuing: I do not seek that which you reveal to the world and the people of the world. I seek out the real you that hides beneath the exterior, so that I can find the things I can help you with; the deep, hidden things that you can't see; that no one can see but us who want to see. That is why I said you are very strong in the power of the Cross. I don't mean a crucifix. I mean a cross of light. I think many people think of the Spirit, or the Christ Spirit, in the past tense, when it is ever present. You know? Of today, and of tomorrow, and of all the tomorrows. Jesus was a wonderful person, because he mastered all weaker and baser impulses, do you see, through experience. Therefore one knows that he is still active, and we know that he comes to see people when they need him the most; not for selfish reasons but because they want to do what is right. So it is my privilege to tell you of His blessing upon you.

Ruth: Yes. Thank you.

Snowdrop: You know it is truly said, 'A little child shall lead them', and the little one who **was** a little one, who has now grown so much in spiritual wisdom, has led you and guided you, to give you strength, and to know that there is so much in life to do; much more than even the things that people normally do in earth life. She is so happy and so gay to come and talk about these things, and to say: 'Take no thought for the morrow, for what ye shall be fed. For your Father knows the need, so that if you do His will, then everything will be all right.' There are naturally fears of the material, of the misunderstanding of other people. Well, they are blind, and they do not want to see. And you can't make them see if they do not want to see. But remember, if you fear the crucifixion, there is always someone there, and you will not be crucified. You will only be crowned by glory; and not for self-glorification, but only that men shall see the wonders of God's power, as he works through his angelic forces.

*　　*　　*

115

Snowdrop continuing: . . . For many years there have been plans which have been made by discarnate minds, by the scientists in spirit. These plans have been made, and they are waiting for fulfilment until the whole members of the body were drawn together in order that these could go forward. I think you listened to the conversation that we had before on the tape, and it is there that you will find that we talked about the members of the body, which you are. One uses the talent. The talent which you have is for helping the sick and that kind of thing, **but it can be more perfect once you break down the barriers of the past.** In this way you can come more fully into that field of activity.

Comment: The recurrent theme throughout this whole, long and extraordinary series of communications from the discarnate world is of the existence of the great plan for humanity, in which we are all involved. This seems to mean the healing of mankind through the use of spiritual power and spiritual energies. These are to be displayed at least as much for the conversion of mankind towards a more spiritual way of life as for the actual alleviation of suffering. It was comforting to know that one was a part of this, and that there was purpose behind the agonies which we had suffered.

Snowdrop continued at some length to explain that mental illness was very often treated with distaste because it was so little understood. It was important, she said, that people who do not understand the diseases of the mind should understand that this was something which was quite separate from the brain, which was merely the instrument by which the spirit made its impact upon the physical body. Where does the body begin, she asked, and where does the spirit begin? People came for messages from spirit but they did not ask questions like that. So it happened that there were many confused souls around at the present time, inhabiting bodies which they did not understand. The physical body was, like a house, just a temporary home. But just the same way as if you have no roots, you feel unhappy in a house, so the spirit was unhappy when it entered a body that was foreign to it. This was the case with those who were called homosexual. They were confused souls inhabiting unfamiliar

116

bodies. It was important that people should understand this so that they might be helped to adjust to the life in which they found themselves.

After this Vicky came to talk to us, and we had a conversation which began like this:

Vicky: Hallo Daddy.

Self: Hallo darling! Lovely to hear you!

Vicky: You know Daddy, you are going to be in charge of something – in a sanctuary. . . . You are going to be in the sanctuary of healing, a hall of healing. . . . Do you see?

Self: I think so.

Ruth: Perhaps not quite yet in this world.

Vicky: Yes, Mummy. In this world.

Self: Do you mean, Vicky, that I am to use my hands in healing.

Vicky: Yes. I do.

Comment: At this moment my 'healing' was confined to the normal practice of medicine in the way in which I had been trained. I was actively engaged in my family practice within the National Health Service. Though interested in 'spiritual healing', and trying to find out all I could about it, I still retained the traditional reservations of the medical profession, and had not yet dared to attempt it for myself. There was no question of a healing sanctuary at this stage. Some four years later, as I shall presently relate, I was to start a healing and meditation group for cancer patients at my house. Subsequently, after Eric had finished building his new bungalow and healing sanctuary, the group moved there, where it still meets at regular intervals. As has already been remarked, our discarnate friends not infrequently become rather vague over matters relating to earth time, presumably because time and space are part of the material environment, and have no counterpart in the spiritual world of the discarnates. Later on I did start to use my hands in healing, even within my NHS practice, though it was not often that I allowed my patients to know what I was doing!

Vicky: You know, Mummy, before I came to be your little girl, I was a spirit, and I knew that I was coming to be your little girl.

Ruth: Yes. I understand. You told Daddy that, didn't you.

117

Vicky: Yes. But I wanted to talk to you about it.

Ruth: Tell me then. You knew you wouldn't stay for long, didn't you?

Vicky: Yes. I knew. But it was all chosen so carefully – so carefully.

Thus Vicky knew, although not consciously, that her incarnation with us was only to be a short one. It was all carefully chosen and arranged. As we learned later, this was a mission voluntarily undertaken for special reasons. She went on to tell us how she had had a previous incarnation in this world. In spite of this she still wanted to call us Daddy and Mummy, and for us to think of her as our little girl. But long, long ago, she had lived in the East. In those days, she said, when she was alive in ancient Egypt, things of the spirit had been plainer. She remembered about having communication and how they used to be able to 'free the spirit from the body'. Unfortunately then, just as today, materialism was rampant and had spoiled many lives. She, however, had always known that it was what you had within you that was important and that you could not take earthly treasures with you just because you had them with your body. She spoke of Jesus, saying that He too had been in Egypt, as had Snowdrop and many others. What Jesus said about not laying up treasures for oneself upon the earth was true, and it was important to realise this. We could not take them with us. 'We take with us the memories;' she said, 'the good memories and the bad memories, we take them with us. But I thank you because I only have good memories to take with me on the next stage of the journey.' She told us that she knew that she would 'come back' to us because our journey together had to go on. We should come to join her, but we all had something to do here first.

She went on to tell us how sometime previously, before she had been born as our little girl, our medium had seen her as she had been in Egypt. At that time she had had a crippled foot, and she demonstrated this to the medium and her husband by taking control of the medium's body and manifesting the crippled foot. She made him and the other members of the group (circle) examine the foot and test it. If we asked the medium about it, she would remember, though she still did not know that it was Vicky who had controlled her. We asked her if she remembered anything about her life in Egypt, and she replied that she had been the bride of one of the Pharaohs,and that her mummified body was in Egypt today. As she told us this we realised what a tiny part of her total life she has spent with us, but this tiny part, she said, was very precious to her.

Ruth: You did a lot of things dear, didn't you?

Vicky: Yes. I did what I had to do. And I am doing what I have to do now. But sometimes it is difficult, because one becomes in that state that one remembers. So when I am, I cry. I am not really sad, not really . . . I am very happy; and more so because you are here, with whom I have shared precious moments of life – and especially, Mummy, because **you** are here.

Comment: This throws an interesting sidelight upon the question of memory and reincarnation. The various 'lives' or 'states' as Vicky puts it, are quite distinct, like beads strung together on a thread, or differing roles played by a single actor. But just as an actor can move from one role to another, so the human soul can remember past lives, and, in recalling, enter once again into the emotions of those lives. No doubt this is a cogent reason for the shrouding of the memories of those lives in the mists of forgetfulness. Full memories might well be too painful for us to handle in our present state, and be productive of all sorts of problems additional to those of ordinary life. Striving to reawaken those memories through hypnotic regression merely to satisfy our curiosity is not to be encouraged.

Vicky: You know, Mummy, some people come into the world, and they come with various purposes. Some are the ones who can do one thing, and some another. But none are more important than each other. Everyone has something to do.

Ruth: Yes. They all have a job to do, however small.

Vicky: Some people are very impatient, and don't want to be just a power station! They want to be able to do the things which will make people think how marvellous they are. But that isn't being true, when you say, 'Nevertheless, Father, not my will but Thy will be done'.

Self: That is wrong thinking; to do things for power.

Vicky: Yes. One can only do what God gives one the power to do.

119

Self: And one must do it for the right motive.

Vicky: **Not to be seen of men, and not to receive acclaim.** Do you know what Paul said? . . . I mean Saint Paul; people call him St Paul. It is not important.

Ruth: Do you mean by St Paul the Paul who lived in the time of Christ.

Vicky: Yes. I am sorry if I jump ahead.

Self: You forget that our experience is so small in this world.

Vicky: No, I don't forget. But I do tend to get rushing ahead!

Ruth and Self, in chorus: You always did! Go on. What did Paul say?

Vicky: He said that if you do things, when you pray, you should say: **'Take me, and use me acording to Thy wisdom, for within me is part of Thy creation. Therefore am I created. But if I were to use Thy creative power to the detriment of Thy people, then take away Thy creative power, lest I harm others, and harm myself more.'** He is very wonderful. He too was in Egypt.

Comment: Paul's prayer should be inscribed in every scientific laboratory throughout the world and written deep in the hearts of all investigative scientists! So many of the present day problems of the world can be traced back to the misuse of this divine creative power. A deeply sobering thought for scientistis and politicians alike.

Vicky: I hope you will not have any doubts that God is working out His sovereign will for all things. Not just for this world, but for all time. You know, people ask some very funny questions. Not from me, they don't, because I don't talk to many people. But they do. They want to know 'Why this?' and 'Why that?' But they have got a very narrow view of things. . . . They only think of the earth planet, don't they? There is more than a tiny earth. There are other planets, and there are the souls who have evolved. The come back, and they communicate.

'In my Father's house are many mansions: if it were not so, I would have told you. I go to prepare a place for you.' (John xiv.2) Our growing knowledge of the cosmos helps us to understand. Far-off planets in far-off galaxies may well provide our future home – or homes! We must not allow our minds to be bounded by the

limitations of our present horizons. But it is equally important that these distant 'mansions' are not the Kingdom of Heaven, and to free ourselves from the sensory delusion of attempting to locate Heaven spatially! The Kingdom of Heaven, as Jesus said, lies within each one of us, at 'the deep heart's core'. Thither we must learn to find our way.

At the conclusion of this sitting, I took Vicky at her word and spoke to Mrs D about 'the Egyptian Episode'. Although this must have taken place more than fifteen years previously (it must be remembered that it had taken place before Vicky was born in 1955, and it was now 1970), Mrs D remembered the incident perfectly. Unlike many of the souls communicating through her, 'Vicky' had never visited her previously, nor attempted to communicate. She had come as a complete stranger. The occasion was evidently a small private circle held at Mrs D's house in Hull with not more than four or five people present in addition to Mrs D and her husband. It took place exactly as Vicky had told us. 'She came through, this one,' said Mrs D relating the incident to Ruth and myself, 'and my husband asked her who she was. The only information she gave was that she was a bride of a Pharaoh in Egypt, but they told me after that that she had, as she sat there, a deformed foot. She asked them to sit still while she took me up and walked me to them, as a cripple, on this foot. Then she put the foot up and asked them to examine the foot, which was absolutely rigid. She didn't think they were testing it enough, so she told them off about it. She told them off, you know. 'You are not going to hurt the medium, because we have built up the power. Otherwise you wouldn't have been allowed to touch her anyway. So please test it.' Well they did, and of course, the foot was absolutely rigid. There was no give in the foot at all. She didn't say any more. She just took me back to my seat and then left me. I was perfectly all right. The foot was perfectly normal and everything. I had no ill effects from this. It was just one of our experiences, which we didn't bother about.'

Quite some time later, Mrs D was speaking to a woman whom she did not know at that time, but who was a member of the developing class at her local Spiritualist church, and who was going to Egypt to visit her daughter, who had married an Egyptian. 'But,' said the woman, 'I have a very strong feeling that that isn't the main reason for going.' On her return, another friend of

Mrs D, whom she had known for years, and who had a strong interest in Egypt and who had done a great deal of reading on the subject, expressed a desire to meet the returned traveller and hear about her impressions of Egypt. So there began a discussion on Egypt, to which Mrs D, who knew nothing about Egypt and had very little interest in the subject, listened with only half an ear. All at once she heard her friend say: 'And do you mean you can actually see these mummies? You can actually see this?' 'Oh, yes,' came the reply. 'I went into such-and-such a place, and, do you know, there was a bride of one of the Pharaohs, and,' she went on, 'do you know, you could actually see her deformed foot!' Mrs D said that she nearly shot out of her chair with astonishment at hearing this. To add further interest and confirmation to this remarkable story, I met the lady in question when I was speaking in 1981 at the Scarborough conference of the Churches' Fellowship for Physical and Spiritual Studies, and she was able to confirm the incident, and remembered Mrs D very well. Although I knew nothing about it at the time, and I am perfectly certain that Mrs D did not either, I later learned that clubfoot deformities were by no means unusual in ancient Egypt, and that several examples are indeed preserved among the mummies.

Though I had previously been inclined to accept the concept of reincarnation intellectually, as being the only way that I was able to reconcile the varying conditions of earthly life with the sense of justice that I felt must run through the whole of creation, the idea that my darling daughter had once been anyone other than **my** daughter; that she had had other parents, and another home; that she was more than **my** daughter alone; that she was, in fact, another soul, with quite separate and different experiences, whose path had crossed with mine; this was something that, at this stage, I found totally repellent. These feelings of revulsion became even stronger following our next sitting with Mrs D, at which Vicky repeated the incident, by appearing in the personality of the long dead Egyptian princess.

At this sitting, following a preliminary discussion with Snowdrop, Vicky again came through, but this time, as I said, as the Egyptian princess, deformed foot and all, controlling the entire body of the medium, and with her right foot distorted into that form of clubfoot which is known as talipes equino-varus. In this deformity the ankle joint is held with the foot flexed rigidly inwards, and the ankle joint extended in such a way that the person is forced to walk out the outside of the foot. Vicky insisted that I should carry out an examination of the foot just as I would have done with a patient in my consulting room. The ankle joint was held absolutely fixed and rigid, as if frozen solid in this distorted position, and no effort of mine could induce the tiniest degree of movement. Then, following my examination of the foot and confirmation of the condition, even as she was speaking, and almost as though a switch had been pressed, the condition suddenly passed off, and the foot returned to normal.

However, perhaps an even more interesting feature of the sitting was that both Ruth and I felt that this personality to whom we were now talking, while remaining essentially Vicky, was a much older and rather different spirit. The voice was quieter and more subdued, with a subtle change in accent and intonation, and there was, both about the voice and her way of speaking, a curiously indefinable and intangible feeling, almost impossible of description; an aura, as it were, of great wisdom and even holiness surrounding the spirit with whom we were talking.

Vicky: Mummy! I am so happy! Are you happy? Look Daddy, it is all right now! Chung Ling – he is the doorkeeper of the medium – said that I would be allowed to bring this as evidence to you. He said that you would not hurt the medium; that there is a complete wall of power built up around her. But the test must be made, because, he said, we must for the sake of the medium, bring our proof.

Self: This was important. Yes, this we understand.

Vicky: I understand she always asks that evidence may be given. You think I am talking quite well?

Self: You are talking beautifully, darling.

Vicky: It is wonderful to be able to talk to you in this way. Yes, it is true. I met the medium a long time ago.

Self: This was before you came to us as our little girl.

Vicky: Before I came to you as your little girl. It is wonderful to meet you again. You will always have a very special place in my heart – always – because you have been to me such wonderful links of love. I could only remain here for a short while. Yet that was a time of great happiness. For you helped

123

me to progress; and for this I will eternally be grateful to you both. You understand?

Self: And you are going to – you **are** helping us to progress?

Vicky: I am helping you now. And as I hoped that that which was the gateway through which you would investigate – you see all things are planned with more than one purpose. That purpose was not only that I should enter into experience on the earth, but that through my transition you too would make the investigation for yourselves. If it seems a little harsh to you that you must suffer in order to seek, remember that when things are easy on the earth, when everything goes well for you, then you do not seek to understand God. You merely accept His gifts and take them for granted.

Self: I am afraid that's true.

Vicky: Therefore it is that God, in his wisdom, gives you the experiences which you come to understand are your greatest blessings, although they appear to be sorrows. Yet out of them, which appear to be darkness, comes a great light, and I rejoice with you for these moments which we spend together. To come back to you gives me great joy.

Ruth: It gives us great joy.

Vicky: But there will be moments when I do not appear to be the little girl, you know, you loved and lost. For you never lost me anyway. I merely went on a little journey, in order that you would miss me perhaps and try to find me. You understand?

Self: Yes, we understand.

Vicky: Will you accept my lily-of-the-valley?

Ruth: Thank you. Lovely.

Comment: Discarnates often bring gifts of flowers as a token of love and affection. For the most part these are in the spiritual realm, and do not materialise. At times the gift is accompanied by the characteristic scent of the flower in question, and this is sometimes used by the discarnate as a means of identification, or by way of announcing their presence. At one period Eric's son, Roger, regularly used to bring the scent of carnations to his father as a kind of visiting card. On this occasion nothing so dramatic happened, but later in the year the ground outside the entrance to my workshop in the garden became carpeted with lily-of-the-valley, which flourished there for a number of years!

Vicky, continuing: I give them to you with all my love and my gratitude for the time we have spent together. You have worked so hard, and it has not been easy. But you will find that the revelations will come to you if you will be but still, and know that HE is God, and we are just tiny rays of light from His love. You understand?

Self: Yes. We understand. And you are going to be able to remain and teach us, are you not? You are not going to go on ahead and leave us?

Vicky: I have already told you, I have committed myself to this mission. When one commits oneself, one says, 'Father, I subject myself to what is Thy will.' And, if one promises, one is promising God. So I will remain to teach you. May I still call you Mummy?

Ruth: Yes, surely. Why not?

Vicky: It sounds so strange, when my mind is travelling so far.

Comment: Vicky is plainly asking whether, in the light of the revelation of her previous incarnation, we can still continue to think of her as 'our little girl'. It was a great shock to me personally, from which it took me weeks to recover, and, with her intuitive perception of what this revelation meant to me, she is looking to give reassurance that she can still think of us as 'Mummy and Daddy'.

Ruth: You can always call us by our Christian names, can't you? Some children do.

Vicky: I don't want to do this.'If I do this, then you will feel you have lost something (that is exactly what I was feeling even at that moment, and this feeling intensified after our return home), and I don't want you to feel that. I want always for you to remember me as you have always known me. It is necessary to speak words of truth to you. I could not remain in the darkness, or keep you in the dark of the truth. But I want you always to retain your hold upon that memory too. You understand?

Self: We understand.

Vicky: This is important. If I have had to reveal things to you, it is that you have to know.

Ruth: Well we are not disappointed. We are very interested. We think it is very wonderful.

Vicky: You know:

'Deep in unfathomable mines
　Of never failing skill,
He treasures up His bright designs,
　And works His sovereign will.'

and He has ordained that our lives should touch each other, and that the links should be forged between us which can never be broken. So I am not going to go away, and neither am I going to enjoy – or otherwise(!) – a new incarnation. I will be with you from spirit. I am not reincarnating. You understand?

Self: Yes. We understand.

Vicky: I am here to remain with you as long as you need me to help you.

Self: Until we come to join you.

Vicky: Until you come to join me. I am NOT reincarnating.

Ruth: Well, we will remember. We will remember.

Vicky: Now don't forget what I have told you.

Ruth: No. We shan't forget.

Vicky: There is a reason I have told you this. I would not speak words which have no meaning. Remember what I have told you. I am not reincarnating. I have no desire to reincarnate at this time; only to help and to serve you. I owe you a debt of gratitude for the love which you have given me, and I must always remember to fulfil my obligation to you in love. Remember.

Ruth: Yes. We will remember.

Vicky: You may have moments when you will doubt very much. You will doubt because of the irresponsible attitude that some people have. But remember my word to you. Do not believe all the things you hear. Sometimes they are born of subconscious reaction. We do not judge them. They are perhaps insecure people, and because they are insecure, they seek to find a little illumination through someone . . . seeking perhaps to give them encouragement. Maybe it is that they are needing people to think they are good and clever. Yet how frustrating it can be when one has to overcome these things. But I have brought my proof to you.

Comment: This is plainly a warning against being naive and gullible, and accepting 'messages' from other sensitives which might appear to conflict with what we have learned.

Vicky, continuing: The medium is perfectly all right, as you see. There is nothing wrong. **It is good to examine.* Paul said 'Test the spirits. See if they be of God.' And what Paul really meant is, 'Test the spirits and see if they are real, and if that which they say is true.'** So you have tested, and I pray to God that you have found, and will find, much more. . . . Now I must go. It has been wonderful talking to you. I am so glad that I was able to communicate. Communication is not just words, you know. Communication is something when one comes and vibrates love to each other. And **it** communicates, and you find that you take this with you and feel happy. This is communication. All is healing; **everything is healing, if it is done with love.** Words of themselves are as nothing. It is what we give is important. . . . May the Grace of God be with us all to help us that we may become more in tune; that you may hear me and, God willing, may see me.

Ruth: Thank you for coming, dear.

Vicky: I am so glad that it was a day that you should be joined together. Happy anniversary.

Ruth: Auf wiedersehen!

Vicky: Auf wiedersehen! May I say *Merci Beaucoup!* .

Comment: *The reference to St Paul is plainly incorrect so far as recorded writings go. There is no record of St Paul having said this. But – he was a master of the psychic dimension, and plainly would have known and understood. He may well have said these words. The famous reference to testing the spirits actually comes from the fourth chapter of the Epistle of St John and runs:

> 'Beloved, believe not every spirit, but try the spirits whether they are of God: because many false prophets are gone out into the world. Hereby know ye the spirit of God: Every spirit that confesseth that Jesus Christ is come in the flesh is of God: and every spirit that confesseth not that Jesus Christ is come in the flesh is not of God.'

Vicky's extreme insistence upon not reincarnating at this particular moment did indeed have a special reason. My eldest son and his wife were expecting the birth of their first child in five months time. When the baby was born, it proved to be a girl, and not all that unlike Vicky in appearance. But for this warning we might easily have thought that this was Vicky returned to earth again to make up for her short incarnation, and to be with us for a further period. Had we believed this, it would, of course, effectively have inhibited any further communication between us. The reference to the anniversary also is interesting. Ruth and I were married on 25th March – her birthday. This sitting took place on 25th February, just exactly four weeks earlier. It bears out, I think, what I have already said, that dwelling in the next world, which is an environment beyond the confines of time and space, which are mere dimensions of the material world, discarnates not infrequently have problems relating to earth time. For them, all time is NOW, and all things, both present, past and future, are already and eternally in existence in the ever present 'NOW'.

Although the whole question of reincarnation is discussed in some depth in the Appendix, I feel that it would not be out of place, at the conclusion of this chapter, to introduce to the reader the train of thought which arose in me as a result of this unusual experience. The spirit of each of us is immortal, without beginning and without end. It neither starts nor finishes here. It has clothed itself in matter for the duration of this lifetime, and what it has done once it can surely do again. I believe that this spirit is, in truth, a minute part of the Divine Creative Power, being God, which has descended into the density of a material environment in order that it may undergo experience, and that it may impregnate and uplift the denser spheres. To this end, it becomes clothed first with a personality (or soul), and then with a physical body. Slowly but surely it is making its way back to the Creator from whom it sprung. I believe that there is within each one of us a divine spark from the fire of God, and it is this which is the essential ground of our being. I believe that this has come down for His own inscrutable purposes into the super-dense and heavy material atmosphere of this world in which we live, and that it is slowly, slowly making its way back to Him. I believe that it is necessary for that spark to go back, enriched with all the experiences of living – the experience of joy, the experience of sorrow and suffering, the experience of success, of guilt and of failure – so that it becomes refined and purified through its repeated lives until at the last (and there is no need to be in a hurry over this, because there is all eternity in which it

128

can be done), like the drop of rain, which has fallen from the heavens upon the mountains and trickled down the mountain streams to the great river, finally to make its way into the mighty ocean, the spark rejoins the eternal fire from which it came; bringing with it all the richness of its many experiences, bringing with it the readiness to surrender its own identity, and yet, para-doxically, with the surrender of that identity still to keep it, there to enrich the Godhead with the wealth of that experience. I believe that this act of descent into the density of the material spheres to impregnate and uplift their density is an intrinsic part of an act of continuing creation by the Father Power; that in so doing each creature leaves behind – or so it is intended – some-thing finer and more glorious because it passed that way; thus it participates in the Master's work and shares in some small part in the continuing act of Creation. This redemptive act upon matter is seen in its apotheosis in the divine incarnation of Jesus, the Christ. This, I believe, is both the glory and the destiny of Man.

CHAPTER TEN

PAUL

It is difficult for us, with our limited horizons and overpowering concentration upon our own individualities, to accept that anything so traumatic as the death of a child could possibly be an integral part of God's planning for Man. But this is because we, who are here on earth, tend not to look beyond the earth, and are thus inclined to consider that life on earth is the main, and perhaps, the sole object of Man's existence. About this our spirit teachers had other views. Here is Snowdrop speaking on this subject on an earlier occasion.

Snowdrop: Now if I may say this (I hope you don't think I am being rude, talking like this), but, if I may say this, it perhaps took something of sadness to bring you to this realisation. Well, nothing is wasted, and you too will come to the time when, when you pray, you can say with all truthfulness: 'I thank you, Father, for the blessings of my joys. But I thank you more for the blessings of my sorrows, for out of them has come an understanding.' You see, it is through this – you were chosen before ever this happened anyway, so there was nothing you could have done about it you see? The little one, that was lent to you for a little while, was an evolved soul, chosen for a purpose: and that purpose was to touch your lives and to quicken the love that was within your heart. Through that, then one knew that you would seek to find that one. Do you understand? One does. If one loves, one seeks to find the loved one. It doesn't matter where they are. We still seek to find. Through this, then comes the opening of the door, which is spoken of so many times: 'Knock and it shall be opened.' This is the beginning of the revelation of the ultimate plan, which has to be, and **must** be fulfilled.

We are inclined to forget, even when we know better, that this material life of ours, on which we set such store, is no more than a single paragraph in the saga of each human soul. The greatest and most important thing of all is that the soul **is immortal**, and that the crucial thing about life is not the fact of life, but the way in which it is lived. Spiritual growth and evolution of the soul through experience are what life is all about. Little as we realised it during her lifetime, our Vicky was already a highly evolved soul, with an important role to play in the great spiritual plan. Because our memories are for the moment confined to the events of one particular life (though it would appear that in some there is an ability to recall past lives), we are unaware of the state of evolution in which we stand. Perhaps this is as well. As has already been hinted, to be burdened with the knowledge of past failures and misdeeds to be redeemed, or with the sense of the overwhelming importance of the mission upon which we embarked at birth, might well be too heavy a load for us to carry. It could in fact serve to distract and hinder us upon our way through life. We are allowed, mercifully, to know just as much as is necessary for us to carry out our mission in life. Not even when we reach the other side does this rule appear to be relaxed. We still see only a part – that part which is necessary for us to see. But, as we progress and evolve still further, that part becomes increased. Our horizon expands and our depth of vision increases together with our capacity to handle the broader view. The idea that passage into the life to come automatically brings completeness of knowledge is totally false. Total knowledge belongs only to God, the Creator. We still see and know only in part, but the glass through which we look darkens the view a little less than that through which we peer at present.

Snowdrop: Some people have some peculiar ideas. They say, 'Well, if they are real spirit, they should know everything.' That's ridiculous! We don't! We don't know everything!

Ruth: No one can know everything.

Snowdrop: No. Because we are only a part, and like a member of the body. So we can only know what we are allowed to know of whatever state of evolution we may be in. Vicky is a very evolved soul.

Ruth: Yes. So we have been told.

Snowdrop: You know, it is all part of the plan which has been in operation for a long time. My medium was in contact with the one you call Vicky before she came to you anyway. . . . You see, when Vicky was discarnate before, it was then she made contact with my medium. Because everything was planned out, you see, even to this time.

Ruth: That's amazing, isn't it?

Snowdrop: To you it is, and to many people it is. But, you see, these things are not just of the moment. They are things which are organised quite a while beforehand. Although we speak in modern English, many of us are not – well we are not English anyway. But there is one common language. Do you know what that language is? The greatest language is love. One knows that one plans things (not just one person, but many), and it is because there are times when we know that people are going to have to pass through certain experiences (and) we know that it will be difficult for them when that time comes. We know that they will need very much reassurance, particularly when a loved one that has been lent to them is concerned.

So all these things are planned, you see. All you do is to accept when the time comes and do something about it. If you don't, then you are only denying yourself the help that is there. We can only reach out our hands. We can't make you take them.

Comment: All things, indeed, ARE planned. But Man has been given free will, so that, despite the plan and the intention, the right to choose is always his. But with that right goes the responsibility to make the right choice and the requirement that he accepts the consequences of that choice. Inevitably mistakes are made and wrong choices made. But through Grace abounding we are granted the opportunity, perhaps in a further lifetime, to redeem our past mistakes.

Self: We have got to reach back.

Snowdrop: You have got to reach back. I think that Vicky was extremely clever, you know. Sometimes some of the things we do are our own ideas.

Self: Are they?

Snowdrop: Oh yes. We enjoy certain liberties, you see. What Vicky did was to prove herself to you in a most wonderful way. This was all part of her own planning, her own thought.

Ruth: Are you talking about a special incident?

Snowdrop: I am talking about the special incident of her first communication. She had this idea that it would be wonderful to be able to say this is conclusive proof; one is not in telepathic communication. This is definitely spirit. Do you see what I mean?

Self: Yes.

Snowdrop: **There is always the question that is arising in the minds of your people here about telepathic communication. Well, we have to do certain things which will rule out any telepathy; so no one could say, 'Oh well, that was telepathic. She was picking up their thoughts.'** So you see Vicky was extremely clever about this, and one has to give credit for this to Vicky herself. You see the organisation behind all these communications is very vast. But at the same time you always get that individuality of the communicator. So you see you cannot lose out on Vicky, because you can never lose her. Do you see what I mean?

Self: We do indeed.

Snowdrop: That individuality which is her; the desire to do things perfectly, which is part of her, which has always been a part of her, and always will be. So you see always that determination to do everything right. One could maybe say 'This is ambition', but I don't think so really. I think it is really this wonderful essence of perfection.

Ruth: This is the impression she gave.

Snowdrop: And this is HER; always to be perfect, to be at the top with everything. . . . You see, in Vicky herself you would see that there was something special. Not just because you were her earthly parents. It has nothing to do with that. But there was that patience and that calmness, and yet that grim determination to get there, which come from all souls who have been striving towards this goal. With each one of us – and this is what we have in common – every link that we can get is important. Every soul that is travelling on the earth at this moment that can be reached, we are reaching them and welding them together. You see, if you have got two lights, two bulbs, and they are in different parts of the room, that light is not so strong. But if you blend those two lights together, then that light is greater. So it is important to draw

133

the lights together, so that they become blended. That way the power becomes stronger, and then it can overcome or break through the barriers that are there.

Comment: The desire for perfection in all that she attempted was an integral part of Vicky's character. It did not make her an easy child to live with, for desire constantly outran performance! The fact that she was five years younger than her brother Andrew, the next nearest in age in the family, and was, after the immemorial fashion of all small girls(!), constantly striving to emulate him, did nothing to ease the situation. The references to her first communication were, of course, in respect of her appearance to Eric on the day when I was prevented from going with him. As I have already pointed out, this amounted to the classical 'proxy sitting', for long accepted by psychic researchers as being the strongest form of evidence, and the least likely to be influenced by telepathic factors. As far as I personally was concerned, both at the time, and whenever I have dispassionately considered the matter, this has always been the final and conclusive factor amongst the evidence.

Up to this time I was still unclear in my mind as to exactly what was being asked of me. I was being gently led along in the direction of spiritual healing, and through my friendship with Gilbert Anderson, a well-known healer, who later became administrator of the National Federation of Spiritual Healers, and was a personal friend of Harry Edwards, I was gradually beginning to learn more about the subject. I was still, however, part of the National Health Service, in which I was practising as a family doctor. Although my personal doubts about survival and the future of life beyond the veil had now been resolved, I still had a very long way to travel, and much both to learn and to unlearn, before I was ready for the task before me. However, the fact that Mrs D was now safely esconced in her own home in north London, and that contacts no longer had to be made at 33 Belgrave Square, had made the way clear for both Eric and myself to receive teaching from an even more highly evolved source than had so far been possible. The first instance of this occurred on 12th January 1970, when Eric went up to visit Mrs D in her new home.

Voice – a deep, resonant and plainly masculine voice: Good day to you! I am very pleased to have this opportunity of speaking to you. I have waited for the time when our plan would be complete, in order that I should come and speak with you in this way. . . . In order that we could bring this child into the present condition to which she now lives. My name is Paul.

Eric: Yes. I've heard of Paul.

Paul: It gives me great joy to come into your conditions to speak with you of the things that must be accomplished.

Eric: This is what I have been looking forward to.

Paul: Indeed, we have looked forward to the day when we could come and speak with you for a little. There are those things which it is not easy for you to understand, but in the very near future we will take you out of your body, and we will reveal to you through your friends, the doctor friend, whom we also know and have included in our plans.

Eric: Yes. When you say you will take me out of the body, could you please clarify that?

Paul: Indeed I can. As you are looking at the child we use at this moment, you see but the shell, and we are the substance. This, indeed, is how it shall be with you. **But it shall be in order that the truth of healing through medical science in spirit shall be revealed as a positive fact.** As you know, there are many who doubt and many who ridicule. But as medical science has progressed on earth, so also has it progressed in spirit. As you will understand, my friends, nothing stands still. Therefore there is progress with those who have the well-being of humanity at heart in our world of spiritual consciousness. And to the chosen ones, that have the ability to respond, we are prepared to bring forward through their organism the evidence of our knowledge of sickness in the body and in the mind. You follow?

Eric: I follow.

Comment: Mrs D was, at the moment of speaking, in deep trance. When this happens, the soul and the spirit of the individual are completely withdrawn from the physical body, retaining connection only by the so-called silver cord – as happens in dreams, out-of-the-body experiences, and anaesthesia – leaving the physical body free to be controlled by the discarnate entity. This is what had happened when Vicky materialised the clubfoot of the Egyptian princess, and also takes place when the discarnate communicates directly, as Paul was doing at the moment. Under these circumstances the medium has no faculty of recall of what has taken place during the sitting. It is unclear at this point whether Paul is suggesting that Eric will be controlled by a discarnate 'doctor' who will teach of new forms of physical therapy to be embodied within orthodox medical therapies, or whether he will heal in trance. Eric himself rather expected that this would take the form of communication of new therapies. In actual fact – and the term 'in the very near future' is a trifle misleading, because it took years to achieve – his healing appears to take place under discarnate control while in a state of light trance. As the years have passed, however, his trance ability has deepened, and the discarnate controling entity now communicates verbally on certain occasions.

Paul continuing: In order to do this, we must of necessity firstly subject the instrument, yourself, completely to our will. It will become very natural to you after a little while to allow yourself to become the absolute subject of spirit at these moments. Naturally, one does not endeavour to take away your will in life, for you have to live in a material world of matter, and are an individual spirit. We would not want to, nor could we, take away that which is your individualism. But at the times when we do desire to impart some evidence which can be helpful, we can and we will subject that will for that particular time. You follow?

Comment: Notice again the insistent desire to impart evidence. All of this, it seems, is not just an exercise in the healing of sickness, but part of the grand design to bring Man back from his obsession with the material towards a realisation of his own true nature as an immortal spirit. The pattern is gradually becoming clearer.

Paul: So it is important that you accept this responsibility to spirit, to keep that channel clean and pure. Anything that comes from the intelligent forces of spirit that is of a high order, can only come under those conditions which I have stated. We appreciate the qualities which we see in you as a person.

Eric: Thank you.

Paul: When you work with spirit, you work with spirit; not as something that you desire for yourself, but only in order that you may receive the benefits of that which you have proven for your own satisfaction as positive proof of intelligence outside of earth conditions which have progressed beyond the normal activities of humanity. I hope I have made myself clear?

Eric: Yes.

Comment: Notice again the ever present emphasis on evidence, both here and in the passage following. Proof of higher intelligence outside of earth conditions – with all that that implies for Man – appears to be the all important thing at this point.

Paul: The doctor is invaluable to us in this way.

Eric: Is it possible for you to tell me how he will help in this plan?

Paul: That is what I was going to talk about now. He has medical knowledge. Therefore he is no one's fool. He will know the truth of the statements that are made to you. He will understand within a little that which we are imparting. Therefore we have a good foundation on which to start. To those who are on the outside, (of healing), yourself, it (i.e. what comes through) cannot be coloured by that which you know already. Therefore you will see that we are very wise in our choice of instruments. One complements the other according to the knowledge which they have. If you had been linked with the medical profession, we could not have used you in this particular way, because it could have become coloured by the knowledge which you already had. Therefore it is important to choose very carefully the instruments one wishes or desires to use. **The doctor is a different proposition entirely. He has certain knowledge because of his profession on earth. Therefore he can, as it were, dissect that which comes forth through you as a channel. Do I make myself clear?**

Comment: This passage, as spoken, seems a trifle obscure! I think what Paul must mean is that it is better for their purposes of demonstrating the reality of discarnate knowledge of healing

137

for that knowledge to be transmitted through a channel without any prior knowledge of healing.

Eric: Yes. I think so.

Paul: So it is vitally important that we go a step at a time. Were we to impart too much to you in a moment, you, being what you are, your make up being what it is, would then place barriers in the way, because you would then say, 'Ah! But this has got into my mind. Is this therefore a subconscious reaction?' You do understand?

Therefore you must see that there is wisdom in the fact that we do not impart too much information. **We desire a clear channel**, or a clear field of action. We do not wish to delay the work which has to be done. We wish only that it should go smoothly and well. But were we to impart to you too much knowledge, you would block us at every turn through this conscientiousness, (which I appreciate very much), and this desire to know that this is true and not just some wishful thinking on your part.

Comment: The important thing in spiritual healing is the nature of the channel through which it comes. Too much knowledge is a dangerous thing! It is very difficult for left-brain dominated intellectuals to achieve the essential simplicity needed to accept the things of the spirit. They tend always – as Paul points out – to be asking questions which can undermine the whole process, and lay too great an emphasis upon the personality of the individual. I am reminded of Jesus' words, 'Except ye become as little children ye cannot enter the kingdom of heaven' and we must remember that his disciples were chosen from among the ordinary people and not from among the intellectual elite of the day! Most of the best healers and sensitives are remarkable for this quality of childlike simplicity and trustful obedience.

You will note that during this period of time, in which you have had certain revelations, each one has confirmed the other. Therefore have no doubt as to the outcome of these things. Do not take any thought of the morrow, but know that all things will work together for good. We are not insensitive to the conditions in which you dwell. We know of the difficulties of earth life. Therefore realise this: **that all things are to be taken care of.** There is no need to have any doubts or fears on this matter.

Comment: Paul's assessment of Eric's personality was very shrewd. He was, indeed, a deeply sincere person and the very last person to allow the wish to be father to the thought. Wishful thinking and self-conviction were totally foreign to his nature. To my mind, this shrewd assessment is yet further evidence of the genuine nature of these communications. Paul's comment about the 'difficulties of earth life' rings very true. Eric was much concerned at this time over the problem of suitable premises in which to carry out his healing mission. At that time he was the proprietor of a small, high class shoe shop, which was situated as one of a row of shops in a very busy and noisy main road. Eric himself still lived above his shop in a two-storey maisonette This was approached by an outdoor, concrete stairway giving access to an open corridor serving the row of maisonnettes above the shops. It is difficult to conceive of an environment less suitable for carrying out a ministry of healing. Access was awkward even for the able-bodied, and accommodation severely limited. The road outside was a main traffic artery, with heavy lorries passing noisily by throughout the twenty-four hours of the day and frequently coming to a standstill at times of peak traffic flow. The whole ambience was totally wrong for anything involving association with the higher powers. However, Paul spoke the truth. Within a comparatively short time Eric was able to negotiate a loan at a purely nominal rate of interest, and to build a modern bungalow on a pleasant village green, remote from the problems of traffic and parking, and with space to indulge his hobby of gardening. The surrounding atmosphere is one of complete peace and tranquillity and entirely suitable for spiritual work of all sorts. It has since become the centre for my own work, in association with Eric, for the group healing of cancer patients.

Paul: You know, my friends, many people on earth do not realise that we are not saints. They call us saints. In reality we have passed this way the same as you. We have had our doubts and our moments of great weakness, and, if it is any comfort to you to help you to understand how much we realise your difficulties, then I too had my moments. We too sat in the silence and asked that we be given guidance what we had to do; in other words, 'Whither goest Thou?' And many times there was no answer. We could not hear. We could not see. Like yourselves, many times we were discouraged, disheartened, lost confidence. **But you know, my friends, it is when you are on the edge of the precipice that God makes His purpose known. It is then that you begin to see the next step. The ground is there before your feet. You cannot fall.** Everything is in HIS hands, and we work according to HIS wisdom. And the pattern of your life since its inception has been prearranged. It has been a preparation. Tomorrow you too will see a little clearer according to your capacity, or the wisdom of your seeing.

May I take this opportunity of wishing the members that are attached to your organisation the manifold blessings of the spirit? I send my love to your dear families, who will be taken care of. There is no necessity for anxieties. You will eventually, my dear friends, become as the child I use at these times, with great confidence in our abilitity to take care of the things that matter. It is a great joy to speak with you.

Eric: It is a great joy to speak with YOU.

Paul: It is also wonderful to know that those who are suffering through the ignorance and limitations of your earthly people will be able to receive the benefits of the work which can, and must, and SHALL be done. *The mind is a very complex thing, and, indeed, the understanding of the mind is absolutely nil as far as earth people are concerned.* You would agree with me?

Eric: Yes. I agree.

Comment: Paul is perfectly correct in his assertion that man is woefully ignorant of the powers of the mind, which are only now starting to be studied. The study of parapsychology is vital to the understanding of the mind. But it is important to realise that there are different levels of consciousness in the mind which range all the way from those connected with immediate consciousness to those buried in far memory. There are also powers which relate to the material environment as well as to states of consciousness in other minds. The important light that these throw on the constitution and working of the mind is that they appear to be outside the laws governing the physical realm. This leads us to postulate the existence of another, equally real but non-physical, realm in which the mind exists. (This subject is fully discussed in the author's previous book, *The Gate of Healing* [C. W. Daniel, 1983]). This, in its turn, has important connotations for the continued existence of the mind (personality) following physical disintegration.

Paul: But, you know, **there are many sicknesses that can be helped, once the barriers of orthodox medicine have been overcome.** I wish you well, and pray that you will feel, as you have today, our presence more and more strongly as you respond and subject yourself.

Eric: This I want.

Paul: And this shall be.

Comment: Although over fifteen years have now elapsed since this conversation, neither Eric nor I have yet developed the unique ability of Mrs D for complete withdrawal of consciousness from the body, and the ability to enable it to be used by discarnates. Indeed I am beginning to question whether this is what Paul really meant at this point. As far as I personally am concerned, I think he was probably meaning the development of complete trust and 'confidence in our ability to take care of the things that matter'. That I have certainly developed in full measure. Eric is gradually beginning to develop the ability for trance mediumship, and I think that there is little doubt that when healing he is 'controlled' by a discarnate spirit. There are also an increasing number of occasions when he speaks under light trance and appears to be being used as a vehicle by a discarnate communicator. Now that he has finally been able to retire from his retail business work, it is probable that both these facilities will deepen and increase in power and effectiveness. For myself, I have never experienced the most elementary capacity for going into trance, and I think it likely that such gifts as I have lie in another direction, possibly that of inspirational or mind-to-mind communication.

At this point Paul is concerned with the healing mission which seemed to lie before us both. His remarks appear to be addressed at least as much to me as to Eric, and have gone a long way in guiding the development of my own thinking in the intervening period. It is interesting to note that the pattern of both our lives was already determined from the very moment of their inception, confirming what Snowdrop has already told us: 'You were chosen for this, anyway, so there was nothing that you could have done about it.' Paul returns to this at the conclusion of this remarkable communication, when he spoke about those who had been our children in these moving words:

Many times I have spoken to the one who came into the world to be your earthly son. It may have appeared to have been a great tragedy that his earthly span of life was so short. But, you see, it has all been a part of the plan. Human people would think of this as being a cruel thing to do. But, indeed, you will grow to understand, and to be able to say with all sincerity: 'I thank you, Father, for the blessings of my joys: but I thank you even more for the blessings of my sorrows, for out of them has come a wondrous understanding, and an illumination of the knowledge which lies within my soul'.

He is a wonderful soul, this one who was your earthly son. He has had wonderful results simply because he was a wonderful soul. He did not find it difficult to talk with you. People do not understand. They seek for communication with those who are dead, instead of seeking to communicate with those who are living. They do not realise that it is according to our state of enlightenment how we can communicate. And, in the words of our medium, 'There can be no communication unless there is a communicator'. And then the communication is not with one, but with many.

Comment: Communication seems at all times to be very much of a team effort. Note, too, that ease of communication seems to be greatly influenced by the state of spiritual evolution of the communicator. However, highly evolved discarnates require a medium of a similar degree of evolution whom they can utilise. Perhaps this accounts for the paucity of communications which are of real spiritual value at the present time. Those highly evolved souls, who are incarnate at this moment, are concerning themselves with more pragmatic matters than mediumship, presumably because the present climate of thought is unfavourable to mediumship and communication. Highly evolved souls are not willing to waste their energies in knocking on permanently closed doors! They have better things to do, and other ways of serving humanity.

And so I say to you that these, who have been children in your understanding of earth conditions, are indeed wonderful people. They have co-operated with us. They have helped to bring you together – the members of the body that we have needed. Therefore I salute with all love your dearest son and the doctor's dearest daughter. For they are good and faithful servants, and, to us who know them even better than you, they are born of the spirit of love. If one could only realise the import of these words more fully, then you would realise and understand, when they speak to you of the universal family consciousness, they are not leaving you behind. They are taking you along with them. There is no need to fear being left behind, while they march on to brighter things. They are reaching out their hands to you. And you are reaching out to them, which is good. Therefore you are going on together, and by the grace of God we shall overcome the ignorance which has kept the truth hidden from the minds of mankind. May the Grace of God be in your thinking – and in your understanding.

This communication was given to Eric on 12th January 1970, just four days before Vicky first told us about her Egyptian incarnation, and a month before she confirmed this by 'appearing' as the Egyptian princess. About this time I heard of a week long pilgrimage to the Isle of Iona by members of the Churches' Fellowship for Psychical and Spiritual Studies, of which I was now an enthusiastic member. Shortly after putting my name down to go, I was invited by Colonel Reg Lester, the founder of the Fellowship, to contribute to this by giving a talk. I had felt right from the start of the Odyssey that these revelations were not given to Eric and myself just for our own edification, but that they were meant to be shared in some way with others at the right moment. I therefore felt that this pilgrimage, where I would be surrounded by people who shared my feelings about the spiritual nature of life and the nearness of the afterworld, and where we would be living in a place which had been a centre of

143

spiritual power for many hundreds of years, was the right occasion on which to reveal what had been happening to us. I accordingly prepared a talk, which I entitled 'One Man's Odyssey', which told the story of our adventures, and which was illustrated with extracts from the recordings which I had made at the various sittings. When I was considering what to include and what to leave out, however, I was in the deepest doubt about the propriety of including Paul's words from this previous sitting. They seemed to be putting the spotlight on me in a way which I felt was not very desirable, and could readily be seen as presenting myself as seeking to be seen of man. These doubts continued until a couple of weeks before we left for Iona, at which juncture I went up to Mrs D for a final sitting before I presented my talk, in case there was anything that my spiritual teachers particularly wanted me to include. At this sitting Paul actually appeared again and came and talked with me. It is difficult to describe my feelings on this occasion. I was by this time quite convinced that this was indeed he whom we had known as 'St Paul, the Apostle'; one of the great spiritual masters; the 'Great Lion of God', who had done so much to promote the spread of his Master's message throughout the world, and whose words were daily read in our churches and places of worship. Yet he had deigned to come down and talk with me, a humble neophyte upon the path, with everything to learn. Yet so it was. Ruth and I, two very ordinary denizens of the twentieth century, were sitting and talking with one who had lived and worked in the times of the Master. Words still fail me, when I recall my feelings upon this occasion.

Voice, deep and commanding in tone: Dyi kyum!

Self: Greetings.

Voice, solemnly and with great feeling: Greetings! By the Grace of God we meet!

Self: I am glad to meet you.

Voice: It gives me great joy to speak with you.

Self: And I with you.

Voice: My name is Paul, as you have realised already. It is essential that we take care of the instrument we use. In all things which are of the flesh there are always weaknesses. The spirit may be of great strength, but the body can be very weak.

Comment: Mrs D was evidently not very well this morning. The sitting had started with Tania, but Mrs D had come round from her trance before Tania had finished speaking, due to an attack of catarrhal choking. Unusually, however, while she was talking about Tania, and telling us something of her background, she was 'taken over' and went into trance, when Paul came through.

Paul: . . . There are times when it is essential that people realise only the fact of survival. Who or what the communicator may be or may have been is not important. The greatest thing we know is to reassure people as to the fact of survival, the continuity of life, **in order that they shall understand that it is vitally important to the way they live.**
Ruth: Yes, it makes all the difference, doesn't it?
Paul: It is indeed, my child, a great step forward when one passes through the valley of shadows in order to come into the light. Yet many times people cry out against God. They condemn Him for His lack of charity for the suffering which is caused through the death of a loved one. But they understand so little that God is granting them a great blessing – as you have been blessed. For out of the darkness cometh a light, and the light eliminates the darkness. Is this not a true?
Self: Yes.
Paul: Indeed it is important always to remember that that which you create today is that which you will see tomorrow. **Therefore, whatever one does, one must also understand that one is truly going to reap whatsoever one sows.** I hope you can hear me quite clearly?
Self: Very well.
Paul: I am of necessity having to be extremely careful. If we were not what we are, we should not be able to use this channel at all. We have to completely subject the physical matter in order to talk with you. But I do reassure you that there is nothing that we would not do in order to express our great love for you. If one loves a child, one chastises a child. It is not done to hurt, but to help. So I say to you, it is good to learn to walk before one learns to run. If one tries to run before one learns to walk, then one will eventually learn that one hurts oneself through trying to move quicker than one is capable of doing.

145

Self: You fall down.

Comment: Paul is gently warning me against impatience, a besetting sin of mine, and against frustration that my healing powers and healing mission were not moving more rapidly. Seen with hindsight, I can endorse his warning! Neither I, nor conditions around me, were ready yet. I had yet to learn the true meaning of the spiritual law that 'All Things in Due Season Come'.

Paul: You fall down! It is so difficult to climb the mountain of life, is it not? There are many hard places. And everyone has to learn to climb that mountain. This is the law, that no one can climb that mountain of life for us. But there is one great blessing, and that is that one gains experience. And how does one use the experience that one gains, except by saying, 'Here is my hand, my brother. I have passed this way before you. Therefore let me help you. I cannot climb for you, but I can help you out of my experience to climb that mountain with less difficulty, with less hurts.' But you must listen. You must obey. If you cannot obey, then you are not coming in complete subjection and completely taking my hand, but are saying, in the words which I used so many times:'Thy Will be done. But Oh Father! Let it be my way!' How many times, and how many voices have said these words without understanding or realising the great import of the words which are spoken. They become as nothing. They mean nothing. They are merely words. They are lip service, but indeed they are not coming in absolute subjection to God's will, and that we must eventually come to understand that alone we are nothing.

We need each other. Therefore go forward. Have no fear or doubt in your mind. Anything that is worth having is worth striving for. Everything that you do that is bringing you closer to the realisation and the consciousness of the great creative gift within you will always bring you into contact with rough patches, trials, times when you feel, 'Is it worth while?' What am I doing? Am I really about my Father's business? Or am I seeking something of a sensation? Is this my own desire? Or is it really the Will of God?'.

146

Self: I have been asking just that!

Paul: I know! Why do you think I have come? For all things are known by the discarnate ones. It is vitally important that you lay hold on the Truth. Only the Truth can set you free; free of your doubts. There will be moments when you can hear nothing. You know, many times, like you, we sat together, we had our dissensions among us. We differed in our opinions, and our opinions very often interfered, just as yours do. We are no different to you, my dear brother; no different. We have merely passed through experience. Let our experience help you. We are only too happy to give you our help.

Paul spoke further of his own doubts and experiences during his life. Many people, he said, on reading the Bible, thought that everything had been made easy by a moment of revelation which had changed everything. Speaking slowly and with the greatest emphasis he said.

It was NOT! Many times like you I looked back, and I would have reverted to my former way of life. Make no mistake. I was no saint! I was a man, the same as you. So remember, if they speak of 'the great Paul', I am not great. I have received the great blessing of the revelation of the truth, but alone, I am nothing.

He went on to say that each one of us had been given our own experience, but that we were a family who had gone out into the world. Our paths had lain in different directions and we had walked away from each other for a little while, but we were part of a family and it was good to see each other again. I asked him whether we had known each other before. He replied that indeed we had, and that in a little while I would begin to have remembrance of that experience. This might only be a vague remembrance, but it would be there, because it would bring me reassurance about the things of the spirit, and this was important for me.

Paul gave his blessing to Ruth and to 'those whom you call your family', reminding us both that while God had given us the power to create the body, He did not give us the power to create the spirit. For this reason, he said, there might be moments when our children would appear to be beyond our comprehen-

147

sion, since there were facets of their characters which we did not understand. We tended to regard our children from the physical point of view as *our* children, but the spirit of each was individual and would act in accordance with that individuality. It could be very difficult in certain circumstances to know the right thing to do. Naturally those who had families on earth wanted to do everything they could to help them, but there were times when this caused hurt rather than help. At this point, and for the second time in this sitting, the medium broke into a prolonged fit of coughing, and came abruptly out of her trance state.

CHAPTER ELEVEN

PAUL 2

In the last chapter Paul's teaching had been abruptly stopped by Mrs D's coughing fit. When she recovered Mrs D apologised and we talked at some length with her about what he had said to us, and she was most helpful. She said that she felt intuitively that we were meeting certain difficulties with people when things did not seem to be working out. In her experience when we were given great gifts from the world of spirit we were subsequently put through a period in which our faith was put to the test to see how far we had progressed. We have to realise that no one ever gets anything for nothing, and the testing is necessary to see what use we have made of the revelations which we have been given. Unless we put these to work for humanity, we are in danger of becoming like the servant in the parable who buried the talent given to him by his master instead of putting it to work. Psychic curiosity for its own sake is to be condemned.

We spoke about changes that were to come, and Mrs D said that she felt that at the moment things were not progressing as they should, because a change of environment was necessary first. There was an impenetrable barrier created by the present environment. Once this was changed, the barrier would fall away and a talent which was not being properly used at present would be used as it should be.

This was certainly true as far as Eric's healing mission was concerned. His present premises were impossible and the only healing which he was doing was at the local Spiritualist church in Norwich, 20 miles away. Ruth and I had been discussing the possibility that we might lend Eric the money to build a proper place to live which might have a sanctuary attached, and the effect of this conversion was to encourage us to do just this. With this help Eric was able to build a pleasant bungalow on a nearby village green and, after selling his business six years later, to build on a healing sanctuary. From the moment of moving into this peaceful environment Eric began to move ahead both as a healer and as a sensitive in a more rapid and assured manner. Many people received help through his healing powers and eventually I came to work with him in the sanctuary when the cancer healing and support group which had grown up at my home became too large for us to accommodate. So, as Vicky had foretold, I found myself giving healing in a healing sanctuary. But this was not to materialise yet for a number of years.

The other important thing that came out of this conversation with Paul was the feeling that he wished to resolve my doubts about including his message to Eric in the talks which I was to give at Iona later on. I was not to be deflected from this by the feeling that this was seeking to be seen of men, and my intuitive understanding that out of all the messages which we had received this was the highest and most important, was right.

Also from Paul's teaching a remark about the difficulties of people, and things that seemed to be going wrong, proved to be correct. The meat was too strong for some of those attending the pilgrimage to digest. For a number of them this was their first experience of the discarnate, and they shied away like frightened colts! I was subsequently attacked within the Fellowship for laying too great an emphasis upon the psychic dimension, and paying insufficient attention to spiritual matters. The shadow of the traditional church, described elsewhere as 'The Longest Shadow in the World' (MacDonald, Findlay, MacManaway and Pearce: Findlay, Boturich 1978) lay menacingly across my path. **What such people forget is the truth of Paul's words that to very many the most important fact about life IS its continuation – its continuity of being.** Once this has been grasped and accepted in all its implications, it is then possible to start to contemplate the nature of that life. For people such as these an awareness of the psychic level is the first rung upon the spiritual ladder that leads eventually to the All Highest. However in the minds of very many the belief seems to exist that there is a natural progression from the psychic to the occult (i.e., forbidden things) and thence to the daemonic and to witchcraft. It is this belief, based for the most part on ignorance, on fear and superstition, which is such a powerful barrier to spiritual understanding.

There was another and unexpected side effect to these disclosures. The group making the pilgrimage, while residing at the Columba Hotel on the island, held its meetings within the precincts of the Abbey, in a room opening off the cloisters and known as the Chapter House. Iona had been a centre of spiritual power long before the arrival of Columba and his monks from Ireland, and had probably been a centre for Druid worship. Indeed, despite the delightful legend that Columba settled here because it was the first place of landing from which it was no longer possible to look back on Ireland, it is very likely that he chose to settle on Iona just because it was a spiritual centre. In modern parlance 'the vibes were right for what he had to do'. After the landing of St Columba and his twelve companions in the sixth century the island became a centre of Celtic Christianity, and from it the monks set out on missionary journeys, which took them the length and breadth of Scotland as well as deep into Europe. (The Canton of St Gall, in Switzerland, was actually named after one of Columba's monks who helped to Christianise the tribesmen in that area.)

Following a succession of Viking raids in the eighth and ninth centuries, the relics of St Columba and the Book of Kells, an illuminated manuscript of the Bible, written during the eighth century, were removed to Ireland for safety, and the Abbey started to fall into disrepair, both materially and spiritually. After the collapse of the Celtic church in Britain consequent upon the Synod of Whitby, the monastery started to fall into decay, until in the eleventh century Queen Margaret of Scotland, herself an Englishwoman, imposed her faith, which was Roman Catholicism, upon Scotland. Margaret gave money for the building of a mortuary chapel for the monks, which is still to be seen today upon the island, and is known as the Reilig Oran. The island became celebrated as the burial place for the clan chieftains and the Scottish kings, twenty-seven of whom lie buried within the precincts of the Abbey. With the imposition upon it of the discipline of the Church of Rome the Abbey began to pick up again, and at the beginning of the thirteenth century the old Celtic monastery was no longer large enough and was rebuilt according to the established Roman pattern. The Abbey church was subsequently reconstructed on a number of occasions, and in 1499 it became the Cathedral church of the Western Isles.

151

However, following the Reformation, and the backlash against the Roman Church, the monks had to leave the island in 1567, and the Abbey again began to fall into ruins.

This process continued until in 1899 the eighth Duke of Argyll gave the ruins to the Church of Scotland, expressing the desire that the Abbey Church should be rebuilt and made available to any branch of the Christian Church for worship. The rebuilding of the church took place between 1902 and 1910, and in 1938, largely due to the efforts of the Revd (now Lord) George Macleod, the Iona Community was formed and started to rebuild the cloisteral buildings. The rebuilding work was carried on throughout the war and was the subject of international donations until at last, over thirty years later, it was finally completed. The island has indeed now become once again a centre of religious experience for many different sorts of people.

The resurrection of Iona, Phoenix-like, from the ashes of its past and its return to its former glory and eminence as a centre of spiritual power and understanding had been described prophetically by Columba upon his deathbed. 'Before the world shall come to an end Iona shall again be as it was.' In the fifth century Iona had been the centre from which the teachings of the Christian church were taken throughout the length and breadth of Scotland and well as deep into mainland Europe. The teachings, of course, were those of the Celtic Church, which was more mystical and perhaps more spiritual – certainly more psychic – than the pragmatic Church of Rome, When King Oswald of Northumbria, who had been converted to Christianity, sought for someone to preach the Gospel to his people, it was to Iona that he turned. Columba sent Aidan, one of the monks who had accompanied him from Ireland to Iona, and it was he who was responsible for the Christianisation of Northumbria under King Oswald, and through his influence, of much of England even before the arrival from Rome of St Augustine and his monks. Cuthbert, Wilfrid and Bede were also products of this church.

Now although the Abbey is available, in accordance with the wishes of the donor, to any branch of the Christian Church for worship, it is important to remember that it is run by the Iona Community, who are part of the Church of Scotland, and Presbyterians. There is a strongly calvinistic and fundamentalist

152

strain running through it, and, despite the holding of a weekly service of healing, including the laying on of hands, which is carried out by the whole congregation, or as many as wish to lay on hands, the Community has an intuitive aversion to all things psychic. One must also remember that psychic sensitivity is, or was, until it was eliminated by a campaign of systematic persecution and witch burning during the seventeenth and eighteenth centuries, extremely common among the inhabitants of the western isles of Scotland. This campaign, moreover, was strongly supported by the radicals within the Scottish Church. There is therefore a deep distaste through the island for all matters even remotely psychic, and a fixed belief that all such things are, quite literally, the WORK OF THE DEVIL! Although our meetings in the chapter house, at which the talks were given and the tapes played, were private to the members of the pilgrimage, information of 'what was going on' reached the Warden, to his considerable displeasure, and for a time the Fellowship became *persona non grata* at the Abbey.

So there came the testing of faith and confidence of which we had spoken, and it was necessary to proceed with extreme discretion. Even now, more than twenty years later, my colleagues upon the Council of The Churches' Fellowship for Psychical and Spiritual Studies are apt to view me with some suspicion in consequence of these revelations. I see their point. Sensitives of the quality of Mrs D are very, very rare indeed, and over-encouragement of the perplexed to seek guidance through communication can lead to confusion, if nothing worse, through too low a level of communication.

In any sitting the level of communication reached depends partly on the sitter's ability to respond and understand, but mostly on the level to which the sensitive can raise his/her own level of consciousness. The understanding of discarnates on the lower levels is little greater than that which they had while on earth, and communication which fails to rise above these levels is often merely productive of confusion. In *The Celtic Church Speaks Today* (Revd A. W. Jackson. CFPSS 1968) there is an interesting account of communication taking place with a first century disciple of Jesus, who preferred to be known as Denarius. In this instance it was apparently necessary for there to be a chain of mediums, like transformer stations, with one medium on each level extending from the earth plane to the extremely rarified tenth plane upon which Denarius existed. While I take this particular description of the mediumistic conditions with rather more than the proverbial pinch of salt, it does, I think, lend strength to my belief that it is the level to which the medium's mind is able to ascend which determines for many the level from which the communicator speaks. Paul himself was described to me as a 'Master Power', which suggests to me that he is able to lower his own state of consciousness to meet that of the medium.

This aversion to the psychic, of course, is shared by many beyond the Church of Scotland. A patient of mine, whom I had advised to learn how to relax so as to combat a stress situation, was actually advised against meditation by a local vicar, because, he said, 'in the silence, the devil might get in'! While a hostile attitude towards psychic matters, however, is not without foundation, it is **misuse** of the psychic level which constitutes the real danger. Protection both against the temptation to misuse and against the very real dangers which this involves lies in the purity of the motives of the seeker. There ARE mischievous discarnates, and they CAN create danger.

A year following his first appearance to Eric, on 26th February 1971, Paul again appeared briefly to speak with us.

Paul: We have spoken together on a previous occasion. Therefore it is no surprise to you. I am pleased to see you are responding well. The sanctuary has been prepared, and the healing shall take place. There are members of the body which will be brought in to help in service to other people. . . . Therefore it is imperative that you realise that you must automatically respond to changes. You will leave your house. This is not a prophecy. I do not prophesy. I speak facts. But it will be in accordance with the law of change; change which is progressive. Therefore you will take it as it comes. Those who are unenlightened seek for prophecies. We do not prophesy. We speak of that which is fact, which has already been prepared, in order that that which is for the good of the whole may be carried out with the least difficulty. I merely mention this in order that you will realise that you are completely in our hands.

Comment: This remark was, and remains obscure. There has

been no question of our moving house, either at the time or at any time since – and, to date, over fourteen years have elapsed since this message was given. Two possible interpretations spring to mind. The first, and most likely, is that this statement was actually made with reference to Eric, who, as we have seen, moved house some six months later. It seems that he and I are so closely bound together in our spiritual work that from time to time we become identified with each other. (In any case, is it not true that in a spiritual sense we are all members one of another, and that the idea of separateness is but an illusion based upon our sensory dependence?) The other, and to my mind less likely, explanation refers to my place of work. We did, in fact, move from our own surgery, which had been my father's before me, and was attached to my partner's house, into a custom built Health Centre, built by the local health authority, some five or six years later. This certainly was in accordance with the law of progressive change!

The other interesting thing to note is Paul's statement that the sanctuary had already been prepared. At this point Eric had just started on the building of his new home, which was eventually to be the site of his sanctuary. Despite the loan which we had made to him, resources did not permit its extension to include a sanctuary, and at the time he saw no prospect of this coming about. It was not until he was able to sell his business some five or six years later so as to have more time to devote to his healing mission, that the *sanctuary, already prepared and in being upon the aetheric plane*, was able to be built on the earth plane.

*Paul continuing:*All that is done shall be done for the benefit of those who are seeking help and guidance, Many years ago, when we walked in the garden together, we realised the truth that that which had been made manifest through us as a creative power of healing was only a part of this wondrous creative power called God. But (we realised) that Man also must be able to see that he could not escape responsibility for his actions while on earth. But by the same law neither would he be neglected for that which he had done which is good. Therefore in having the realisation of these truths one knows that one is responsible for one's actions. Therefore if we are limited in our experience, it is wisdom to turn to those who have a greater knowledge than ourselves. This is true humility; the acceptance that we are part of each other. Therefore according to the law, we must function according to whatever member we must be; that we need each other, we must work together.

We thank you for your great trust and belief in us; for the times when you speak mentally to us, and ask us for help and guidance. We thank you for your faith, when you could not see, and yet you believed. There is another (Vicky), who would wish to speak a few words, Therefore we, as part of the organisation to further the progress of your particular mission on earth, work together as a band. Remember this, that you come under the star of David, and this is your responsibility, that you belong to a great organisation. Therefore this sign I leave with you. May God be in your thinking.

So Paul spoke again of our previous knowledge of one another, and made reference to a time when we walked together in the garden, and were quite obviously involved in a mission of healing. More importantly, however, for the purposes of this book, it was from this point that I began to understand a little more about what the East calls the Law of Karma, and started to think that this doctrine of responsibility could have a bearing on our state of health. Maybe we were wrong to consider that disease was just an accident: something over which we had no control; the 'slings and arrows of outrageous fortune', or the bludgeonings of blind, malignant Fate. Maybe we brought our diseases on ourselves by the way we behaved in our lives and by how we looked after our bodies. Maybe some diseases, for which there seemed to be no explanation other than chance – developmental and congenital conditions for example – were the result of behaviour in past lives, and we did in very truth reap exactly what we had sowed. 'Be sure your sins will find you out' was the ancient teaching. Perhaps this was literally true; not in a sense of punishment, but rather as part of the law of cause and effect.

It must be remembered when these words are read that this all took place away back in 1971, at a time when the modern concepts of holistic medicine were still in their infancy and proclaimed only by a heretical minority. This was still a time when disease was seen by the majority of people as the enemy from without which attacked the creature, and healing, even by the doctor, as the semi-miraculous intervention by a superior being with heightened powers and knowledge. The idea that we actually had personal responsibility both for our diseases and for involvement in the healing of those diseases, which I have been preaching up and down the world for the past seven years, and at which we shall be looking in more detail later on in this book, had hardly yet emerged in medical thought. This was totally heretical from a medical standpoint. Yet during the following decade such concepts have blossomed in many countries all over the world, and have started to carry all before them. These ideas, I believe, have been fed through by the spiritual powers into the consciousness of Man, and are a part of the great plan to which reference has been made so many times.

Paul appeared again, rather unexpectedly, some six months later, at a sitting on 27th October 1971. Ruth and I had been discussing as we drove up in the car the role played by St Paul in the early Christian Church, and the tremendous importance given to the Pauline epistles in the services of the Church today. We had been agreeing that while there was much of pure gold in his words, such as his teaching about the gifts of the Spirit, and his great hymn to Love, his words had to be interpreted in the context of the time in which he lived, and that in many cases a considerable degree of obscurity was present owing to flaws in the original manuscript and to errors in copying. In any case, we felt, the words of ANY man, no matter how holy and distinguished, were no more than the words of Man, and therefore potentially liable to error. To take such words and dress them up as if they were the words of God, divinely spoken and recorded, was fundamentally wrong. We felt that much of the doctrinal teaching of the Church today, in particular the penitential dimension, and the emphasis placed upon credal belief as a prime requisite for salvation, was Pauline in origin, and had moved far away from the teachings of Jesus as set out in the Gospels. We also felt that there had been a tendency throughout the ages for the scribe, translator or copyist to 'doctor' the manuscript to comply with his own particular beliefs. The emphasis had shifted away from following Jesus, and endeavouring to express God in our daily lives from an awareness of the Kingdom of Heaven within, to an insistence upon the belief of a particular form of words which had grown out of the way in which other men perceived Jesus and presented his teaching. This, we felt, was an over-emphasis upon credal belief, and was due in large part to the prominence given by the Church to St Paul and the weight attached to his writings, which were treated as if they were the very words of God.

After a brief conversation with Snowdrop, Paul spoke to us again:

Paul: It gives me great joy to speak with you for a moment of time.

Self: It gives us joy to hear.

Paul: It is wonderful to be able to speak to those who do not worship a Paul of the past, but a Paul of the present and of the future.

Self, feeling extremely disconcerted at his awareness of our conversation and criticisms: I hope that my remarks were not irreverent to you. They were not intended to be.

Paul: Certainly I would not be what I am – a soul who can read your thoughts – if I could not accept your criticism, which is founded upon fact and not upon fiction. Whatever has been distorted of the Truth, that at least has not been distorted. I am what I am. And though I may appear at times to be very straight in my way of speaking, yet it has the greatest purpose that love can give to it, and that is to stimulate people to a right way of thinking. Therefore of necessity there are times when I may appear to be stern. But, my dear beloved people, remember that I cannot be condemned to die the death of a saint of the past, whose poor words describing his experiences are today offered as the words of God to the people. For we were men and women in the day in which we dwelt, gathering our experiences. But we are indeed not the same today as we were yesterday. God forbid that that pathway of progression should be closed against us! For are we not all given the opportunity to seek even further to understand our personal relationship with each other and with God? Therefore in the epistles, which have been written in the past, there are words, which perhaps today are offered as absolute fact, which were given as the experiences of individuals, and therefore coloured by the environment of the time in which we had those experiences granted to us? You understand?

Self: Yes. I do.

Paul: Therefore the great tragedy of our endeavour to communicate when we were in the physical body even follows us when we are discarnate. We are still combatting the thought of worship, instead of stimulating people to think for themselves. Therefore the sense of failure follows us through many, many experiences of living. When you read your Bible, which is given as the word of God, remember my words: that they are not the words of God, but the words of Man, which have been further distorted by the interpretation which has been placed upon them. Jesus once said, 'Which of you, if his brother ask him bread, would give him a stone?' Offering the words of man as God's is therefore giving him a stone. *But we must seek together to find that relationship with God throughout our time when we perhaps dwell in the physical dimension in which you live today.* Yet are we confused, and the Truth becomes confounded by opinions which are offered, which have no basis upon fact.

*This passage is quoted exactly as it was spoken. The meaning seems a trifle obscure! I think, in fact, that the order of the words has become jumbled up in their passage through the medium, and that what was intended should probably read: 'But throughout our time, when we perhaps dwell in the physical dimension in which you live today, we must seek together to find that relationship with God.' This at least seems to make sense and to be in conformity with what Paul was talking about.

Paul continuing: Know, my brother and sister, there is no death. Neither are there powers of darkness such as have been described.† There are those who have not benefited from the experiences through which they have passed. That is why it is vitally important that each child seeks to overcome whatever weakness may lie within him. Jesus said, 'Know Thyself'.‡ Seek out that which is within you, and if you find a weakness, then endeavour on seeing it to overcome it. Now I must leave you, with great joy in this communication.

Self: It is a great joy in our hearts to hear you.

†Many will probably wish to dispute this assertion. A fixed belief in the reality of the devil and his angels has been a

cardinal point of Christian belief since earliest times. I personally have always had some doubts about this, believing that there is quite enough evil in the heart of man to account for all the evils in the world without necessarily having to invoke a devil. However I **do** believe that under certain circumstances it is possible for unevolved discarnate souls to overshadow, and impress, and even 'possess' incarnates from time to time, and that this may well account for some of the horrors of unnatural behaviour and cruelty current at the present time. Others may say that this is a gullible position to adopt, and that we are here faced with the deception of which the devil is traditionally believed to be capable.

‡There is no record in the gospels of Jesus ever having used these words. They are, in fact, a quotation from the inscription written up above the entrance to the gymnopedia where Socrates taught: 'Man know thyself, and thou shalt know the universe.' Mrs D twice made reference to this; once here, and once when Snowdrop was talking. This could be a flashback to ancient knowledge, or simply a reference to a well-known quotation. Equally we have no authority for saying that Jesus did not use the quotation with His disciples, or that He was unfamiliar with it.

Paul: Know that all things are possible, and remember that even we, who were on the earth with you many years ago, had the difficulties of interpretation that many are bearing today. Therefore I speak not with condemnation, but with great compassion for the confusion that is around those who offer that which is the word of Man for the Word of God. Indeed then we have seen God in action. For is not this communication that part of God which we are? Working, bringing harmony, reuniting, and strengthening in that uniting those lights which shall surely overcome all darkness, all shadows. . . . Peace be with you.

Comment: Notice the *compassion* of Paul as he speaks of the confusion that surrounds so many who sincerely believe that they are preaching the word of God. There is no sense of self-righteousness or dogmatism to be found in the Paul of the NOW. What a difference from the arrogant intellectual who set out upon the road to Damascus to imprison the Christians! Only an immense compassion for those who think otherwise. We must not judge others whose vision is different from our own, but must accept them for what they are, remembering that there are many facets of Truth, and giving thanks for all that is good within them. As I was later taught by my unseen friends to pray, 'Give us the compassion neither to judge nor to condemn those with whom we disagree'. (See *A Prayer for All Seekers*: could this have come from Paul? An interesting thought.)

With these concluding words from Paul the substance of this series of communications from the discarnate world really came to an end. We still continued to visit Mrs D for a short time longer, but when the messages received started to become repetitive and to restate what we had already been told on several previous occasions, we felt our discarnate friends had said all that had to be said at the present moment. We had received our 'marching orders' and it was now up to us to go forth and translate those orders into action. Not very long after Paul's last message Mrs D was taken seriously ill and had to stop giving sittings. Her husband, too, was in deep trouble, and, having undergone two operations, had had to give up his work. As soon as they were able, the couple returned to their own background in Hull. After a considerable period Mrs D started to work again in the Spiritualist churches in the area and continued to do so until her death last year.

It would be arrogant and egotistical to suggest that this whole exercise was designed specifically for the enlightenment of Eric and myself, for there must have been many others who received help, perhaps just as crucial and vital, during her short stay in north London. 'All things are planned with more than one purpose in mind', as Snowdrop said. But it is suggestive, to say the very least, that almost as soon as Paul had completed his message, and the arrangements made by the spiritual workers were no longer necessary, Mrs D was compelled to return to her own environment. We will consider the implications of that message both for our individual selves, and for mankind in general, in the following chapter.

CHAPTER TWELVE

AFTER PAUL

With this final communication from Paul the major part of the preliminary teaching seemed to have reached its conclusion. The message had been put across, and it was left to us to make what we could of that message and apply it to our own particular situation. However, before considering the authority for the message, which must obviously include some consideration as to the identity of 'Paul', it is appropriate at this moment to summarise what it all meant. Just what was it that we had learned from this astonishing series of happenings? Was any reliance to be placed upon the experience at all? Was it, as it purported to be, a genuine experience of communication from another world, with higher powers and different standards from those to which we were accustomed? Or were we the victims of fantasy and our own delusions, mere grief-stricken victims of circumstance, frantically seeking comfort from any quarter however impossible?

Before making these considerations one important fact has to be kept in mind. Knowledge is of two types: rational knowledge, which is logical and scientific, dependent upon repetitive experiment and quantifiable data; and intuitive knowledge, which is not subject to logic or experimental verification. Each is equally real and valid in its own sphere and at its own level. The one applies to the realm of the material, while the other applies to the realm of the mind. **To attempt to apply the criteria for one to the other is an open invitation to error.** The phenomena which we have been considering belong properly to the realm of the mind. It is therefore inappropriate to attempt to apply to them the same rational criteria as we might apply to a series of scientific experiments. The two belong to different dimensions of being, so different laws apply.

When we start to consider the series of events described in the foregoing chapters, it is necessary to take into consideration the starting points for both Eric and myself. Both of us were extremely reluctant starters. Eric was a conventional and profoundly honest businessman, who had recently moved to a new environment and was intent upon setting up his own business there and making a success of it. Apart from his grief at the loss of his son from an incurable disease, which had taken place seven years previously, he had no interest in healing. Nor was he a dabbler in psychic matters. The whole thing had arisen as the result of a chance remark at a supper party for a group of friends, and initially seems to have been started as a form of after-dinner entertainment.

For my part, though completely thrown by the loss of my daughter (three months later I went into a state of profound reactive depression, which required active medication, and which persisted for many months), I was a conventional though somewhat lazy Anglican Christian, and an entirely conventional family doctor. I was, in fact, the last person who might have been expected to become involved with mediums and seances for communication with the dead. Nor had I gone out to look for such experiences. I had, indeed, owing to the things related to me by 'Pat', my psychic dispenser/receptionist, an open mind as to the possibility of such things happening, and, perhaps, a healthy curiosity about psychic matters, but it went no further than that. The whole thing was, as it were, dumped in my lap. Indeed, on a number of occasions I felt as if I had been taken by the arms on either side and was being frog-marched rapidly down a path which was not one of my own choosing! Moreover each happening seemed to lead logically and inevitably towards the next in what, when seen with hindsight, seems to have been a deliberately planned series of events, involving all four of us, Eric, Cath (Eric's wife), Ruth (my wife) and myself. Now the important thing that has to be grasped is that if this series of events is, as it would seem to be, a **deliberately planned** sequence, then there has to be a mind behind the plan, and that mind was most certainly not that of Eric or myself. In fact, since it was neither of us, it seems to me that we are forced to assume the existence of a discarnate mind. Leaving entirely aside for the moment the arguments about mediumship and the source of such messages and communications, which we shall consider in a later chapter, this has always seemed to me to be a most potent argument for accepting the whole series of events at their face value.

Perhaps before considering just what it is that we have learnt, it is appropriate to consider the authorities for this information. As I have suggested, the whole affair seems to have been too highly organised and coordinated to have been just the work of chance. At every turn we find purpose and method, with each event leading naturally on to another. From the almost casual beginning with an after dinner party of friends lightheartedly playing with the glass and the letters, on through the very persuasive evidence of communication provided through a classical example of a proxy sitting and the 'machinations' which had to be undertaken in order for the sitting to take place, to the final and purposeful removal of Mrs D to an environment suitable for 'Paul's' communications, every happening smacks of order and method, of design and strategy. Add to this the way in which each revelation complemented the last, adding each time a little more, and yet never too much, detail to the total picture, and it is very hard to believe that this was the work of chance. The sequence appears to be self-authenticating.

It would be easy to say that much of the authority for accepting, and therefore believing, what we were told rests upon the identity of the final and greatest communicator. My identification of the Paul of these communications has been seriously questioned by members of the ecclesiastical hierarchy. Leaving aside the importance of this, do the words stand up on their own as worthy of St Paul? The critics say 'no', and use this as a method of decrying the whole sequence of events. But we have to take into account Paul's reasons for coming to talk to us. Firstly, perhaps, he came as an old friend and comrade: 'We are part of a family. We have gone out into the world . . . and it is good to be with you again.' Secondly, he came to promote the spread of true healing in the world, and especially what we would now call 'spiritual healing'. This is part of the great 'plan' in the discarnate world to call men back to God. He came to me because of my profession as a doctor, and because the involvement of a trained doctor appears to be an important part of the plan. (Perhaps to give added credibility?) Therefore he spoke to me about healing. He did not come to teach theology. If he had, he would undoubtedly have come to one who was trained in theology and able to appreciate the impact of what he had to say. He did not come to preach. If he had, he would have chosen an occasion when there was a larger audience. Thirdly, it is being said by a number of people with mystical and spiritual insights that the great ones are drawing close to earth at the present time because it is in such desperate need. I think the dismissal of this identification of Paul by academics is too facile a response. To deny the authority and the power of his words is impossible to one who was there. The message stands upon what it is. Paul himself is the last person to claim authority from his personality. 'Who or what the communicator is or may have been, is not important', he said on his first meeting with Eric. (Incidentally, this is typical of St Paul, the Apostle. 'Not I, but the Grace of God', as he said so many times.) Is he indeed what he claims to be, the 'great Paul' (though he would deny strenuously all claims to greatness: 'I am not great: I have received the great blessing of the revelation of truth; but alone, I am nothing.')? Is he, as has been asserted by one staunch follower of the Church, the devil himself or another spirit of darkness, masquerading in robes of light to deceive the unwary, and lure them to destruction? ('Know, my brother and sister, there is no death. Neither are there powers of darkness such as have been described. There are (only) those who have not benefited from the experiences through which they have passed.') Or is he, as would be maintained by most classical psychiatrists, a secondary personality of Mrs D, an offshoot of herself?

Personally I incline to the belief that Paul is genuinely what he appears to be. I know the difficulties in accepting this view. But – **I was there!** I FELT the force of his personality! And, as I said at the outset in this chapter, we are dealing here with the realm of the mind, in which the laws of logic and science do not apply. We are in the realm of intuitive knowledge, and intuition tells me that this is true. If we are to consider the possibility of a secondary personality, then I think we must compare the language and phraseology of Paul with that of Mrs D in conversation. Paul is grammatical in his use of language, and his sentences are well constructed. They vary in length like those of a practised orator, and the emphasis is always in the right place. Mrs D, on the other hand, is often the reverse of grammatical.

Her sentences run on and into one another, often with shifts of the subject and omission of vital verbs. The 'feel' of the two is completely different. Some may be tempted here to quote the case of Sally Beauchamp as authority for saying that totally different personalities, each of them offshoots of the central personality, may manifest through the same individual. To this I would make two answers. The first is that it is still a matter of considerable argument whether 'The three faces of Eve' were (a) examples of discarnate possession; (b) examples of 'far memory' i.e. a flashback in consciousness to previous incarnations; (c) examples of secondary personalities of the one individual. The second is this: if Paul is indeed a secondary personality of Mrs D, who was not a reader and had had little of the advantages of education, where did she acquire both her mastery of the English language and of oratory, and the philosophical wisdom behind her utterances? To me they seem to be incongruous. Finally, one must take into account the authority with which they are delivered and the tones of the voice. Just as Tania's voice embodied tenderness and compassion in rich but unmistakably feminine tones, so Paul's voice, which was deep and definitely masculine, rang with age-old authority and vigour. Even in the recorded version that authority is clear and compelling. To have experienced it live was completely devastating. One was simply forced to believe. That being so, I must accept the substance of what was imparted to me as being truth, and act upon it.

Another argument, which has been put to me in respect of Paul, and is one which is often advanced in similar cases, is that Paul's words to Eric and to me do not match the profundity of his writings. But here I think we have to take into account the purpose of the whole exercise. This purpose – the great 'plan' referred to by Tania and Snowdrop so often – is to bring forward convincing evidence of the existence of a discarnate world by restoration of the physical body through the exercise of a different form of healing. Healing, by which I mean reharmonisation of spirit, mind and body, is to be used once again to bring back to man an understanding of his true and essentially spiritual nature; in a word, to make him God-conscious. To this end the instruments have ben chosen for their own, intrinsic qualities and experience; Eric, because of his capacity for transmitting the healing energies; I because of my medical knowledge and ability to interpret and to set non-physical or spiritual healing in the framework of Man's triune nature. Had the purpose been to impart theological teaching, then the instruments chosen would have been of a different nature, and capable of understanding and interpreting theological profundities.

So what indeed has been the content of the messages? What have we learned from this experience? First and most importantly, if we accept the messages as being genuine, **we have convincing evidence of personal survival of death as a fact.** No longer need we fear that death of the physical body amounts to extinction of the person. The mind and the soul go on. Furthermore, not only do they go on, but it appears that they take with them the accumulated memories of their earthly life experience, both the good and the bad. Still further, not only do they take with them those earthly memories, but they take with them the consequences of those earthly lives, the good and the bad, the pluses and the minuses. We cannot escape the consequences of our deeds, and we reap precisely whatever it is that we have sown. 'Tomorrow we shall stand in the shadow of today', as Paul so dramatically phrased it.

Secondly, we learn that there is a purpose to life, and that purpose is the gaining of experience, that through that experience we may grow. Moreover the experience must of necessity contain many contrasts, riches and poverty, male and female, joy and suffering. Sometimes, we learn, the most important lessons are those to be learned through suffering. We shall reach the time when we too shall learn to say 'I thank you, Father, for the blessings of my joys, but I thank you even more for the blessings of my sorrows, for out of them I have learned so much.'

Thirdly, and most fortunately, we learn that we are not confined to one appearance upon the stage of life. It is not possible in one short life to run the whole gamut of all the experiences necessary for fullness of spiritual growth. It is even hinted that these experiences of living may not necessarily be confined to this earth upon which we now are living, but that there are other worlds and galaxies where life goes on. We learn also that we seem to have some control over the circumstances of our incarnation. 'I chose you and Mummy,' said Vicky, 'because I knew what you were, and that you believed in God.' We make the

167

earthly beds upon which we are to lie – and in more than one sense too, because the nature of those beds, whether comfortable or full of stones, is determined by the influences generated in previous lives which we bring with us. We choose, it seems, the life before us according to our spiritual needs.

This whole process is magnificently described in Robert Frost's great poem, *Trial by Existence*, part of which I quote below:

> And from a cliff top is proclaimed
>   The gathering of the souls for birth,
> The trial by existence named,
>   The obscuration upon earth . . .

> And the more loitering are turned
>   To view once more the sacrifice
> Of those who for some good discerned
>   Will gladly give up paradise. . . .

> And none are taken but who will,
>   Having first heard the life read out
> That opens earthward, good and ill,
>   Beyond a shadow of a doubt; . . .

> Nor is there wanting in the press
>   Some spirit to stand simply forth,
> Heroic in its nakedness,
>   Against the uttermost of earth. . . .

> But always God speaks at the end:
>   'One thought in agony of strife
> The bravest would have by for friend,
>   The memory that he chose the life;
> But the pure fate to which you go
>   Admits no memory of choice,
> Or the woe were not earthly woe
>   To which you gave the assenting voice.'

And so the choice must be again,
    But the last choice is still the same;
And the awe passes wonder then,
    And a hush falls for all acclaim.
And God has taken a flower of gold
    And broken it, and used therefrom
The Mystic link to bind and hold
    Spirit to matter till death come.

'Tis of the essence of life here.
    Though we choose greatly, still to lack
The lasting memory at all clear,
    That life has for us on the rack
Nothing but what we somehow chose;
    Thus are we wholly stripped of pride
In the pain which has one close,
    Bearing it crushed and mystified.

Robert Frost

Nor are we separated from those we have known and loved in previous lives, but rejoin them, although sometimes in a different form of relationship. At one moment we took Andrew, my youngest son, and Vicky's adored elder brother, to visit Mrs D. Vicky came through in radiant form, and it was plain from her conversation that those two souls had shared in a previous life, apparently in Rome during what seems to have been the eighteenth century, though not in a brother and sister relationship.

The next important thing which we learn is of the existence of the Great Plan. It is possible to criticise this view, and say that while we have been told that there is a plan involving Paul, Tania, Vicky, Eric, myself and others, how can we be sure that this plan is of **God**? Is this really a valid conclusion? In any case, what is this that we call **God**? Are we to conceive of **God** as a separate and super Mastermind who plans? It is dangerous to subject the Infinite to the scrutiny of the intellect. It is dangerous to try to think of God in human terms. Intuition rather than reason must be our guide. As long as we dwell in a finite world of time and space we are incapable of comprehending the Infinite. To attempt to subject the Divine Infinity of the Creative Force to the analysis of the time and space-bound human mind is per-haps the ultimate in blasphemy. I only know that God really does exist, and has to be experienced in such small way as our puny souls are capable of doing. He has a plan for all humanity in which each one of us has a small and humble part to play. Each one of us is a tiny cog in the machinery of the Divine Plan. Alone, we are nothing. Together we ARE that plan. Whether we join in and play our part in it is ours to choose, and ours alone. But still we are called to participation, and the circumstances surrounding that call, whether we like it or not, are preordained. Yet still the nature of our response is ours. *We are not forced to join in*. But, whatever our answer may be, we shall reap its consequences. The workers in that plan, we learn, are present on both sides of the dividing veil, incarnate and discarnate alike, and, in the discarnate world, linked together by bonds which shall never be dissolved. Owing to the nature of Time and Space as dimensions of the material world, a number of links already in being in the discarnate world have still to come into existence in our world of matter. We have to learn the lesson of patience and the truth of the eternal law that 'All Things in Due Season Come'.

Plainly the Plan involves the recall of Man to the realisation of his essentially spiritual nature. There is no death for the spirit is immortal and cannot die. What we call death is no more than birth into another life, a transition from one environment to another. In the immortal words of the Bhagavad Gita:

'Never the spirit was born; the spirit shall cease to be never,
  Never was time it was not; end and beginning are dreams.
Birthless and deathless and changeless remaineth the spirit
    forever.
  Death has not touched it at all, dead though the house of it
    seems.'

It is because Man has grown away from God, and, sunk in the lethargy of matter, has moved away from the Light into dark-ness that he is in such a desperate plight. The plan is to recall him to that state of God Consciousness in which he can again be his Father's child. Inherent in the plan appears to be the role of healing, which is again to be used, as it was two thousand years

170

ago by Jesus, to draw Man to God. Spiritual healing of disease, both psychological and physical, is to be demonstrated as a fact, and as evidence of powers that exist beyond the material plane. No longer are the psychic phenomena of physical mediumship to be the major instrument for breakthrough. Healing is to be the key to unlock the fast closed door of Man's understanding of his essentially spiritual nature. It was in this area that I, because of my profession (and presumably also because of my unknown past), was called to work, together with Eric, the sensitive and the healer. I had been given my marching orders. Whether I obeyed them or not, and how I obeyed them, was up to me. I had no excuse for not doing so. The evidence which had been set before me was utterly convincing as far as I was concerned. Each one of us was an immortal spirit, temporarily enshrined within a physical body. Once that knowledge was ours, we neglected it at our peril. Nor was I to be left alone upon the journey, or in the task laid upon me. Unseen friends were close at hand to strengthen and to inspire. The knowledge needed to carry out the work would be given once I had learned to be but still. All that was needed was commitment, faith and courage. These, indeed, have been given to me in abundance, and, together with the never failing and unstinting support of the Unseen, have brought me to the position in which I find myself today, and from which we started out in chapter one. Through this wonderful series of experiences and revelations I can truly say that out of the blessings of my sorrows I have learned so much. I can only pray that I be given the strength and the inspiration to use this knowledge and this experience aright, and can truly come in subjection, knowing that God is indeed in control at all times.

May God be in your thinking – and in your understanding!

CHAPTER THIRTEEN

FURTHER STUDIES

The events related in the preceding chapters by no means constituted the whole of my learning process, which has proceeded uninterrupted ever since those early days. They did, however, serve to give me a firm sense of the direction in which I was travelling – which has never left me – and a foundation upon which to build. I was nevertheless pitifully ignorant about many things, and aware that I had a great deal to learn before I could start upon the task with which I had been entrusted. Much of this learning process became centred round the Isle of Iona. John Walters, the owner of Iona's two hotels, the The Columba Hotel and The Argyll Hotel, who was a keen member of The Church's Fellowship for Psychical and Spiritual Studies, and an old associate of the late Tudor Pole, had started to run conferences on matters spiritual at the Columba Hotel. The first of these had taken place around the time of our visit with the Fellowship and had concerned itself with 'The Life to Come'. In fact I learned about this too late to attend, but I heard later that it was a resounding success among the participants, though the islanders were less than happy over the subject matter! The following September 1971, the theme for the conference was 'Medication as an Aid to Healing'. The conference was under the direction of Major Bruce MacManaway, and the chief speakers were the Revd Dr Kenneth Cuming and Canon Roland Walls. To one like myself, who was seeking to learn more about spiritual healing, and who had been told that knowledge would be given in the stillness, this seemed like the answer to prayer. And so it proved to be! I had already besought my friend and mentor, Michael Parker, to teach me how to meditate, without success. Though a healer of proven ability and one of the best preachers from the pulpit it has been my good fortune to hear, this was something he was unable to do. Maybe he was not meant to be my teacher in this respect, for had he been able to teach me meditation, I might well not have made the long journey to Iona, and I should then have left out what has proved to be a most important element in my onward progression and spiritual growth.

At this conference I really began to learn what meditation was all about. **What was perhaps even more important for me, coming as I did from a basically Christian background, I learned about meditation in a Christian context, which I was able to accept. Had it been presented to me in an Eastern context, as it well might have been, I should probably have rejected it as 'not for me'.** Meditation, of course, is an integral part of all the great religions of the world, but it tends to be sadly neglected by Western Christianity. Although it is coming very much to the fore amongst a certain section of society today, the traditions from which it appears to spring tend to be presented as being of eastern origin, and therefore as being fundamentally non-Christian. It has always been practised in the Eastern Orthodox Church, where it has been an essential part of Christian practice since the first century. The highest form of meditation, indeed, is identical with what is called contemplative prayer in Christian terminology. It is therefore extremely important that meditation should be seen as being in the mainstream of the Christian tradition, particularly since the regular practice of meditation is a powerful adjuvant to the exteriorisation of the gifts of the spirit, especially that of healing.

I began to learn, too, more of the importance of recognising the power and influence of the 'unseen', or 'the general staff' as Major MacManaway liked to term it. I learned about the value of groups for meditation and healing, and of the necessity for harmony and balance in such groups. Part of the tradition which was growing up around the Iona conferences was that they took place at the beginning and the end of the summer season in the hotels. This particular conference was at the end of September and the concluding day was 29th September, the Feast of St Michael and All Angels, a date of particular power and significance for all who walk the spiritual path. The conference terminated with an act of dedication in the beautiful Michael Chapel of the Abbey on the part of all those taking part.

Subsequent conferences followed thick and fast: The Cosmic

173

View; Christian Mysticism; The Charismatic Movement; Healing and the Wholeness of Man; Parapsychology and the Christian Faith; The Role of Meditation within the Christian Faith; Healing and Wholeness (organised by a well known Naturopath); God, Man and the New Age; and others in different parts of the country. Each one contributed something new to my education, and introduced me to new sources of reading and knowledge. By 1974 I felt sufficiently sure of myself to know that I had something to impart to others and I persuaded John Walters to organise the first Holistic Health Conference ever to be held in this country, at which speakers from orthodox medicine, homoeopathy, radionics, spiritual healing and religion shared a common platform and sought common ground in their approach to healing the diseases of man. Such an approach is now familiar, but in those days it was revolutionary. Sadly, although widely publicised, it was totally ignored by my medical colleagues, not one of whom, apart from a homoeopath, troubled to attend.

The framework for the Iona conferences, each of which lasted for a full week, so as to permit those attending the opportunity of experiencing something of the unique atmosphere and beauty of the island, as well as the exploration in depth of the conference theme, was for each speaker to have three separate periods of one hour to present his subject matter. This meant that one had to do a good deal of background preparation to fill the available space.

The first conference in which I was involved as a speaker was the 1974 conference on Healing and Wholeness, which I instigated. For this I had three one-hour lectures to prepare, and it was in the course of the research for these talks and in the meditations which preceded their preparation that my ideas began to form, or perhaps one should more accurately say emerge. It was my task to present the case for orthodoxy, and yet to be a unifying bridge between the different disciplines of healing which were to be presented. I therefore started to look at the history of healing and the way in which primitive healing had developed into the patterns applied by Jesus, and how these had gradually become separated from those applied by the medical profession. In the course of this research I started to become aware that the chief error was one of perception; that Jesus simply did not look either at Man or at disease as did other people. He saw beyond their physical bodies and into their lives, and how these lives were related to the sicknesses from which they suffered. Were we ever to be able to return to the simplicity of His healing, then we had to shift our perception of Man.

So I started to look at Man; at what he really was, and how he related to the world about him. I started to look at the new physics, and its implications for Man; at the electrical discoveries of men like Saxton Burr, who discovered the life field of living bodies; at the researches of the Russians into telepathy and the paranormal; and the work of people like Wilder Penfield and Shafika Karagulla in neurophysiology. This led me to the belief that it was incorrect to think of Man as being just a physical body, with a non-physical soul attached, which was liberated from the body at death. This was a mediaeval view, and a gross over-simplification. It was also the view of Descartes, and, as such, formed the basis for the present-day approach by the medical profession to disease. The reality was a good deal less simple. Man was, in fact, a complex amalgam of energy fields, ranging all the way from the simple electrostatic fields of the atom and its sub-atomic particles, which merged together to form molecular fields, and, eventually, the field for the whole body, to fields of a totally different nature, which appeared to be related to thought and emotion. One saw, also, that although each field was a separate entity, it tended to merge with and become influenced by other similar fields in the environment around it. Thus no one field could rightly be considered in isolation from that surrounding environment.

I started to look for confirmation of these ideas among the patients in my practice. Initially I tried to consider how their individual diseases had come about. Instead of being content with the ordinary process of diagnosis – that is to say attempting to answer the question 'What has this patient got the matter with him?' – a process which informs the physician both of the therapy required and of the likely outcome of the disease, I set myself to try to answer a far more difficult question. 'Why has **this** patient got **this** disease at **this** particular moment?' I call this process 'diagnosis in depth', and I maintain that it is only when this question has been answered in its entirety that the condition has been fully thought through and that the physician is in a position to give real help to the patient. Somewhat to my surprise, although it should not have been, I found when I started to apply this process to the ordinary run-of-the-mill situations with which I was confronted in my family NHS practice, that some three-quarters of the diseases were associated with a condition of stress on the part of the patient. I had already noted that there was a vast variation in the way in which different patients responded to therapy, even when the presenting disease and the therapy were identical. Could it be, I asked myself, that this variation was also stress-related?

So I started to think about stress. I came to the conclusion, as I have said many times, and with which those of my readers who have heard me speak will be very familiar, that this again was a matter of individual perception. Everybody was faced on their journey through life with certain stressful combinations of circumstances. These did not of themselves constitute stress any more than does the force applied to the metal bar constitute the state of stress fatigue within the bar. The stress fracture in the metal bar takes place as the result of certain changes in the crystalline lattice structure of the metal resulting from the force to which it has been subjected. The stress is something which has taken place internally within the metal. Similarly in Man it is how he perceives and responds to the stressful circumstances in his life which determine the presence or absence of stress. This perception will be influenced by many factors, including his background, his upbringing and character, his memories of what has happened previously, and his expectations of the future. All of this can be termed the environment, or the total life situation of that particular soul, and it includes also the particular stressful circumstances of the moment. Stress itself, I concluded, is a state of mind which is dependent upon the reaction of the individual to that environment. It could be simply expressed in the equation STRESS = REACTION × ENVIRONMENT. Any variation in the quotient, stress, can only be brought about by varying one or other of the factors, the reaction factor or the stress factor. Most of the environmental factor is out of reach. Background, past memories, upbringing, and most of the present environment are unchangeable. Only the perception of the challenge, upon which depends the response, and the expectations for the future can be said to be subject to treatment. Only so can the stress quotient be reduced.

This set me to considering how much of our response to our stress-creating challenges was conditioned by our personal, philosophical and metaphysical beliefs. How could we learn to change our perceptions of challenge? What did it really mean to us? This led me back to the words of Paul about climbing the mountain of life; about learning and benefiting from the experiences through which we pass; and how, when considered in these terms, and in the perspective of ongoing existence, our greatest sorrows were indeed our greatest blessings.

The meaning of all this became greatly intensified when I started to move into cancer care. One of the offshoots of the 1974 Healing and Wholeness conference at Iona (which I instigated) was that I there heard for the first time from Gilbert Anderson, who was presenting the case for spiritual healing, about the Harry Edwards initiative for cancer healing and the parallel work being carried out in the United States by Dr Carl Simonton and his co-workers in Fort Worth, Texas. This was the year of the May Lectures in London, at which papers were presented on:

Biofeedback and Voluntary Control of Internal States. Elmer Green PhD.

The Role of the Mind in Cancer Therapy. Carl Simonton MD and Stephanie Simonton.

Is Primitive Medicine Really Primitive? Lyall Watson PhD.

Man, Mind, Matter and Fields. E. Stanton Maxey MD.

Do Plants Think? Cleve Backster.

Interpersonal Communication between Man and Plant. Marcel Vogel MSc.

Bioenergetics in Healing. Dr Sister Justa Smith MD.

The Role of Psychics in Medical Diagnosis. Norman Shealy MD.

(Those people who are interested even at this late date in learning what went on at an epoch-making conference can read in depth of the material presented in 'The Frontiers of Science and Medicine', Edited by Rick Carlson, published by Wildwood House 1975.)

At the conference I learned about the cancer healing group which grew out of the view of Harry Edwards that cancer was a psychosomatic disease. As a result of this view the National Federation of Spiritual Healers had commissioned a Literature Survey of the Psychosomatic Aspects of Cancer Research by Yehia Raef MSc, PhD and following this had circulated a large number of cancer patients with a detailed questionnaire into the emotional antecedents of their disease and into their personal backgrounds. The questionnaire was also sent out to a number of patients suffering from conditions other than cancer. When the results came in, they were fed into a computer, from which it was made plain that while nearly everybody had stressful circumstances in their lives, the stresses from which cancer patients suffered were of a very special type, revolving around undischarged states of negative emotion and unsatisfactory interpersonal relationships. In the majority of cases there had been the loss of some central and meaningful relationship in life and a failure to find a satisfactory substitute. A pilot group of seven patients was formed, who were taught a system of deep relaxation, encouraged to visualise their bodies attacking and overcoming their cancers, and at which they received regular healing from attendant healers. All the patients in the pilot group were terminal patients; that is to say they had each been told that there was nothing more that medicine could do for them. The average expectation of life among the members of the group was three months. At the time of the conference the group had already been meeting for over a year, and apart from one woman who had died before they could start meeting, all the original members of the group were still alive. When Gilbert Anderson heard of the work of Dr Carl Simonton, he at once made contact with him, and was able to meet and exchange experiences while they were both in London. It appeared that both men were working along very similar lines at which they had arrived totally independently. On my return home from the conference I lost no time in joining the group, which Gilbert Anderson started at his Suffolk home, as an observer. Though I was not yet ready to undertake such work on my own account, such an approach fitted in with my developing views on the nature of Man and of the relationship between spirit, mind and body. It was an important milestone in my spiritual journey.

My contribution to the Healing and Wholeness conference, although delivered with knocking knees and great trepidation

178

had been hailed as a considerable success by those attending. I was in consequence invited by John Walters to be one of the speakers the following year at a conference on Parapsychology and The Christian Church. The lead speaker was to be Father Geoffrey Curtis, CR, the Senior of the London Branch of the Community of the Resurrection, Mirfield, otherwise known as the Mirfield Fathers. Together with Father Curtis were to be The Revd Max Magee, Senior Chaplain, Strathclyde University, and Secretary to the Working Party of the Church of Scotland on Parapsychology, and the Revd Anthony Duncan, at that time Vicar of St John's, Newcastle and one time diocesan exorcist to the diocese of Worcester. Here was a challenge indeed! The theme of the conference had been stated by Father Geoffrey Curtis in these words:

'The future of mankind depends upon the development of a new level of consciousness. This must include an honest awareness of the facts within and around us. There is a range of phenomena of great importance too long ignored by churchmen and by the vast majority of scientists. These include the phenomena of mysticism; extra-sensory perception; new ways of healing; alleged evidence as to the survival of the dead and of communication from them. We hope to examine without prejudice and in a Christian and therefore impartial spirit these faculties of man, real or supposed, which appear to be inexplicable on any generally accepted hypothesis.'

This was throwing down the gauntlet with a vengeance – and in the sacred Isle of Iona too! I thought long and hard about my contribution. My role was to cover the field of paranormal healing, but obviously with three hours of lecture time to fill, it had to go far further than that. Equally obviously it would be highly inadvisable to start revealing my own journey into the field of survival and communication. There was going to be enough inflammatory tinder about on the island without deliberately importing high explosives! All the ancient shibboleths would again be raised by fundamentalist objectors, and we should be lucky if, in a land which still practised the burning of witches as late as the eighteenth century, we escaped without being burnt at the stake, metaphorically if not literally. It was while I was meditating on how I was going to handle this potentially highly explosive conference that the following very beautiful prayer was dropped into my mind. It is comparatively well known now, for it has been used many times, often by persons other than myself, as well as being quoted in my writings. I call it 'A Prayer for All Seekers', and I am perfectly certain that its origin is discarnate.

A PRAYER FOR ALL SEEKERS

Almighty, All loving and Omnipresent God!

Deliver us from the stubbornness of mind that clings to preconceived ideas, and from the arrogance of spiritual pride that thinks it knoweth all:

Give us the strength to cast off the fetters of the past:

Give us the courage to follow wherever it may lead:

Give us the humility to examine without prejudice new sources of knowledge:

Give us the wisdom to discern clearly between Truth and error:

And give us the compassion neither to judge nor to condemn those with whom we disagree.

In the event, the prayer was read out at the very start of the conference, and at several intervals later when the atmosphere was growing rather warm! In fact, within the conference hall itself, this was reasonably harmonious, despite the presence of at least one member of the episcopacy, with whom I crossed swords on more than one occasion! Outside on the island, however, it was a very different matter. What was going on at the hotel was imagined by some to be witchcraft of the deepest dye, and in another age the whole place would doubtless have been set on fire with the inmates locked inside. As it was, however, objections were in the main confined to the media (fortunately Iona is so difficult to get at that there was virtually no media coverage) and to personal disapproval by individual members of the island community.

My own contribution, which involved the giving of the opening talk on the Monday morning, following a broad over-view of the Church outlook on parapsychology given by the Revd Max Magee on the Sunday evening, involved me in a good deal of research and background reading. It was essential, if paranormal (i.e. spiritual) healing was to be made credible and acceptable to any except fanatics, that an attempt should be made to set it in a framework of the natural 'Whole', of which the supernatural and miraculous was an integral part. Since Jesus had sent his disciples out to heal the sick, and had told them that 'greater things than these shall ye do', it had to be an attribute of humanity as well as of divinity. Jesus healed, not because he was God, but because he was perfected Man. The psychic gifts, subsequently outlined by St Paul in 1 Corinthians xii, were part of the nature of Man, though their manifestation was often marred by his imperfections, and were to be seen in their full flowering in the person of Jesus, who was the example of perfection to which all must strive.

When I look back on this phase of my life and analyse it for the purpose of writing this book, it becomes apparent to me that these two conferences – or rather the contributions which I had to make to them – were really the catalyst for my spiritual growth and understanding. It was the research needed to present my subject which provided the seedbed for the growth of my subsequent ideas. Like all growth, this was for the most part quiet and secret, unseen and unrecognised at the time. Nevertheless, it was to prove the foundation for where I stand today.

Following the 1974 conference on healing, at which I had learned of the Harry Edwards initiative and the work being done by Gilbert Anderson and Dr Ann Woolley-Harte, who was herself a healed cancer patient and a research worker on the field of bio-energies at St Bartholomew's Hospital, I started to become involved in the cancer scene. Initially this amounted to no more than sitting in on Gilbert Anderson's group as a medical observer, and learning what it was all about. After a fairly short period, however, Gilbert had to move to London to fill the position of Administrator to The National Federation of Spiritual Healers. This meant that unless the group were to fold up for lack of leadership I had to do something about it. So I found myself involved in the running of a cancer support group, which inevitably involved a further period of study.

Other influences came into my life. I was invited to become a member of the prestigious Medical and Scientific Network, an organisation drawn exclusively from those who held a medical or a scientific degree, and which was primarily concerned with expanding the horizons of those involved in education, science, medicine and religion. It provided a meeting point for like-minded persons who had an understanding of the unseen dimensions and might otherwise have felt isolated and smothered in their beliefs.

I came into contact with Sir George Trevelyan and the Wrekin Trust, whose many conferences became nearly as important an influence in my onward development as did Iona. In particular I remember a conference on Reincarnation in 1975 at which I heard my old school fellow, the Revd Patrick Blakiston MA, who had been a contemporary of mine at Lancing College, deliver a scholarly address upon the attitudes of the early Christian fathers towards reincarnation. Regular conferences entitled Mystics and Scientists were organised each spring at King Alfred College, Winchester by the Wrekin Trust. These were mammoth affairs, with upwards of 500 people attending, at which the speakers were drawn equally from the top scientists and the most distinguished mystics of the day. Incredible as it may seem, both groups found themselves saying precisely the same thing, very often in similar language. Here I had the good fortune to meet men like Fritjof Capra, Lawrence LeShan, David Bohm, Pir Vilhayat Khan, Tungku Sogyal Rimpoche, Metropolitan Anthony Bloom and many others. From contact with men such as these it was inevitable that I should grow in wisdom and understanding, and each of these exercised a profound influence upon my thinking.

So, gradually and almost imperceptibly, I found myself walking along the spiritual path. It is only when I am questioned as to how I got here and start to look back upon the journey that I realise quite how far I have travelled. Yet, when I listen again to the words of my spiritual mentors; when I hear again the tender, compassionate tones of Tania, the authoritative voice of Paul and the much loved sound of Vicky, it is then that I realise quite how far there still is to travel, and how much work has yet to be done. Yet am I not alone in this work. Vicky has many times been seen behind me on the platform, casting about me her lovely aura of blue and gold; strengthening and inspiring me in what I have to say. And there are others too of whom I am con-scious from time to time. I have had to learn to still the intellec-tual mind; to leave the mind open as an instrument upon which the helpers can play; to trust the intuitive guidance which is given. Anything less is not to come in subjection and take the outstretched hand. I have had to learn, too, that while I have been given the power to bring healing to those who truly seek it, that this healing is different from that which I sought to give in my days in the NHS. That healing was confined to the physical level. It was, in fact, cure, and not healing, and, because it left the inner person untouched, was often followed by relapse. **This** healing is making the person whole – at all their levels. This means the reharmonisation and rebalancing of the energies of which those levels are composed, so that they interact and inter-relate in a positive, rather than in a destructive, manner. It means helping the sick person to correct the negative forces which are destroying his body so as to allow the divine self-healing power of life full play. Often, of course, the body has been so damaged by the ravages of disease and the destructive nature of the physical therapies which have been applied to it, that it has passed the 'point-of-no-return' and physical healing is no longer possible. Here, where physical cure lies beyond the limits of the natural laws which govern the healing process, and the most that can be achieved at the physical level is a reduction in physical suffering, I have had to realise that death itself is the ultimate healing and that my task is to prepare the person for and to aid that passage. So I have reached the position in which I stand today and can say to those who ask, 'This is the road along which I travelled'.

CHAPTER FOURTEEN

THE NATURE OF HEALING

'There are many sicknesses that can be helped once the barriers of orthodox medicine have been overcome.'

Paul to Eric, 12.i.70

Paul's words to Eric, quoted above are a profound challenge to any conventional and orthodoxly trained doctor. Even today, when a new vision of healing is beginning to raise its head, there are many, both within and without the medical profession, who find such thoughts intensely disturbing. When I first heard them, back in 1970, long before the spreading of ideas of holistic medicine throughout the country, they were deeply shocking. The idea that all those weary years of study, all the knowledge of the mysteries of the human body, all the experience of disease acquired, were barriers and not aids to healing, struck at the very foundations of one's being. That spiritual healing should succeed where learned physicians and skilful surgeons have failed is not a concept which commends itself to the conventional doctor. When faced with it he all too often reacts as did one well-known scientist when confronted with the idea of precognition, and fights tooth and nail to disprove it, lest he be forced to go back to square one and rethink his philosophy.

I was more fortunate than most, because the way in which the concept had been presented, in communication from a discarnate personality whose power and authority compelled respect, allied to the fact that I was by now in close contact with two proven healers of considerable ability, was gently urging me down a path from which most doctors shied away at that time. Moreover I was deeply aware that there **were** many diseases which I was powerless to cure, and I desperately wanted to be able to do more to help these patients. I believed totally in the truth of the healing miracles recorded in the gospels, and, while I still tended to look on these as the miraculous intervention of a divine person, the stories told me by my healer friends (one a Methodist minister, the other an associate of Harry Edwards) were inclining me to the belief that healing power was not the sole prerogative of Jesus, but that when he said to his disciples 'and greater things than these shall ye do', this was no more than the literal truth. If these powers were granted to Man, then I longed deeply that they should be granted to me too, that I might be able to help the helpless sick. I prayed deeply and sincerely that I might be granted this healing power, and I started to sit in healing and development circles, and to attempt to meditate, as best I could at that time.

Very soon things began to happen. The first was that a patient of mine, who was diagnosed as having a secondary cancer, received a complete healing shortly after I had asked my Methodist healer friend to put her on his list for absent healing. The story of this is interesting and instructive. Mrs P, who was then in her middle seventies, was married to a man with whom she had little in common. She herself was 'psychic' and had had more than one extra-sensory experience. She was a member of the Churches' Fellowship for Psychical and Spiritual Studies, and believed firmly in life after death and in spiritual healing. Her husband did not share these beliefs. For him death was the end of everything, and there was nothing to follow afterwards. He was also a heavy drinker, and he spent much of his time sitting brooding in his chair over a bottle of whisky and lamenting that his sister had left her property (of which he had no need) to someone else instead of to him. Mrs P felt that life was a burden, and while she accepted the responsibility of caring for him, she found no joy in the task.

One day she appeared in the surgery with an enlarged gland in the neck. Since this was very hard and strongly suggestive of a secondary cancerous deposit, I immediately referred her to a surgeon friend of mine for a biopsy. The report came back confirming my suspicions, and Mrs P was given a booking to be admitted to hospital for investigation. In the meantime I had passed her name to my healer friend for absent healing. Before she could go into hospital she had a remarkable 'dream'. She 'dreamed' that while she was lying in bed in her room, she saw two men in white standing by her bed. One she recognised as

185

being a doctor who had previously looked after her before she moved to Diss, but who had since died. She had always been deeply attached to him. The other figure she did not recognise. 'Have no fear!', they said. 'We are going to heal you.' She awoke in the morning filled with an immense happiness and a feeling of certainty that she had been healed. This feeling remained with her, so that when she was finally admitted to the hospital, she immediately asked to go home, saying to the surgeon, 'I am afraid you are wasting your time! You are not going to find anything. I've been healed, and there is nothing there!' However, as might have been expected, no attention was paid to this, and she went through a series of exhaustive tests, all of which were negative. This was over fifteen years ago, and she is now nearly ninety. She lives just along the road from me and I see her nearly every day as she goes down the town to shop. Her husband is long since dead, but she goes on perfectly happily. It is said by the experts that cases of proven secondary cancer **never** regress spontaneously. But in this case it happened, and the biopsy report is there to prove that this was no mistaken diagnosis. No cancer treatment of any kind was ever given to Mrs P, who remains a medical mystery.

Not long after this another incident occurred, which was an important step in my further progress. A lady came into the surgery one morning complaining of a lump in the breast. She was an attractive woman in her early forties, who was the second wife of a husband considerably older than herself. When I examined the breast, I found that there was indeed a lump present. This was in the lower and outer quadrant of the breast. It was very hard and completely unattached either to the skin or to the deeper structures. There were no glands to be felt and there were no other lumps in either breast. I felt fairly certain that this lump was a cancerous lump, and I immediately referred her to my surgeon friend at the hospital. However I knew that she would be deeply distressed at the prospect of losing her breast. (This was before the days of 'lumpectomies', when mastectomy was the preferred first choice of treatment.) I therefore thought I would try to see whether my hands could help her. Without telling her what I was doing, I took rather longer than usual over my physical examination, and while I was doing this I tried to make a mental link with my discarnate friends, and to visualise healing power entering into me and flowing out through my hands into the affected area. I tried to keep my mind tuned to the unseen help, and focused upon the transmission of energy from a higher source entering into the patient. When the patient subsequently attended the hospital clinic, the report came back that there was no lump in either breast, and that both breasts were completely normal. The conventional explanation of this sort of occurrence is that the diagnosis was wrong; that the lump was probably a cyst, and that its appearance and disappearance related to the patient's menstrual cycle. It is difficult to refute that sort of statement, but I **know** that in this case it is incorrect. I was there. I felt the lump, and I know that it had the feel of a cancer and not of a cyst, and I am far too experienced to make a mistake of that sort, whatever unbelieving colleagues may say!

Shortly after this I began to find that I could relieve the pain of sprains and tendon injuries by holding the affected part in my hands while talking to the patient. I used to be told that my hands felt 'so warm and comforting'! On another occasion I was called to see a woman who was thirty-six weeks pregnant and had an acute pain in the abdomen. The pregnancy was a first pregnancy and the baby very much wanted. She was not in labour, but as I laid my hands upon the abdomen I knew, without any shadow of doubt, that there was something very seriously wrong, and that I must send her into hospital at once where a Caesarian operation would be required. I did not know precisely what the cause was. I merely knew that the baby's life was in danger. When I arranged for the hospital admission – it was fairly late in the evening – I insisted on speaking personally to the duty obstetric surgeon and telling him what I felt. With some reluctance he accepted what I had to say and duly operated. At the operation they found that the umbilical cord was twice round the baby's neck, and that it would have died within a couple of hours had relief not been afforded! Needless to say, those people became my most faithful patients.

None of this, of course, was due to me. It was the consequence of unseen powers flowing through me, of unseen help at hand. I had to accept this. (Dorothy Kerin, I believe, once described herself as a 'little pipe' for others to play upon.) There ARE other powers which operate through us if we will allow them to do so. Patients CAN be helped when medicine says this is not possible. Thus gently and slowly the unseen helpers began to lead me along the path which I walk today, the path of holistic healing.

A good deal of misconception surrounds the word 'holistic'. To many people holistic medicine signifies something which is different from conventional medicine; a form of treatment which is alternative and is able to take the place of traditional medicine. This is quite incorrect, and it would be helpful to step aside for a few moments and to consider just what is meant by this word.

Conventional medicine, and indeed almost the whole of western science – with the exception of mathematics and physics – is rooted and grounded in the Cartesian maxim that 'The Whole is the Sum of its Parts'. This implies that the study of each object, or 'whole', is bound up with the study of its component parts. According to this way of thinking, to understand anything, whether it be an inanimate object or a living creature, it is first necessary to break it down into its smallest components, study these, and then attempt its reconstruction from an understanding of these component parts. We are currently witnessing this approach, being carried to its extreme, with the modern practice of spare-part surgery.

The current Western medical model is founded upon this view, in which an organism is viewed in terms of its parts, both organs and cells, and all of its properties and functions are considered to be the consequences of the activities of these component parts. Medicine has always studied the parts which comprise the human body. Students start in the dissecting room and physiology laboratory, learning to look at organs and cells. For the most part this is done in the cadaver, so that life and behaviour are absent from the material studied. Up until forty or so years ago, the process of study ended here. Now it has travelled far further – right down into the component parts of the cells, the cell nuclei, the genes and chromosomes of which they are composed, the proteins, which in their turn make up the genes and chromosomes, and ultimately the aminoacids and atoms which make up the proteins of the cells. It has been found possible to induce variations in the behaviour and properties of the cells: to cause certain cells to be replicated artificially in the

188

laboratory before being reintroduced into the body: artificially to conjugate male and female cells in the laboratory and then culture and preserve the resulting embryo: to stimulate the body into creating its own defences against certain diseases through the production of antibodies specific to particular antigens. Thus it is hardly surprising that many doctors have come to view man as a mere collection of organs and cells and to believe that nothing exists outside that collection; that nothing which cannot be touched or weighed and measured has any reality; that the information presented by their five senses and their instruments is total and complete. Such a model is inevitably mechanical and reductionist. It is in the starkest contrast to the Holistic Model.

In the concept of Holism, the Whole is considered to be greater than the sum of its parts, and the extra dimension beyond this sum to be the consequence of the interplay, inter-relationships and interconnections both of the parts with one another and of the whole creature with other whole creatures in the surrounding environment. Thus man, even at the phsyical level, is comprised not just of the organ parts and their cells, but of the way in which each works alongside and in harmony with the rest of the body. Every part and every creature is not only an entity in its own right but also an integral part of larger and yet larger systems. None can be considered in isolation from the larger whole of which he is a part. To this is added another concept; that man exists at a number of differing levels, of which the material, physical level is only one, and that just as the physical level is comprised of the cells, organs and their complex inter-connections and inter-relationships, so also the finer levels of Man interconnect and inter-relate, both with each other and with those of others around them, to comprise the total man. However, since these finer levels of feelings, thoughts and spiritual qualities are not subject to being weighed and measured, they are disregarded by orthodox medical and scienfitic thinking, and considered to have no true reality, but to be mere epiphenomena of the brain.

This narrow, traditional view of man, which is held by many western scientists, is responsible for most of the world's ills today. Such a view of Man as a machine, analysable in terms of his parts, and restricted in the entire sum total of his being to his physical body, is totally incompatible with acceptance of survival of death, or continuity of the personality after the disintegration of the physical body. Where mind and intellect are considered to be the consequences of the material body, the product of the cells of the brain, and all our noblest thoughts and ideals no more than the chattering together of the cells of the brain like a tribe of monkeys, there can be no longer view. Yet this longer view, this wider horizon, is crucial both to our health and to the problems which beset the world. Once one can begin to conceive of consciousness as lying outside the brain; of the brain as being no more than an instrument – like any microphone or television receiver, which changes one form of energy into another – for the conversion of the energies of thought into the energies of the body; that the brain is the part of the body which forms the link between the mind, existing in a different realm, the spaceless, timeless realm of the ALL, and the body, which exists in the space-time continuum of the senses, it becomes possible to conceive of an ongoing pattern of existence, of which physical life in the material world is only a part. Such a concept, as we have seen, has the profoundest implications for conduct and behaviour in the world.

The reductionist, Cartesian view of Man is thus diametrically opposed to the concept of Holism, and its concepts of disease and healing are equally dissimilar. In the western medical model, to which nine-tenths of the medical profession and a large proportion of the general public subscribe, disease is mostly seen as the attacker which comes from without; the arrow of a malignant fate, whose flight is unforeseen, and for which the innocent victim bears no responsibility. 'Theirs not to reason why; theirs but to do and die.' These words might almost have been written to express the attitude of the public towards its health. Similarly, just as the public sees no responsibility for its sicknesses attaching to itself, so it sees itself as having no part to play in the healing of those sicknesses. It is the passive recipient of the skills of others, and its only task is to suffer as uncomplainingly as possible whatever is done to it.

Were the causes of disease truly to be confined to the material realm, were soul and body truly to be so separate that neither could influence the other, as Descartes used to teach, then this would be a logical approach, and it is noteworthy that many of

190

those who follow it are either materialists or adherents to Cartesian dualism. However, Man is not so simple a creature. It is not possible, so long as life continues, to separate soul from mind from body, for all are intertwined and relate together, What happens at the physical level, in the way of sickness, or health, or healing, is deeply influenced by emotions, attitudes and beliefs prevailing in the 'finer' levels of being.

I first started to become aware of this when I embarked on the process of 'extended diagnosis'. When I set myself to try to answer the question, 'Why has THIS patient got THIS disease at THIS moment?' instead of trying merely to discover what was wrong with him/her, I found that mind, body and spirit were indeed very closely related, and that it was not possible to consider one to the exclusion of the other. In my first, rather groping, enquiries into this area I found, to my considerable astonishment, that something like 75 per cent of the ordinary run-of-the-mill sicknesses with which the average family doctor is confronted at the daily surgery had their origins in a state of stress within the patient. Of the remaining 25 per cent the majority were brought about by sheer wilful disregard of the ordinary rules for healthy living. A very small number did not fit into either category, and seemed to have occurred for deeper and more esoteric reasons.

I remember the first time that this was brought home to me. I was sitting in my surgery one cold April evening when a man walked in whom I had known for over twenty years. Normally he was a bright, cheerful and happy extrovert, who had troubled us remarkably little over the years. But tonight he was clearly most unhappy. He sat down beside me with a look of complete dejection on his face. 'Doctor!', he said in sepulchral tones, 'I think I am getting rheumatism.' He thrust his hands under my face. Sure enough there were the tell-tale spindle-shaped swellings of the finger joints, and the commencing distortion of the wrists, which signified the beginning of small joint rheumatism. In those days I knew a lot less about the relationship of mind and body than I do today. Psychosomatic illness to me was something that existed in the mind so that the body **behaved** in an abnormal way, but it did not mean that there was anything physically wrong. One had only to reassure the patient that nothing was really wrong, and, provided that he/she believed

191

one, all would be well and the disability would disappear. (It makes me blush today to look back on my naivety then.) However, I did recognise that some of my colleagues believed that there was a stress element in this particular condition and I started to talk to the patient. (I am going to call him Bob, though, of course, that is not his real name.) Bob very soon shut me up!

'But I don't worry, Doctor,' he said. 'You know I am not a worrier.' (This was true. Bob was the last person to worry about things.)

'Sure, Bob,' I replied. 'I know you are not a worrier. But, you know, there are a lot of emotions which can affect your body besides worry.'

Here I ran off a little stock list of negative emotions, such as anger, resentment, frustration, jealousy, doubt and so on. They could perhaps best be summarised in the classic words of the Book of Common Prayer as 'Envy, hatred, malice and all uncharitableness'. At this Bob sat very quiet for a while. At length he said,

'Well, I'll tell you something doctor. You know I used to work for . . . .' and here he mentioned the name of a local public utility company.

'Yes', I replied.

'And you know that not long ago we were all amalgamated into a much bigger concern.'

'Yes.'

'Well, the other day I was going through the office, and I happened to see on the table my personal file. Now I know I shouldn't have done this, but I just couldn't resist looking inside to see what they said about me. And what do you think I saw? There in capital letters on the front page – and in RED INK too –' (as if this underlined the enormity of the whole occasion!) 'I saw the words "No potential for promotion here", and I have been so angry that they should do this to me after all the years I have worked for them that I haven't been able to get it out of my mind or think of anything else since.'

'When did this happen?' I asked.

'Just after Christmas' came the reply.

'And when did your rheumatism begin?'

'About six weeks ago.'

'Well,' I said. 'There you are. That is the cause of your rheumatism. You've been so burned up with anger at this insult to you that it has been burning up your body!'

Now it is not much good making a pronouncement of that sort, no matter how true it may be, without doing something to try and help the patient. So I proceeded to administer a little correction.

'Are you any worse off as a result of this?' I asked.

'No', said Bob. 'I'm earning the same money and doing the same job, working the same hours. Nothing has changed.'

'Would you have expected to be promoted, if there hadn't been an amalgamation?'

'Oh no. There would have been no room in the establishment.'

'And were you thinking of going out and looking for a better job at which you could earn more money?'

'No. I was quite content. I have enough for my needs.'

'So,' I said, 'You are no worse off. You are working the same hours, and getting the same money. You had no reason to have expected to have been promoted, and you were quite content with what you were doing and what you were earning. You know, the only thing about you that has been hurt is your pride! And', I went on, 'you know there is always the possibility that if you had been promoted, you might have found the load of responsibility heavier than you could carry!'

'Oh,' said Bob, 'I never thought of it quite like that!'

So Bob went out with a prescription for soluble aspirin and butazolidine tablets and a lot to think about. (It is important to realise that neither of these have any curative effect in rheumatism of this type. All that they do is to relieve pain and discomfort. These days I should probably have given him massive doses of vitamin C!) He also had instructions to come back in a month and report progress. In fact I was away when he came back, and I didn't see Bob until the autumn. It was not in the surgery either. I found him in the barber's shop at the far end of the town, leaning up aginst the door, with a broad grin on his face, looking the picture of health and swapping yarns with the barber.

'Hallo, Bob!,' I said. 'How are you? How is the rheumatism?'

'Oh, I am fine, Doctor', he replied.

'What? No rheumatism?'

'No,' he replied excitedly, 'Look! It's all gone away.'

He thrust his hands under my face again. It had totally disappeared, without trace. Bob had been lucky(?). He had switched off the injurious flow of emotion while the self-healing power of his body was still able to reverse the situation.

This is just one of the many examples I found when I started to look more deeply into how disease originates in the human body. I have told of others in the chapter on the genesis of disease in *The Gate of Healing*, and have outlined there the hormonal and neurophysiological links whereby emotions interfere with or reinforce the processes of self-healing in the body. The baleful influence of negative attitudes and emotions becomes even plainer when we start to deal with cancer. What we have to consider at this moment is how all this fits into and becomes part of the holistic model for healing.

As has been stated, many people view holistic healing as an alternative to conventional, orthodox medical treatment through drugs and surgery. In fact it is nothing of the kind. Holistic medicine depends upon four major principles, the lack of any of one of which is sufficient to destroy the element of holism.

1) Man is a creature of different levels of being, all of which work together – in health – in a state of harmony and dynamic balance. These levels can be thought of as being different forms of energy. The energies, at the different levels, interconnect, interact and inter-relate both with each other and with the similar energies of other creatures in the environment around. Sickness and disease occur when the energies are out of balance.

2) The state of dynamic balance, which is the natural state of the healthy creature, is a homoeostatic state. That is to say, if the state of balance is disturbed by a disrupting force, whether arising inside or outside of the creature, then the system always attempts to return to the previous state of balance, once the disrupting force has been neutralised or removed. This implies that there is an innate power of self-healing in every living creature, which is forever striving to restore health. This power, to which the ancients gave the name **Vis Medicatrix Naturae**, is an expression of the life force within the creature, and as such is divine in origin and in nature. All healing, whether conventional in nature, or in response to spiritual healing, takes place through the operation of this power. It is this which is responsible for the maintenance of

the body and its protection against environmental hazards. Unless it is active and functioning, it does not matter what conventional treatments are employed to help disease. They will fail. (This is plainly to be seen in the problems which appeared over AIDS in the mid-1980s.) The mechanisms through which it works can be damaged or destroyed by external forces such as radiation or chemicals. When this happens the power has no mechanism for expressing itself at the physical level, and no healing takes place.

3) The healing act, whether conventional or 'alternative' or spiritual, is a partnership on equal terms between the patient and the healer. Each is a specialist in his own right and upon his own subject; the healer or doctor a specialist in his subject, the patient a specialist in him/herself, knowing things about him/herself which can never be known to the other. There is no longer room for the authoritarian/victim stance on the part of the therapist, or for the didactic attitude on the part of the doctor. Patient and doctor are equal partners in working out together what is the best course for the patient to follow. The patient must therefore know and understand exactly what is being done or recommended, and be encouraged as far as possible to play an active part.

(I came across the other day an almost classic example of how NOT to proceed in this way. The patient, one of my cancer patients, had had a lump in the breast. The surgeon wished to carry out a complete mastectomy, but the patient refused, struck out the relevant parts from the operation consent form, and insisted on only the lump being removed. Subsequently the surgeon wanted to carry out X-ray treatment 'just in case'. The patient again refused. She said that she did not wish to disturb the self-healing power within her body, that she knew why she had got her cancer, and that she could handle herself through techniques of meditation, imaging, life-style and nutrition. The surgeon was FURIOUS! 'Madam,' he said, 'when you take your car into the garage, you don't tell the mechanic what to do. You let him get on with it!' 'True,' she said. 'But my body is rather different from my car. My car can't tell me what is wrong with it. Neither can it heal its own scratches. My body can do both!' This attitude of the 'mechanic' is very characteristic of reductionist medicine in some quarters today.)

4) Each patient is a unique and a precious individual, and must be met and treated as such. We cannot label a patient with a particular diagnosis, and then assume that this label contains all the necessary and relevant information about them. In practice this means that we have to move away from our old habits of 'treating' diseases; we have even to stop thinking about disease *per se*, and start instead to think about people. Rather than concerning ourselves primarily with the disease state, we have to view the sick person as a person with a problem, of which the sickness is the physical manifestation. We find that instead of proceeding on stereotyped lines that the treatment of a particular disease is this or that, and adhering slavishly to the protocol of this treatment, we have to tailor the treatment to the particular patient, recognising that all are individuals, and that what is right for one is not necessarily right for another, even though the disease may be the same in both instances.

In the holistic model of sickness we recognise that disease may originate on any of Man's varying levels, and if the sick person is to be healed, then help has to be given at the level at which the disease originated, as well as at the physical level. To do less than this is to leave the cause of the disease still operating and to invite relapse or further breakdown in another area. Holistic healing is giving help to a sick person on all the levels simultaneously, and recognising that all methods of helping are valid at their own level, but **only** at their own level. Conventional, orthodox medicine and surgery are perfectly valid **at their own level** so long as they are not destructive of the self-healing power of the body. It is only when the treatment is limited to the physical body, and when it is of a nature to damage the body's powers of healing and maintaining itself, as happens with radiation therapy and many modern drugs, that it becomes wrong. The need is not to eliminate orthodox therapy, but to refine it, so that it no longer damages the body, and to extend the area to which it gives help so as to include the other levels at which the person exists. Thus holistic healing includes orthodox healing, which it then complements by filling in the gaps and extending the help that is offered into those areas which orthodox medicine does not reach.

This applies equally to the other forms of therapy which lie outside conventional medical treatment at the present moment.

196

It may be equally damaging, and often downright dangerous, to concentrate upon a so-called 'alternative' therapy to the exclusion of what orthodox medicine has to offer. Such behaviour can be every bit as blind and reductionist as is the worst of conventional medicine. An example from my casebook will make this plain. J. was brought to me by his wife, who was an enthusiast for New Age teachings, and believed firmly that doctors were unnecessary, if proper use was made of other modes of healing. J. was suffering from cancer of the prostate for which he had been taking an artificial hormone, stilboestrol, for a considerable period. Though he still had his cancer, this was under control, and was not spreading or causing him major symptoms. His wife hoped that if he would agree to a dietary regime, would learn to meditate and visualise, and generally change his life-style, it would no longer be necessary for him to take a drug, which, while controlling his cancer satisfactorily, was not altogether free from side-effects. When I interviewed him I found that he by no means shared his wife's enthusiasms, and certainly did not want to change his diet or his life-style and 'waste time meditating and all that'. (He was an importer of French wines. He enjoyed a high standard of living, and he certainly enjoyed his wines!) He was, in fact, on a completely different wavelength, and there was no way in which he would have accepted the holistic approach which I advocate. Notwithstanding, on his next trip to Paris to see about his wine business his wife went with him and insisted that he should see her French homoeopathist. Though this man was a trained homoeopath, he was not a doctor. J. was told by the homoeopath that there was no need for him to continue to take his stilboestrol tablets, but that he, the homoeopath, would prescribe some homoeopathic tablets for him, which would have just the same effect and would be free from the side-effects. J. took the advice of the homoeopath and abandoned his stilboestrol. The result was that his cancer flared up and he became very seriously ill. Any person with an understanding of the way in which stilboestrol works in the control of prostatic cancer would have known that suddenly to stop taking the drug to which he had been accustomed, and which was controlling his cancer, was simply asking for a reaction. It was a tragic example of the dangers of the restricted approach to disease.

We hear a good deal about stress these days, and I have already given one example of the influence of a stressful situation in creating disease. I am not going to go into the ways in which stress affects the body or to discuss the physiology of stress. I have done this at some length in *The Gate of Healing*, and those who wish to know more of this subject should study the chapter there on Coping with Stress. The point I want to dwell on here is that stress is primarily a state of mind, and it arises out of the way in which we view the various things that happen in life. We all have to face potentially stressful circumstances. They are the challenges of life; the lessons in the text-book of life which we came here to learn. Furthermore, every person is different. What creates stress in one is a stimulating challenge to another. It all depends upon a person's past experience, and their attitude towards the challenge. Nor is it possible to avoid the challenge. If it were, we should never learn anything. As long as we are able to measure up to the challenge, to handle the difficult situation with which we are faced, we shall not create a state of stress within our minds.

Now as stress is a major factor in producing sickness, then anything that can help to lower the stress level, and thus neutralise some of the flow of negative energy which disrupts the smooth working of the body, must help in the healing process. So it is in learning to change our attitude to life, to others, to all about us that true healing, as distinct from mere cure, really begins. We need to discover how to discharge negative emotion, or how to change it into some force which is positive and creative. When we do this, we start to change our lives and to embark upon a process of transformation and spiritual growth. True holistic medicine, besides its willingness to make use of other therapeutic approaches not yet recognised by conventional medicine, also embodies teaching and training in methods of mental and spiritual disciplines able to stimulate and nourish the growth of the evolving spirit. These will include music, dance, colour, eurhythmics as well as counselling, psychotherapy, and various forms of meditation and contemplation.

In all of this, spiritual healing, both through the hands of the healer and through absent healing by means of prayer and healing/meditation groups, is of the highest importance. Many people see such healing as being some form of 'miraculous' intervention from a higher level, and attribute to the healer powers which verge upon the divine. This is an age-old outlook. Even when patients accept the concept of spiritual healing, so often this is seen as something which is *done to them*, the miracle which is worked upon them and in which they have no part to play. As we have seen, Paul suffered from this response and had regarded it as the greatest sorrow of his life. It is also completely in accord with the mechanistic, twentieth-century view of disease and healing, in which the cure of the disease is sought through the intervention of the skills of the scientist and the doctor, and is something which they 'do to' the patient, and in which the patient plays no part. It becomes 'a magic' worked upon them by the healer, or by God through the healer.

This, again, is one of many misconceptions about healing. ALL healing, whether at the level of conventional cure, or taking place through the hands of the healer or as a response to the prayers and intercessions of others, is an expression of the divine force of life within the creature, and operates in accordance with the laws governing that expression. It acts through the encouragement of the natural self-healing, acting perhaps as a catalyst to stimulate it into activity, and then amplifying and accelerating the healing energy. At all times it functions within the framework of the laws governing natural healing. George Bernard Shaw once remarked that Lourdes was the most blasphemous place on the face of the earth, because with all its claims to be a place of healing, there were no glass eyes or artificial limbs to be found amongst the memorabilia of healing. But this is only to be expected. Nature, in Man at least, does not include the regrowth of severed limbs or enucleated eyes. Such things lie outside the phenomena of healing. A few nights ago I watched a spokesman for the British Medical Association being asked about a trial which was to be made within the National Health Service of the efficacy of spiritual healing. 'Well', he said, 'of course it might be able to help people suffering from nervous conditions, but will it make a leg grow again?' No more could orthodox medicine. Such regenerative capacities lie outside the laws which govern healing in the mammalian kingdom. The earthworm can regenerate a severed body; the starfish a severed limb; some lizards a severed tail; but mammals cannot do these things. Such a reply illustrates a total lack of understanding as to what healing is all about. God – and the healing energy is part of God – works at all times through the framework of His own laws, and though from time to time one law may become temporarily over-ruled by the operation of another and higher law, at all times the processes of healing are law abiding.

An interesting example of this is related in *Man the Unknown* by the Nobel prizewinner, Alexis Carrel. Himself a doctor, and a meticulously accurate observer, Carrel describes the healing of a skin cancer after the patient had received spiritual healing. Occasionally cancers of this particular type had been known to regress (i.e. heal spontaneously), and since they were on the skin and thus easily accessible to investigation and study, the precise changes in tissue structure and the different stages through which the healing cancer passed, were well known and easily recognised. This cancer was seen to pass through precisely the same sequence of changes as did the spontaneously healing cancers – but, said Dr Carrel, at a rate which was many, many times faster than he had ever heard of it happening before. **Spiritual healing, too, works through the natural self-healing power of the body.** It is accomplished by the channelling into the energy system of the sick person energies coming from a higher source. Although the originating source of all these energies is the divine Creator, God, the level at which they are, as it were, tapped into, depends upon the level to which the healer is able to raise his own consciousness just prior to and during the act of healing. The higher he/she is able to reach up, the purer and stronger are the energies into which he/she is able to tap and the greater the intensity of the boost to the self-healing system of the sick person. Moreover, together with the heightening of the consciousness of the healer, there comes a breaking down of the barriers of individuality which separate him/her from the sick person so that the healer, in raising his own consciousness to the point at which he becomes lost in the totality of the Creator, takes with him the sick person, so that he/she too becomes merged in the Oneness of the Creator. Judged in temporal terms this may last for only the smallest fraction of earth time – though as we are here outside the time/space continuum the moment may seem endless to the one who experiences it – but in that fraction of time all the energies which sustain the cosmos may flow. In that moment of union the healing takes place, the cancers disappear, the shattered bones unite, the stricken bodies become remade.

However, healers come in all shapes and sizes, and only a very few can scale the heights described above. Many would be scorched by the intensity of the flame. So it appears that a system of filters seems to operate at the interface between the different levels of consciousness, which protects the healer from exposure to a light too bright for him to bear. Readers of Helen Greaves' book, *Testimony of Light*, will recall how Frances Banks, after passing over into the world to come, sought to rise above the plane at which she was living and enter the Halls of Learning, only to be struck unconscious by the brilliance of the light, and to recover consciousness again in her own environment. Others may recall the impassioned cry of Gerontius, 'Take me away, and let me in deepest Hell be laid', when brought before the throne of God. In a number of cases the 'filter' takes the form of a discarnate mind, channelling through the precise nature and degree of energies appropriate to the individual persons. Sometimes the healer is aware of this, and may permit him/herself to be taken over, and to operate in a state of trance. Often, I suspect, he/she is not aware of anything more than he/she is a channel for the transmission of the healing flow. It does not matter. All that matters is that the heart is pure, free from any thought of self-aggrandisement or personal gain, and that the channel is kept clean and pure.

For all of this, as we have seen, Love is the key. Jesus, the Master, made this clear, and, because he loved so deeply, his power of healing was greater than has ever been seen in another, before or since. 'Thou shalt love the Lord thy God with all thy heart and with all thy soul and with all thy mind and with all thy strength. This is the first and great commandment. And the second is like unto it: thou shalt love thy neighbour as thyself. On these two commandments hang all the law and the prophets.' It is love that releases the healing power, both within and outside the patient: love of God; love of one's fellows; love of oneself. A woman came to see me two days ago. She was suffering from cancer and had been given little hope of survival. All her life she had suffered from lack of love. Her father had left home when she was eight years old, and she had spent her life looking for one who would replace him. She married and had three children. With each child all that she wanted was to be a mother and to nurse and care for her child. With each child her husband insisted that she should return to her work as a teacher of handicapped children. At length in despair she walked out and left him – and then proceeded to torture herself with guilty feelings at having done so. Finally she married again, developed a cancerous lump in the breast and became pregnant again. The lump has been removed, and she has been advised that X-ray therapy is necessary, and also that the pregnancy should be terminated. (Without this there is a very grave risk of subsequent spread of the cancer following the birth of the baby.) She refuses termination on religious grounds, and she knows that radiation is likely to be a dangerous threat to the developing child. Sadly she belongs to a strict and fundamentalist religious group, who consider that spiritual healing is the work of the devil. Healing could help her, perhaps protect her entirely against future spread. But her religious scruples, which are based on fear, forbid it. 'Perfect love casteth out fear', said the Master. 'Love is letting go of fear', says a modern master (Dr Jerry Jampolsky). How can such a one be helped? Only through love, expressed, in this case, at a distance in the silence of meditation. 'Be still: and know that I am God'.

1 Corinthians 13.
Paraphrased for physicians by Dr Ernesto Contreras MD

1. Though I become a famous scientist or practising physician, and I display in my office many diplomas and degrees, and I am considered an excellent teacher or convincing speaker, but have no **Love**, I am just a sounding brass or a tinkling cymbal.

2. And though I have the gift of being an unusual clinician making the most difficult diagnoses; and understand all the mysteries of the human body; and feel sure that I can treat any kind of diseases, even cancer; but have no **Love**, I am nobody.

3. And though I invest all my money to build the best facilities, buy the best equipment, have the most prominent physicians for the sake of my patients; and I devote all my time for their care, even to the point of neglecting my own family or myself; but have not **Love**, it profiteth me nothing.

4. **Love** is an excellent medicine; it is non-toxic; it does not depress the body defence, but enhances it.

5. It can be combined with all sorts of remedies, acting as a wonderful positive catalyst.

202

6. It relieves pain and maintains quality of life at its best level.

7. It is tolerated by anyone; never causes allergies or intolerance.

8. Common medicines come and go. What was considered good yesterday, is useless now. What is considered good now, will be worthless tomorrow. But **Love** has passed all tests and will be effective always.

9. We now know things only partially, and most therapies are only experimental.

10. But when all things are understood, we will recognise the value of **Love**.

11. It is the only agent capable of creating good rapport between patients, relatives and doctors, so everybody will act not as children but as mature people.

12. Today many truths appear as blurred images to us as physicians, and we cannot understand how the things of the Spirit work to maintain life; but one day we will see things very clearly.

13. And now remain three basic medications: **Faith, Hope and Love**; but the greatest of these is **Love**.

(Quoted with acknowledgements to my friend, Ernesto Contreras, MD).

CHAPTER FIFTEEN

CANCER

'The cure of a part should not be attempted without treatment of the whole. No attempt should be made to cure the body without the soul, and therefore, if the head and body are to be healthy, you must begin by curing the mind. That is the first thing. Let no one persuade you to cure the head until he has first given you his soul to be cured. **For this is the great error of our day in the treatment of the human body, that physicians first separate the soul from the body.'** *Plato 'Charmides,' 156 (circa 480 BC)*

Of all the multiplicity of influences tending towards disease in modern times, none is more potent than stress, and learning how to handle the stress creating areas in life is a vital and necessary constituent of the healing process. Nowhere is this more plainly to be seen than in patients with cancer, and nowhere is the finding of tranquillity of greater importance towards healing.

Up until the last two years (since when it seems to have been supplanted by AIDS) cancer has been the most feared disease in western society. It is the second commonest natural cause of death, being surpassed only by cardiovascular disease, and has become so prevalent that according to a recent statement from the Imperial Cancer Research Foundation one family in four will experience cancer among its members, and one in three of those who develop cancer will die from it. Indeed, it is this association with death in the minds of the public, and the inevitable fears of those who have little understanding of the temporary and ephemeral nature of material life, that is largely responsible for the dread with which it has been invested in the minds of so many. So strong is this association with death, and so great the fear engendered by the very word, that it has been said with some truth that the word cancer kills more people than the disease!

There are many factors associated with the development of cancer. Amongst these are genetic influences, viral infections, cancer producing substances in the environment, faulty feeding habits, as well as a general deterioration in the standards of nutrition consequent upon the commercialisation of the agricultural, horticultural and food industries, However, it seems likely that by far and away the commonest and most potent influence for cancer is the personality of the individual cancer patient and his/her ability to come to grips with the problems and the challenges of life.

Successful management and control of cancer in the patient involves giving aid to the patient at each and every level of being, and it epitomises all that has been said about holistic medicine in the preceding chapter. The control and the eventual elimination of cancer from mankind will involve overcoming and finally removing the destructive factors both from within each individual and from the totality of the environment. (By the phrase 'totality of the environment' I mean not just the physical environment, but also the psychological, social, political, cultural and spiritual environment. All of these need cleansing, if cancer is to be finally overcome.) Indeed, I see cancer as being an agent sent by God for the cleansing of the world, just as for so many individuals it has been a catalyst for personal transformation.

Since this book is largely the account of a personal odyssey, and my name is now considerably associated with my work for cancer sufferers, I make no apologies for devoting part of the book to a consideration of how the truths with which we have been entrusted relate to this most chilling of diseases. There are, as Paul has said, many diseases that can be helped once the barriers of ignorance and suspicion have been cleared away. Cancer is prominent among these diseases. Moreover, the lessons which the cancer patient learns, as he struggles to overcome his disease, apply equally to almost all chronic and degenerative diseases, and are relevant to all of us and contribute towards our spiritual growth and evolution.

Without going into too much detail, it is necessary to understand that there are probably cancer cells present in all of us, if not all the time, for a substantial portion of the time. One authority has estimated that there may be as many as 100,000 such cells at any one moment. (This sounds a lot, but relative to the total number of cells in the body, it is the equivalent of three persons among the whole of the population of western Europe!) According to this view, which is generally accepted by most cancer specialists today, the essential difference between the cancer patient and the person who has not got cancer lies less in the presence of the abnormal cells, than in the failure of the body of the cancer patient to deal with them. It seems likely that this is the result of a failure of the immune system.

That this is so, is evidenced by a number of observations. One is that cancer is more common in persons in whom the activity of the immune system has had to be artificially suppressed, as when an organ transplant has been carried out. (The incidence of cancer in persons who have received kidney transplants varies from 2.5 – 4 times higher than it is in the rest of the population. The higher figure is when cancers of the skin are also included in the count.) It is also significant that post-morten examinations of persons dying from causes other than cancer reveal a higher incidence of small, unrecognised collections of cancerous cells than the proportion of the population who actually develop cancer. Further strength is added to this view by the fact that cancer is one hundred times more common in persons born with an immune deficiency than in normal people. Moreover the incidence of cancer is many times higher in older people, (although we are are now tending to witness a lowering of the age incidence in some cancers), and a weakening of the body defence mechanisms is one of the natural consequences of ageing.

The reasons why the immune defence system fails to cope satisfactorily in certain people probably vary. Genetic factors, though rare, undoubtedly can play a part. We frequently see families in which successive generations have suffered from cancer, very often in precisely the same organ. Excessive production of abnormal cells, as occurs when the body is exposed to noxious substances, such as asbestos, tobacco smoke, certain hydrocarbons, gamma radiation and so on, may swamp the immune system. Deficiency in certain essential vitamins and minerals may cause the immune system to be functioning at only part of its potential efficiency. All of these can, and probably do, play a part in the production of cancer in some individuals. However, by far the most potent force interfering with the smooth working of the immune system appears to be the influence of personal stress within the mind of the sufferer.

Many authorities, including the Imperial Cancer Research Foundation, with one of whose directors I had a lengthy discussion on this subject recently, refuse to accept this. 'Yes', they say, 'stress is present in cancer patients, but it is the result, and not the cause of the cancer. In any case, we are all subject to stress, but we do not all get cancer. So this view cannot be true.' People who argue so, merely advertise their ignorance of what stress really is. They confuse stress, which, as we have seen, is the state of mind resulting from exposure to certain combinations of 'stressful circumstances', with the stressors, the stress inducing circumstances to which the mind is exposed. In any case, when one starts to examine in detail the stressors to which the cancer patients have been exposed, one finds they are of a very particular nature, which is different to those found among persons who do not develop cancer. Persons who argue in this way are doing no more than proclaim to the world that they have not taken the trouble properly to research the facts behind that which they announce so confidently. The result is, that in seeking to identify the cause of cancer at a purely physical level, they neglect the enormous potential of the mind both in the creation of and in the healing of disease, and by focusing the impact of their therapies solely upon the tumour, leave the influences which cause the tumour still in operation. It is therefore scarcely to be wondered at that attempts at therapy which regard the appearance of the tumour as primary, and concentrate entirely upon its removal, especially when carried out without reference to the underlying deficiency of the immune system, though often strikingly successful in the short run, are so often followed by the reappearance of the tumour at a later date, since the primary deficiency which allowed the appearance of the tumour has never been tackled and is left still operating.

If cancer is ever to be conquered, there will need to be a basic switch in emphasis by conventional medicine towards a more holistic approach, which will address itself equally, or even primarily, towards the underlying cause. It would seem that the tumour should be regarded more as a *symptom* of a basic underlying immunological malfunction than as a disease entity in its own right, and that, following the ancient maxim of treating causes first, and symptoms only secondarily, the main thrust of therapy should be directed towards the restoration of the efficient functioning of the immune system.

What then are the stresses so peculiar to the cancer patient? How do these differ from those of the rest of us? What is there which makes the cancer patient such a special case, and why is peace of mind and tranquillity of such importance in cancer? The answers are to be found in the work and writings of Lawrence LeShan. After studying the literature about the influence of the mind in cancer, and especially the work of W. H. Walshe, LeShan embarked upon a monumental study in an attempt to answer two fundamental questions, These were:

1. Is there a particular type of personality more prone than others to develop cancer?

2. If there is such a personality, how does the person acquire that personality?

In a study extending over some seventeen years, in the course of which he worked with over 250 cancer patients, who were interviewed from two to eight hours each, and with a further 200 cancer patients who were referred for counselling and psychotherapy, LeShan found there did, indeed, seem to be a 'cancer personality', and that no less than three-quarters of the cancer patients whom he interviewed had passed through a very similar basic life history. This was found in less than ten per cent of those who did not develop cancer. Basically the cancer personality was as follows:

1. Cancer patients were extremely prone to self pity, and tended to brood upon their sorrows and their disappointments.

2. Cancer patients had a very poor opinion of their own worth. They valued themselves mainly either in terms of personal success, or in what they were able to do for other people, and needed to justify themselves through success or good works.

3. Cancer patients tended to feel rejected both by society and by those around them. They felt emotionally isolated and lonely. They had difficulty in establishing and maintaining long-term stable personal relationships.

4. Cancer patients had great difficulty in discharging or expressing negative or hostile emotions. They had difficulty in forgiving, both others and themselves, with the consequence that they were apt to brood upon their injuries and to feel guilt-ridden at their own failures. *A tendency to self-blame was an intrinsic part of their make-up.*

5. Frequently the patient's life, due either to parental pressure or force of circumstances, was a way of life, which was unfulfilling and unsatisfying. When this involved the suppression of a strong creative urge towards artistic self-expression, the situation was particularly dangerous.

LeShan considered that the basic emotional and psychological difference between cancer sufferers and other people could be summed up in one word – despair. This despair was NOT the result of having contracted cancer, though that certainly increased the depth of despair. It was, he believed, a fundamental ingredient in the personality of the cancer patient, a kind of 'bleak hopelessness about ever achieving any meaning, zest or validity in life'. My own experience with cancer patients tends to confirm these findings. There is a basic loneliness, incapable of being bridged by love or even by feelings of anger, resentment or jealousy. Three subsidiary factors contribute to this basic aloneness. First there is a failure to be able to believe that any outside object can ever bring real satisfaction in life. Whatever relationship may be achieved, it is only temporary, and is bound ultimately to disintegrate in pain and disappointment. Next, the sufferer is unable to believe that anything, whether time or personal growth, can bring about a change in his underlying situation of despair and hopelessness. Finally, he believes that no matter what he does, no matter what action he takes, his basic aloneness is incapable of change. Rejection is certain – because he is what he is.

Set out thus baldly, all of this would appear to add up to a pretty sick personality, with the sickness reaching out to invade the spirit as well as the body. But most people who develop cancer are beautiful people. They are often described in such terms as 'Such a saint', 'He/she was such a really **good** person'. Idealism, self control, responsibility, a sense of service to others, feature largely in their lives. But if these truly admirable qualities are so firmly maintained that there is no room for self-expression and the release of deep-felt feelings, part of their essential self has been cut off. When deep-seated tensions and emotions are denied expression, when anger and resentment are stifled, they do not go away. They begin to gain in intensity from their lack of expression, and, as we know very well from the development of other diseases such as ulcers and high blood pressure, they start to interfere with the smooth functioning of the body and to strike the body at its weakest spot. In the case of cancer patients this would appear to be that part of the immune system concerned with the destruction of abnormal cells.

In many cases the emotional patterns which eventuate in the cancer personality have been laid down early in life, very often through events which take place in the first seven years of life. Commonest among these is a basic lack of love towards the child within the family. Sometimes this may be associated with one particular member of the family, one particular parent from whom the child has become separated through divorce or bereavement. Sometimes the arrival of another child, monopolising the parents' attention, has left the child feeling hurt and unwanted, starved of love, even when this is not truly the case. Drug and alcohol problems; coldness and failure by the parents to understand the basic emotional needs of the child; sheer economic necessity or greed, resulting in the farming out of the child to a substitute parent or nursery; all have been seen to play a part in patients who have come to me for help. Frequently the failure of the relationship is seen by the child as being 'his/her own fault', rather than attributable to force of circumstance or the fault of others. The result is a deep and in-built sense of guilt and self-blame, together with a feeling that they are not worthy of love. Very often the loveless child, feeling that it is his fault that he is not loved by the desired parent, will try to buy the love that he so deeply needs by seeking always to please the parent, and by sinking all his own wants and personal desires, in the hope of making himself acceptable to the parent. In time he may come even to deny that he has any personal wants, or if he does admit them, to see them as selfish and morally wrong. Such people generally grow up to be the servants of everyone else but themselves. They are always giving way to the wants and needs of others, and cannot bring themselves to believe that they have any right to personal satisfaction or personal wants, or that they can possibly be right and others wrong in a given situation. They suffer, in fact, from what I call 'the-after-you!-syndrome'. They find it incredibly difficult, if not downright impossible, ever to say 'No' to a request, yet often feel guilty at wishing to say 'No' but resentful at not having done so at one and the same time.

Sometimes there is no actual lack of love within the family, but the child is expected to achieve certain targets, either at school or socially, which may be outside their range of attainment. Whether the response to such failure is scolding or loving reproach, a sense of unworthiness, of failure and guilt is engendered. Such children grow up with feelings of personal inadequacy and emotional loneliness and isolation. No matter what success is achieved at school, they still feel themselves to be failures in life. Sometimes this sense of inability is accentuated by parental over-protection, and by constantly being told not to do this or that for fear of getting hurt.

As they grow up and reach late adolescence or early adult life, circumstances frequently arise that offer them a chance of forming stable and long-term relationships with others. Sometimes this may come through the development of some special interest or skill, which takes them into the company of others with similar interests or skills, with whom they are able to relate. Sometimes there may be a sense of vocation or mission in life. Frequently it comes through another person, such as a spouse or the arrival of children in a family. Occasionally it comes through an identification with a particular environment or lifestyle, in which they feel totally integrated and at home. They have, in fact, found a substitute object for the relationship which never had the chance to flower during childhood.

In this, the all 'important substitute object', they find at last their *raison d'etre*, and into it they pour all their strength and energies – physical, psychic and spiritual. Life has meaning and purpose at last, and they feel alive and fulfilled. It becomes their sheet anchor in life. As long as this sheet anchor remains, all goes well. But when, at a later stage, the central focal point becomes lost; when the children grow up and move away; when the time for retirement comes; when the much loved companion moves away or passes on; when the environment and life-style have to be left, the effect is devastating. Unless something can be

211

found to replace that which has been lost, they feel deprived of all that gives life meaning. The sheet anchor has been cut and they are aimlessly adrift on a sea of loneliness. Nothing seems worthwhile. Though many try desperately hard to find a substitute and to develop a new focus for their energies, their underlying sense of personal worthlessness prevents them from doing so. They seem to themselves to be predestined to failure. Once the central object has been lost, the attachment to life has been lost. Death seems the only way of escape.

The difficulty that many cancer patients find in discharging or effectively expressing emotions of anger, hostility, grief or resentment is also a potent force for destruction. Although they can often become extremely angry over the wrongs of others, and very ready to involve themselves on their behalf, when it comes to doing anything which will express their own personal feelings of anger or hurt, their deep rooted feeling of diffidence due to their own feelings of unworthiness gets in the way and prevents them from expressing what they feel. Somehow it seems to them to be morally wrong to be angry at what has happened to them, since this is only the natural consequence of their own basic worthlessness. Very frequently such emotions become so suppressed that they are never recognised as such by the individual, or, if they are recognised, become a cause for guilt, which merely compounds and intensifies the emotion. Such suppressed emotions, however, do not disappear. Having no means of expression at the conscious level, they become driven down into the subconscious, where they continue to bubble away, like a subterranean volcano, only to erupt when the normal defence mechanisms of the body have been so impaired by their influence as no longer to be able to contain the processes of disease.

Closely allied to this failure of emotional self-expression, and arising from the same underlying cause, their own ingrained sense of worthlessness, is an inability to go out and reach for their own personal wants and desires. Very often these have been so suppressed as never to be recognised, or, if recognised, have been relegated to a position of minor importance in their lives. LeShan exemplifies this with a story about a man who in his middle fifties developed a cancer of the pancreas. He had had a distinguished career as a gifted psychiatrist and the two men

212

had been students together many years before. The normal course of this type of cancer is that it responds to no form of orthodox treatment and runs rapidly and progressively downhill to end in death in from three to six months. While he was lying in his hospital bed, LeShan came to see his old friend, who had by this time resigned himself to the inevitable. Talking together, it transpired that he had never really wished to be a psychiatrist. Indeed, he had never wanted to become a doctor at all. What he had wanted to do was to be a sculptor. However, his father had been a cleric, and considered that all artists were an immoral set of persons, and that no son of his was going to lower the tone of the family by descending to such depths of moral degradation! Medicine, however, was an honourable profession in the service of humanity. Furthermore, his marriage had been made for social and professional reasons rather than because his heart was involved. During their conversations together it was gently suggested to the sick man that when he got out of the hospital he might like to spend the time remaining doing what he had always wanted to do and had never allowed himself the chance of doing: in short, that he should turn his back on his profession and devote his time to sculpture. Against all the odds, and totally at variance with professional expectations, his cancer began to regress. He was discharged from hospital, and thereupon took himself off to Italy, where he spent two blissful and satisfying years doing 'his own thing' and immersing himself in art and sculpture. While there he also had his one and only totally satisfying experience of love. At the end of two years, however, circumstances necessitated his return to his native country. His cancer became reactivated, and he went rapidly downhill and died.

One of the questions which I invariably ask of the patients with cancer who come to me for help is: 'What do you want out of life for yourself?' Generally this is something that they find very difficult to answer, apart from saying that they just want to be healed of their cancer. The idea that life should hold anything **for themselves** is something so completely foreign to their thinking that they have never for a moment considered it. Their underlying sense of worthlessness is so great that they feel they have no right to expect anything from life at all.

There are a variety of reasons why people want to be healed

213

of cancer. The commonest and most obvious is, of course, that they do not like being ill. They dislike the symptoms of their illness and the resulting restrictions upon their normal way of life. They do not like the various treatments to which they are subjected, most of which are extremely unpleasant. They dislike even more being forced to contemplate their own mortality. Having to think about death and what, if anything, lies beyond; the prospect of having to bid farewell to those they love; the cessation of life, and all that it holds; all of these are repugnant to modern man. Another reason for wishing to be healed which one often hears is that the sick person would like to go back to what life was like before he became ill. In other words he would like to return to the patterns of life which eventually ended in sickness. Sometimes a cancer sufferer seeks to be healed so as to be able to live to achieve some objective, such as bringing up a family, nursing a sick parent or spouse, or completing a particular project.

The body will not rouse its powers of self-healing for the first two reasons. For the third reason, that of achieving some objective in life it will rouse them sufficiently for the objective to be reached, but, once that has been achieved, it will switch off, control of the cancer will be lost, and it will tend to blaze away like a prairie fire. **The self-healing powers of the body will only be fully mobilised when the sick person is determined to transform his/her life; to find that in life which truly expresses him/herself, and to give expression to it.** 'I want time and space in my life to find my own music in life, and to sing my own song.' For this, and this alone, will the self-healing power in cancer truly flower.

As therapists and healers it is our task to help the sufferer to find this special music. One way of embarking upon this is to change our initial basic question, 'What is wrong with you?' to 'What is right with you? And, what is blocking it?' We are seeking to change the focus of living to life itself. Life is there to be lived to the full, and all the experiences contained within it, even cancer, are gifts from God; opportunities for growth, and not for commiseration. We can help them towards this by teaching 'the spiritual facts of life', so that the events of life come to be seen in a new perspective, as lessons in the textbook of life for which thanks is to be given. 'I thank Thee, Father, for the blessings of my joys. But I thank Thee even more for the blessings of my sorrows, for out of them I have learned so much.' This is indeed true, and there are many walking the streets of life today who will say just that: 'Thank God for my cancer. It is the best thing that could have happened to me, because through it I have been enabled to learn things that I would never have otherwise have been able to learn.'

I recall at this point a radio interview with a young patient of mine a couple of years ago. She was a girl who had developed Hodgkin's Disease when she was seventeen years of age. All her family except herself practised meditation, and meditated regularly. She, the youngest, was the odd one out. When she became ill, I advised that she too should be taught to meditate, and that, in addition to the normal course of chemotherapy employed in Hodgkin's Disease, she should practise meditation regularly as well as go on to a whole food vegetarian diet, with plenty of additional vitamins and minerals. She also had regular spiritual healing from Eric. By the time that she had had two courses of chemotherapy she was much better and in a state of remission. A decision was then made by the parents, in conjunction with myself, to stop the chemotherapy and intensify the meditation. She never looked back. At the time of the radio interview she had been in remission for five years and was completely well. At the conclusion, she was asked by the interviewer how she looked back on her experience today. 'Well,' she said, 'At the time it was absolutely terrifying. But when I look back on it today, I can see that it was enormously enriching.' That young girl had used her experience as a stepping-off point. She had found a central core of peace and tranquillity within herself, and her whole life had found purpose and direction. There are many such people around. I quote here a letter received from another of my patients, a young mother who had developed a cancer following the breakdown of her marriage and subsequent divorce.

'. . . My life is constant source of mystery as well as a joy. Mysterious because, like anyone else, I don't know what the future will bring. Yet prior to having cancer, the thoughts of the future were peripheral ones. The future was something that would always be there. Now I know better. That is where the joy comes in. With each new sunrise there is a beautiful day ahead. A day full of excitment – and humdrums too. Nevertheless it is there for the picking – ripe and full of promise. I like to make my days count. Here is how I have been living.

'Three to four mornings weekly I exercise in my gym. Sounds grand, but my 'gym' is nothing more than an empty room with one mirrored wall, some assorted weights and a rowing machine. My friend, who is an amateur athlete, has designed a two-hour programme which consists of running two miles; lifting weights (for tone and endurance, not muscle bulk); aerobics and dancing. I just love every minute. It is a definite high!

'The other two days you would find me teaching weaving at my daughter, Jennifer's school. It is a volunteer position. With my background as a primary school teacher, it is a job I truly enjoy. A. and I built frame looms, one for each child in Jennifer's class. I will travel with the looms, from grade to grade; teaching fine motor skills, maths sets, patterns, the history of fabric, etc. Next I will do a learning module on honey bees – from the flower all the way to the honeycombs, the production of honey, worker bees, etc. Volunteer teaching is an excellent tool for me – to continue a task which I adore, without the daily commitment. Much like the grandparent who can leave when the grandchild becomes a nuisance. Still in touch with parenting, but at a comfortable distance.

'Jennifer is also a joy. It is often difficult for parents, as much as for children, to separate. Volumes have been written! Relationships are fascinating, aren't they? At five Jennifer is a bright, curious, perceptive sensitive person. We learn a great deal from each other.

'My evenings are active too. I am in charge of fund raising for my Cancer Research Unit. In addition, I started a study group of ten couples to pursue Judaic studies. During the summer months, I raised money for the International Child Abuse Conference that was here in . . .

'Healthwise everything is great and shall remain so.'

Here, indeed, is one who has found her music, and is singing her own song. Often it is difficult to find this music – and this applies just as much to each one of us as to those who come to us for help. Sometimes I will use the following approach in an attempt to find this music.

'You have a fairy godmother, and, as with Cinderella, she has just appeared in front of you, saying, "I have got a most wonderful present for you. It is a once-in-a-lifetime-offer, and will never come again. In six months from now, your life can be any single thing that you want; anything. You have only to tell me what you want, and it will come to pass!" What is your reply going to be? Do you know what you want? If you do know, are you doing anything to help to bring it about? And what are you doing? If you are not doing anything about it, do you think that it is important that you should? What is there in you which is blocking your movement towards this sort of life?'

In our approach towards the sick person we have to help them to see and understand themselves, holding up a mirror to the soul, that they may see and recognise themselves. Most of us are somewhat afraid of finding out what we really are. At the gate of the soul, we find the watch dog Cerberus, and most turn back from the monster. Those who are brave enough to go on find the monster at the threshold to be no monster, but rather a puppy that wants to be loved. Each and every one of us, in finding ourselves, find ourselves both wanting to be loved, and wanting to love. Love, or rather our need of loving and of being loved, is the most fundamental factor in cancer, and it is this which is so often the answer to the question, 'Why did so-and-so die of cancer?' Moreover, as I have already pointed out, this love is something which we must extend to ourselves as well as to others. We need our own love, as well as the love of others; we need to value and respect ourselves if, through God, we are to heal ourselves. ('And the second commandment is like unto it: "Thou shalt love they neighbour as thyself" '.)

Before they can start to heal themselves, cancer patients have to understand why they have got their cancer. They have to be helped to identify the negative emotional patterns within themselves, and then learn how these can be changed into something that is positive and constructive. One way of starting to do this is to review the changes in their lives which have taken place in the period preceding the development of their cancer. These changes must particularly include their changing emotional relationships with others. They must review the emotions which these events produced within them, pondering upon them deeply and with scrupulous honesty. Where there was any negative component in the emotions, such as anger, resentment, grief, jealousy, revenge, or guilt, they must then consider

217

whether any trace of this emotion is still present like a lingering echo, and active at the present time. Where there is, then this must be changed, and it is the task of the healer gently to help to heal the hurt.

A good example of the importance of this is to be seen in the case of H. H. was a young and lovely woman in her early thirties. She came with her husband having had a mastectomy for a breast cancer. This had been followed by radiation and chemotherapy. The cancer however was still active and she wanted to try to help herself. The young couple were obviously extremely happy together and deeply attached to each other. H. had come from a fairly typical background, with emotional deprivation in childhood, a strongly self-critical attitude, and great reticence over her emotional side. She was very ready to embrace the diet, to try to meditate and to visualise, and to take part in the healing group and receive healing. She was a lot less ready to share her thoughts and emotions during the counselling periods, and I felt from the start that there was something very important that she was keeping back. She made very little improvement, and was soon undergoing yet a further course of chemotherapy, to which there was no response. After a very few months she had to be admitted to hospital for terminal care. While in the hospital she was visited regularly by another member of the group, the wife of a healed lung cancer patient. 'God is punishing me for what I have done, isn't he?' she said. And then the whole pitiful story, the story which she had been so ashamed to share, came out. She was the second wife of her husband. She had met him and fallen deeply in love with him while he was still married to his first wife, and she had set out to marry him. She had been the occasion of the break-up of his first marriage, and much as in the story of David and Bathsheba, she had then married him after the divorce. It was not God who was punishing her. It was her own conscience. It was her feelings of guilt and self-blame, which she was totally unable to handle. Had she been able to speak of this when she first came, it might have been possible to teach her how to forgive herself; to explain that marriages just do not break up unless there is already a crack in their structure. Had there been complete harmony and unity in the husband's first marriage, she might have thrown out all the lures she could think of, and he would never even have noticed them. The marriage must have been unstable in the first place for the divorce ever to have happened, and, in all probability, the first wife was at least as much to blame, and probably far more so. Armed with this knowledge she might have learned how to forgive herself. Sadly her disease proceeded apace to its inevitable conclusion. I hope that she is at peace.

Another example, this time of a totally opposite nature, is to be seen in the case of J. J. was a woman of sixty-seven when she first came to see me. She was suffering from a malignant ovarian cyst. This had been surgically removed, and J. had had a course of radiotherapy followed by chemotherapy. At this point she had had all the therapy which it was possible to give. She was suffering from the spread of the cancer cells into the peritoneal cavity and into the pleural cavity, and there were massive effusions of fluid at both sites. She had an abdomen the size of a football and was attending hospital at three-weekly intervals for the fluid to be drained off. Her expectation of life would have been about three to four months.

She first came to me in July, together with her husband. We talked together about the nature of cancer – how cancer cells appear in all of us, and how the body tries to control them, and how, in some people, this control process can be interfered with through emotional stress and faulty life-styles. We spoke about her own life from her earliest days. J. had been a school teacher, and had recently reached the age of retirement. She felt lost without her daily commitment to her pupils, and her life was now centred around her daughter. Here lay the source of her trouble. Her daughter was an epileptic, and like many epileptics she was unstable and unpredictable in her behaviour. She lived with her parents and was unable to hold down a job. J. felt extremely guilty over this, and blamed herself for her daughter's condition. She was also deeply anxious over what the future might hold for the daughter when she was no longer there to look after her and care for her. Guilt and fear predominated in her emotional state.

At her first visit we talked about the damaging effect of these emotions, and how they stimulated an over production of steroid hormones in the body which upset the working of her immune system. We also spoke of how the relaxation response could lessen these effects, and thus help to get her immune system working again. She learned a simple system of meditation and visual imaging, and was instructed in nutrition, vitamin and mineral support therapy. On her subsequent visits we went further into the problems of guilt and apprehension for the future. She came gradually to see that whatever might be the situation today, it could not be helped by dwelling on the past. The past was past and could not be changed, however much she might wish to do so. In any case epilepsy was not brought about by anything that she might have done – or omitted to do, but that epileptics are acutely sensitive to the thoughts and feelings of those around them, and her own very natural anxieties only served to worsen the position. This was something that she had to learn to accept. We spoke, too, of the importance of her own attitudes and beliefs in determining her own future. If she expected that she would progress rapidly downhill towards inevitable death, then her body would programme itself towards this end. We discussed, also, the meaning of death, not as sheer extinction, but as a transition from one environment to another, and how life had to be seen as a series of opportunities for learning and for making personal growth. All the hazards and traumas of life were no more than exercises in the textbook of life, and, rightly approached, became renewed opportunities for growth. We spoke about loving, and how it was necessary to learn to love oneself, since without love for oneself, and respect for one's own true worth, it was impossible to love others. We spoke of God's individual love and care for all his creatures, and how all things, in the end, worked together for good, even though we could not recognise it at the time. We spoke of the necessity for forgiveness, and how it was necessary to extend that forgiveness to ourselves as well as to others.

I also introduced J. to our own cancer support group at this time, and she and her husband used to travel every other week all the way from London to attend. Here she was in contact with others with similar problems, and here she could share her experience with them and learn from the way in which they handled their problems. She found the conducted group meditations to be a tremendous help, and she experienced for the very first time the peace that such meditations can bring, and the power of prayerful healing through the laying on of hands. Little by little J. started to improve. The amounts of fluid drawn off at the hospital became steadily less and less, and the intervals between became longer and longer. Eventually there came a 'dry tap' when nothing came at all, and she heard her surgeon whisper to the nursing sister, 'I don't know what is going on in there, but I am sure it is nothing but good!' Christmas came and went – a Christmas that she had never expected to see. The atmosphere within the family improved and the daughter's behaviour became better as the weeks went by.

By February J. had improved so much and was making such progress with her meditation that I suggested to her that she might like to come to a week-long conference on meditation which was to be held during May on the island of Iona off the west coast of Scotland. Now Iona is, as we have seen, a very special island, and I told her a little about the history of the island and how it had once again become a centre of spiritual power. J. was fascinated by the idea and readily agreed to attend the conference.

Like many such centres of spiritual power, access to Iona is difficult, and the journey there both long and arduous. It entails 600 miles by road, some of it across wild and difficult terrain. There then follows a 45 minute journey by boat, an hour by bus across the island of Mull, and, finally, a further journey in a tiny open boat across the mile wide Sound of Iona. It is, in every sense of the word, a pilgrimage. Samuel Johnson, the great lexicographer of the eighteenth century, is reported by his bio-grapher, Boswell, as having fallen on his knees and kissed the soil on landing, as he uttered his famous words: 'That man is little to be envied whose patriotism would not grow stronger upon the fields of Marathon, or whose piety would not grow warmer amongst the ruins of Iona.'

J. made the journey with her husband. She was still not walk-ing very well, and so they took with them a folding wheelchair in which she was pushed about the island in the intervals during the conference. (The whole island is not more than three miles long, and there are no cars and virtually no roads.) She attended all the talks and meditations, together with the services at the restored but ancient abbey, which are a feature of all Iona con-ferences. When the end of the conference came and it was time to go home, J. did not want to go. What she wanted above all else was to visit the legendary Fingal's cave, which is reported to

221

have inspired the composer Mendelssohn to compose his Hebridean Journey. Now Fingal's Cave is on the island of Staffa, an outcrop of black basaltic rock, sticking out of the sea. It lies six rather stormy miles distant from Iona, and the only means of access is in a small open boat. There is no proper landing stage, just some rough rocks, to which the boat ties up, and often it is not possible even to land. J. was lucky, however, since, on the day that she made the trip, the sea was relatively calm, and she was able to land. She made her way along the narrow cliff path, often no more than half a metre wide, with the sea washing close beneath it, and into the depth of the cave, to hear the echo and to view the stupendous sight of the light coming through the jagged outline of its entrance. She then made her way back to the boat, but, having got there, nothing would content her but that she should climb the hundred and fifty feet to the top of the island to look at the nesting seabirds. (It must be remembered that she had been going around in a wheelchair during the preceding week!) At length honour was satisfied and she returned to the boat, and, the next day, by easy stages, to her home outside London.

It was, by this time, the end of May, eleven months after she had first come to see me, and J. was better than she had been throughout the past two years. She continued to visit me in Norfolk and to make progress, until, sadly, six weeks later, the oil crisis erupted, and the price of petrol escalated so much that they were unable to afford to travel the 200 miles necessary to attend the Norfolk group. She continued with her diet and her meditation, but, lacking the stimulus of the group and the regular healing, from this moment she started to go downhill. In October her condition had deteriorated to such a degree that her husband was no longer able to look after her properly, and she was admitted to the palliative care ward of the hospital she had been attending. She knew that she was dying, but she remained serene and undaunted at the imminence of death. Shortly before Christmas she took part in a television programme along with another patient, two young doctors and two of the nurses, in which she spoke of the approach of death, and of her firm belief that consciousness went on beyond the death of the body. To her death was a door which opened to another dimension of continued being without the inconvenience of bodily impairment. She had no fear; only a serene and radiant tranquillity. This intensely moving programme materially altered the lives of many who saw it and brought a new understanding of the meaning of death.

To many the story of J. would appear as an example of failure; proof positive that the holistic approach to cancer simply does not work. Looked at from a purely superficial level this would seem to be true. But, as has repeatedly been pointed out, we are more than bodies, and just as sickness involves other levels than the purely physical (as we have seen when looking at the antecedents of cancer), so healing has to take place at more than the purely material level. Indeed, healing which is confined to the material level is merely cure, and not healing at all, while in some people, as in J., real healing may take place even when the body has been so damaged as to have passed the point of no-return. In such cases death itself may be the ultimate healing. As we counsel, and as we teach the skills and practice of regular meditation, slowly there comes about a reorientation of the outlook of the sick person; the body begins to be seen for what it is, a suit of clothes, like a diver's suit, to be worn in the physical world as being necessary to exist in that dense, material environment; life becomes a page in the saga of the human soul, and death no more than the turning of the page, the passage from one environment into another. Cancer is seen as just 'one of those things' which are met with along life's journey, a challenge to be faced and handled, and an opportunity for growing and learning.

A good example of this is to be seen in the case of S. S. is another of my patients. She came to me about four years ago with a lump in the breast, in the hopes that surgery might be avoided. The lump was plainly malignant, but there was no sign of any spread of glandular involvement. I told her that in my opinion surgery was necessary, but that provided she was willing to follow the holistic path, it should not be necessary to do more than remove the cancerous lump. She should, therefore, read through the small print of the operation consent form and scratch out anything which allowed the surgeon discretion to do more than just remove the lump. She would probably have a battle about this, but after all it was her body, and she had a right to say what was to be done to it. S. was admitted and had her lump removed. Her breast was spared, and her husband, to whom the cosmetic part of mastectomy was all important, was delighted. Unfortunately (with hindsight) S. was given a post-operative course of radiotherapy to the breast tissue, as a sort of precaution against recurrence, and this was later to prove a minor disaster. (Radiotherapy to the chest area can damage the all important thymus gland, through which the T-lymphocytes must pass, and thus result in a lowering of immune efficiency.)

The background to S.'s cancer was a familiar one. Coming from an emotionally starved family background, she had met and married her young husband while in her early twenties. Physically she was slim and boyish and relatively undeveloped from the feminine aspect. She had no maternal interests and neither she nor her husband had any desire for children. She shared his life and interests and was completely subservient to him, with no friends or interests of her own. She worked as a secretary in a firm of estate agents, where she was the central figure in the running of the office. She had an excellent relationship with her boss, and was regarded with affection and friendship. She was equally attached to her work and to him and found fulfilment in her competent efficiency and the reliance which was placed upon her. Trouble began when this relationship began to deteriorate. Though she did not recognise it at the time, her boss was an immature and somewhat inadequate personality, and with the arrival of another girl in the office, S.'s key position began to be undermined. She was losing her all important role in life, and once this was gone, would have had no individual life of her own, and been left in subservience to her husband. Although she did not recognise this at the time, it was clearly the trigger point for the cancer. Part of her wanted 'out' from this unacceptable life situation. There had to be a change. Cancer, leading to death, was one way of achieving this, though a rather drastic way!

In the course of the counselling sessions, we explored this together, and S. came to see that the office role was, at the moment, of supreme importance to her as a means of expressing her own individuality and worth. She must therefore, instead of feeling resentful at the behaviour of her employer, learn to view this with compassionate indulgence, and seek to rebuild the former relationship of confident trust and reliance which had meant so much to her. Alongside this, however, she must seek to develop a life and interests of her own, and so be less subservient to her husband. She did exactly this, and for over two years things went well and there was no further trouble. Sometime later, however, history repeated itself, and there was further trouble in the office, and S. was threatened with the loss of her job. This fuelled another breakdown in her immune system and she developed another lump in the self-same breast. This time she was not so lucky (or was it the immuno-destructive effect of the radiotherapy which she had undergone?), for by the time she saw me, there was involvement of a lymph gland, and I had reluctantly to tell her that this time I felt that mastectomy was necessary if she was to avoid the risk of future recurrence.

Bravely S. went ahead with this. She is not a very feminine person, and the contours of her breast had never meant a great deal to her. Her husband, however, is devastated, and will, as she puts it, 'have nothing to do with her above the waist!' All the loving tenderness of intimacy has been completely destroyed, (if, indeed, it was ever there, which I am beginning to doubt), and he is unable even to look at what he regards as a mutilated body. S., in the meantime, has regarded this as a challenge to be over-come. She has rebuilt the situation in the office with regard to her boss, and is now content and happy in her work. She has started to take an intense interest in healing and the holistic approach. This has brought her out from the closed environ-ment of her home into contact with others of similar interests. She has started to attend seminars and groups, and in so doing has made friends of her own. She has discovered an interest in music, both in listening to and making music. She has bought a musical instrument and started taking lessons, and she has just passed the first of her grade examinations in her instrument. She has also started taking lessons in the theory of music, and intends later to take a more advanced instrument and try to join an orchestra. In the course of all this she has found an under-standing of life, and a wide compassion which is able to embrace the inadequacies of her husband. The whole of life has taken on a new meaning for her, and she is truly one who says, 'Thank God for my cancer! It is the best thing that could have happened to me. I have learned so much from it and have met so many people that I would never have had a chance to meet and to learn from, had I not developed cancer.' S. continues to be well. She follows her meditation and her diet, and attends regularly at a support group for cancer sufferers, where her example is an inspiration to others just starting on the path. So long as she continues in her present state of calm and serenity, and to express her own essential self in her life, she will, I am sure, continue to be well. But the fact that she had a relapse tells us that she is at risk, and will have to continue on guard for a very long time.

Thus the healing of cancer is something far greater than simply the removal of a painful or unsightly lump from the body, or the curing of a life threatening condition. It reaches deep down into the personality and the soul, and involves a realignment of the whole approach to living. Spiritual healers have long noted that if a healing is to be permanent, then it is necessary for there to be a change amounting to a spiritual reorientation of the individual. There has to have been a healing of the spirit. Such healing cannot take place through material, or even through psychic forces alone. Spiritual power must also be involved, and such power can only stem from God. Those involved in the care and counselling and healing of patients suffering from cancer must, therefore, be truly God-centred in themselves. In Paul's words, 'Anything of a worthwhile nature from the spiritual powers can only come through a channel which is clean and pure.'

Not, of course, that those concerned in this healing ministry should attempt to convert, or to impose their own concepts of God upon those whom they seek to help. I once wrote, in a chapter about how to form and run a cancer group, a warning against attempts to proselytise, which I ended with the words, 'Each person finds his own way to God.' I subsequently received a furious letter from an atheist accusing me of denying to those who did not believe in God the help which I was seeking to give. All unwittingly I had raised an insurmountable barrier for one whom I might have been able to help. The God-centredness of which I speak is for the healers and counsellors. It is **they** who have to remain pure channels for the transmission of the Divine energies, and to be able to raise their own consciousness to such a state of nearness to the Divine that those energies can flow. We are not dealing here with intellectualism and a left-brain approach towards God. 'God is a Spirit', said Jesus, 'and they that worship Him must worship Him in spirit and in truth.' We are working here in the spiritual realm, and it is enough that we do so. The blockage for most, who do not believe in God, is an intellectual blockage. As with healing of the body, the introduction of spiritual energy at the higher level will find its way to and will transform the lower levels. God will perform whatever is right for that individual. We do not have to worry over the beliefs of the patient. It is enough that we offer ourselves as pure channels for the transmission of the healing power.

CHAPTER SIXTEEN

HEALING THE INNER MAN

TRANQUILLITY

'The Lord is my pace setter: I shall not rush.
He makes me stop and rest for quiet intervals.'

Tokio Megashio

We saw in the previous chapter some examples of the holistic approach in action. Two of these would be regarded as failures by conventional standards. One of these failures was undoubt edly due to a failure of full communication between the patient and myself. The other, while not resulting in the healing of the body, was no failure in holistic terms. J.'s life had been enormously enriched by what she learned through practising this approach, and her span of living had been considerably extended beyond what it might normally have been expected to have been in so advanced a case. The intensity of her symptoms had been reduced, and, what is perhaps the most important thing of all, when death came, she was able to leave easily and with dignity. She had found peace and tranquillity, both in life and in death.

In all of this, the most important influence in the healing process is the mind of the patient. It is what the patient really thinks and *inwardly* believes which determines the prospects of healing. The mind is enormously powerful when properly focused and harnessed to a given end, and is able to control a whole range of body functions usually thought to be beyond mental control. An intriguing example of these powers is given in Guy Playfair's recent book *If this be magic*. Playfair quotes a well-known example of the healing under hypnotic suggestion of a boy suffering from the horrible skin disease, ichthyosis. This particular disease is due to the congenital absence of the oil producing glands in the deeper levels of the skin, as a result of which the horny layers of the skin proliferate to such an extent that the skin becomes like armour plating. At every area where movement takes place the skin cracks open and the tissues beneath become a festering sore. It is, by normal standards, completely incurable. With this patient an attempt was made to remove surgically the hardened and thickened external layers and graft other skin in its place. The attempt failed, and the graft rapidly became hardened and blackened like the other skin. The anaesthetist, however, not realising what the condition really was, thought that the patient was suffering from multiple warts. He, the anaesthetist, was a practising hypnotherapist and had successfully treated several cases of warts with hypnotism. He was persuaded to make an attempt with this patient, and duly did so, carefully starting with one limb only. What he expected duly came to pass. Within ten days the blackened and thickened skin had peeled away, leaving beneath a normal healthy skin. The surgeons at the hospital were flabbergasted. 'Do you know what you have done?' they said. 'This is a case of congenital ichthyosis. Go and look it up in the library, for we are presenting the case at the Royal Society of Medicine in two days time!' The anaesthetist had succeeded in doing what had never been recorded as having been done before. He continued to treat the patient, one bit at a time, on subsequent sessions and achieved about 50 per cent improvement overall. Eventually, however, there was no response, and the patient became, in his words, 'Impossible to hypnotise'. The probable explanation for this is that having learned what he had achieved was supposed to be impossible, the hypnotist started to have self-doubts about the possibility of effecting a cure, and that these doubts then communicated themselves to the subconscious mind of the patient. (Also, we do not know at this distance just exactly what was said in front of the patient by the assembled doctors at the RSM, and what was the effect upon his own beliefs.) **It is what the patient believes which is the all important factor.**

This is well exemplified in the following case. A patient suffering from terminal cancer came to learn of a new drug, Krebiozin, which had been reported in the lay press as being the latest wonder drug and as having had excellent results with cancer, and had persuaded his doctor to give it a trial. Within two days the mass of the cancer had disappeared. Subsequently reports published in the daily press that the drug was valueless were seen by the patient. Within the space of three months, the lump had recurred, and he was again attending the hospital. On this occasion the doctor gave him an injection of sterile water, saying forcefully that this was a new and extremely potent form of the drug. Once again the lump disappeared in the space of two days. Finally, following reports by the American Medical Association that the drug was valueless, the cancer again recurred and the patient rapidly died.

Nor is it only the beliefs of the patient which are important. A doctor treating a patient who suffered from severe and persistent attacks of asthma received for clinical trial a new remedy from a drug company, together with a number of glowing reports of its efficacy. He decided that this particular patient was an ideal subject for the trial, and explained exactly what he was going to do. He was going to treat the patient for alternate months, first with the drug, and then with a placebo. Since the patient, would not know which was which, it would be possible in this way to assess whether the drug was really of any value without the patient's ideas having any bearing upon the result. In practice the doctor found that the patient was immensely better, so long as he was taking the drug, but that as soon as the doctor switched him on to the inert placebo, his symptoms recurred. When the time came for a fresh supply of the drug to be sent, the drug company confessed that in order to make the trial truly a 'double blind' trial they had switched the labelling, so that what the doctor believed to be the highly efficient new drug was in fact the inert placebo, and vice versa! The efficacy of the 'new treatment' rested rather in the beliefs of the doctor than in the nature of the drug, and these beliefs influenced the attitude of the patient towards his disease.

This, of course, was common practice when I first started to practise medicine. There WERE no wonder drugs in those days. Chemotherapy and antibiotics as we know them today simply did not exist. We relied upon a few well-proven favourites such as digitalis and aspirin and upon a vast range of different medicines of varying colours and generally abhorrent flavours. Modern research has revealed that most of these had no pharmacological action at all. **But people still got well with these**

medicines. WE believed in their efficacy, and our patients believed in us and in our superior wisdom in being able to select the appropriate remedy for the task in hand. Some of the bright young men of today accuse the physicians of old of perpetrating an enormous confidence trick upon their patients. In fact it was nothing of the kind. We were making use of the oldest healing power known to man, the power of the mind to heal, and were reinforcing it with the potent suggestion of the placebo.

These accounts would seem to substantiate the experience of the hypnotherapist. As long as he believed that he was able to cure the 'warts' – as he believed them to be – he was effective in influencing the mind of the patient to programme the body in that direction. As soon as he began to have doubts, these started to communicate themselves to the mind of the patient and eventually inhibited the healing process. It would appear that, much though many of us dislike the term 'faith healing', this may well be an accurate description of what is taking place, but that it is the faith of the healer in his/her ability to be used in this capacity, and thus to imbue the patient with the conviction that healing will ensue, which is the all important factor. This burning faith in an ability to be a channel of healing power is something that stems from the inner, spiritual life of the healer. Personal spiritual discipline is fundamental, and an active prayer and meditation life would appear to be a *sine qua non* for the successful healer.

Jesus knew this well and taught it to his disciples. 'If ye have faith as a grain of mustard seed and command that this mountain be moved, it will be so'. Peter walked upon the water – until he suddenly realised just what he was doing, and his confidence failed him. But faith is something more than the classic description of the schoolboy: 'Faith is believing what you know is jolly well impossible!' Faith is a deep-rooted conviction that whatever is believed **will be so**. It is the rock upon which stands the temple of healing. Let it be shaken, and the temple crumbles and falls to the ground.

Of course, this is totally at variance with the conventional views of modern scientific medicine, which takes little account of the patient's beliefs and teaches that it is what is done to him from outside himself which determines whether or not he is to be healed of his disease. As we have seen, this approach denies

231

the patient any responsibility or role in his own healing. His body has become 'a thing', to be manipulated by others, a mere biological mechanism at the mercy of the experts. When this mechanistic approach of having things done to one by others is extended to include spiritual healing, as well as the various techniques of orthodox and complementary medicine, all that has happened is that the 'chain of command' has been pushed back a stage, and the responsibility for imposing the healing transferred to the discarnate, and, ultimately, to God. At no time does the patient see him/herself as doing more than submit to the Will of God. Here again faith, in the sense of confident expectation in which it has been defined above, is crucially important, but since the Will of God is often seen as being something which is deep and inscrutable, beyond the ken of Man, and sickness is frequently seen, as it was by H., as punishment for wrongdoing, the certainty that healing **will** take place can become difficult of access. The vision of God as a loving father, whose will for all his children is perfect health of body, mind and spirit, is little understood. Yet so it is. The Old Testament vision of a 'jealous God, who visiteth the sins of the fathers upon the children unto the third and fourth generation', which has been swept away by the revelation of a God of Love, dies hard.

But this belief in sickness as punishment for sin is extremely potent. It is still with us in the minds of many. I remember taking part in a *Man Alive* programme several years ago in which were examined the cases of three patients all of whom had undergone a 'miraculous' healing of cancer. One of these was a woman in her early thirties with three children. Upon being told that her case was terminal and that medicine could offer nothing more to help her, she went to see her local priest, expecting that he would embrace her with the love of God, and that together they would offer prayers for her healing. To her utter astonishment she was told that she must have been very wicked for God to be punishing her in this way, but that if she would admit how wicked she had been, he would pray with her for her forgiveness, that when she died, she might enter the presence of God free from sin! Hardly surprisingly she never entered a church again.

The effect of this abrasive behaviour, however, was crucial. She was so enraged at what she saw as the injustice of the whole affair (although not a regular churchgoer, she was living a perfectly normal family life, and was not in any sense more wicked than any other ordinary person), that she determined that she would not die, but would survive to bring up her three young children. She refused to admit that she was suffering from a terminal disease, or that her various symptoms bore any relationship to this. Every day when she got up and before she went to sleep, as well as many times through each day, she would say to herself out loud, 'I feel good! I have never felt better. There is nothing wrong with me!' This process of self-hypnosis worked. Her body accepted the suggestions being made to it, and her disease regressed. When I spoke with her some ten years later, she was perfectly well, and to the best of my knowledge has remained so.

Although sickness and disease are not to be seen as deliberate punishments by God for wrongdoing, we have to recognise that in just the same way that we as parents have to be willing to allow our children to make their own mistakes, so that they may learn and grow from those mistakes, so God allows us to make our mistakes and rules that we must bear the consequences of those mistakes. It is we who create the diseases from which we suffer, either individually or communally. We are, indeed, the architects of our own diseases. But equally, and owing to the divine creative power of life within each one, it is we who are the architects of our own healing. In the famous words of an American President, 'the buck stops here'. 'Within you lies the power' wrote Thomas Hamblin. Within each one of us lies the power of healing, both to heal ourselves and to help others to heal themselves. But we have to know how to release that power of healing and how to harness it.

The first step in this process of self-healing is understanding just why we have developed the particular disease. Only when we have seen this clearly are we in a position to correct whatever have been the antecedent causes of that disease. Perhaps, as so much of this book revolves around my personal story, an example drawn from my own life would not be out of place and may prove instructive to others. A year ago, I had had a hectic period involving two transatlantic speaking tours, together with patient consultations and a heavy speaking and lecture schedule here at home, including a visit to Eire. Considerably against my

233

will I had become the Chairman of Trustees, as well as the Medical Director, of The Association for New Approaches to Cancer (the cancer charity which seeks to promote the holistic approach to cancer), over which there were immense financial and administrative problems. I am not a born administrator, and I was only too conscious of my lack of skills in this direction. I had also an overwhelming sense of frustration at the lack of understanding and support in this respect from most of my professional colleagues. All of this was intermingled with a stream of desperate patients seeking help for their cancers. I started to feel increasingly unwell. Eventually, and to my utter horror, I was diagnosed as having a cancer of the throat. I understand very well how this had come about. I had for many years suffered from a hiatus hernia, which was a hereditary condition; I enjoyed a glass of wine with my meals and with friends; and I had been a cigarette smoker, though not a heavy one, since my days in Burma during the war. All of these are known to be cancer producing influences. However, it was not until I came home from a weekend away to find my second son paying us a visit to say that after seventeen years of married life he had suddenly left his wife and son and gone to live with another woman, that the real stress was created. Anger, grief and shame warred together within my mind, and were denied expression for fear of making matters worse and raising barriers between us that could not be bridged. Such things just did not happen in **our** family! We read of them as happening to others, but to us – Oh No!

T. was the middle child of three, and as not infrequently happens in such situations, communication between us both had never been easy. The fault was certainly more mine than his. He had been born during my two years absence overseas on war service, and the proper bonding between parent and child, which starts in earliest infancy, had never had the chance to develop as it should have done. Only three months before the family had spent Christmas with us, and I had seen no hint of any breakdown in relations. The shock of the marriage break-up was total, and I felt both angry at his conduct, sorrow for his wife, and desperately anxious at the effect which it would have upon my grandchild. I could express none of this indignation lest it intensify the situation and lead to a total breach between us both. I knew full well what this suppressed emotion could do to me, and I can even remember thinking at one moment, 'This could well be the death of me', and then hastily putting the thought aside as being negative and destructive. The sequel was cancer of the oesophagus, which is well recognised by students of the energy field of man as being associated with a blockage at the throat chakra, which is the centre for speech and communication.

Once the diagnosis had been made, affairs moved with frightening celerity and precision. Referral was made to a surgeon, an examination of the throat was carried out under general anaesthesia, which confirmed the X-ray diagnosis, and a complete body scan was ordered. This confirmed the diagnosis of a small cancer at the lower end of the oesophagus, and that there had been no spread of the tumour outside the walls of the oesophagus. Surgical excision was thus a practical possibility and was the treatment of choice. The decision was mine, and mine alone. For years I had been preaching and teaching the Gentle Way with cancer. I knew all about the techniques of meditation and visual imaging to strengthen and coordinate the self-healing power, the role of diet, and metabolic therapy through minerals and mega-dosage of vitamins. I understood exactly why – as I thought – I had developed my cancer, and the importance of love, of forgiveness, both of oneself and others, of expectations and attitudes to life, and of finding and singing the essential music in life, instead of returning to the patterns of life which had produced the disease. I knew many who had fought and overcome their cancers by these means. Sadly, I also knew many who had tried and failed to do so. The process was by no means infallible. I knew, too, that the operation was exceptionally severe, and carried a definite mortality. I knew no one who had experienced it, and I shrank from it. But the choice was mine and had to be made. Was I to 'stay true' to what I had been preaching, and seek to heal myself by following the Gentle Way, or was I to submit my body to the surgeon's knife, not knowing where it would lead me? For two days I agonised over this. I experienced to the full the fear of the patient who is told that the disease is cancer. I experienced the uncertainty of not knowing that there would be a tomorrow, and that the future, which I had always taken for granted, might no longer be there. I knew

235

what it was to look out at the roses beneath the window and to think 'It's not much good pruning those. I shan't be around to see them.' I knew the agony of leaving the job unfinished, the mission uncompleted, and, in anticipation, the deep, deep sorrow of farewell. I was not afraid to die. I knew that life went on – albeit in another dimension – and that my beloved Vicky would be there to meet me along with my discarnate friends. But I desperately did not want to leave the world just yet. There was still too much which had to be accomplished, and which I felt had to be accomplished by me.

In the end I decided to do both. I would accept the operation, trusting that what had to be would be, and that whatever happened would be in accordance with God's will. At the same time I would use meditation and visual imaging to assist the body to withstand and heal itself from the operation, and I would take the additional minerals and vitamins which I would prescribe to any patient of mine under such conditions. I would also alert my many friends in the healing movement and ask for their help in prayer and absent healing. Prominent among these were the Reverend Donald Reed and his team of healers and helpers at St James' Chruch, Piccadilly, at which I had spoken on a number of occasions, and where I had given advice about the setting up of a Christian healing group for cancer patients, and my friends at The Seekers' Trust. These devoted people, on learning the exact date and time of the operation, set up a twenty-four hour prayer and healing watch over this period, which I am absolutely certain had the most profound influence over the course of events. In addition regular prayers for healing were offered in my own parish church and country-wide prayers and meditations for healing were sent from the many groups and individuals whom I had met in my own ministry. One story of such healing prayer is especially touching. I have always had a special affinity for St Francis, which I shared with Pat, my receptionist-dispenser. Sometime previously she had been given a small figure of the saint, which had been specially blessed and brought from Assisi. This she placed behind the grill at the reception desk in the health centre where I used to prac-tise and from which I had retired six years before. Throughout those anxious weeks, she told me later, many and many a hand would reach through the grill to touch the figure and breathe a silent prayer that I might be healed. Letters, cards and flowers flowed in to my hospital room from all over the world, wherever I had travelled in my efforts to spread the gospel of healing. Even now, nine months later, when all is over and I am practically well again, I am moved to tears when I read these messages of love and healing. No words can express the depths of my gratitude for this support.

Nor was this all that stemmed from my illness. A good deal of the pressure surrounding me was to do with the Association for New Approaches to Cancer, of which I was both Medical Director and Chairman of Trustees. At this time the Trustees had functioned as a Board of Management, as well as Trustees, and it was this process of management which had created the pressure. My vice-chairman immediately took over the functions of the chair, which I was unable to exercise during my illness, thus relieving me of the task of administration and the feelings of inadequacy which I experienced on attempting it. The managerial functions of the Trustees became taken over by a Management Committee, separate from but subordinate to the Trustees, who then reverted to their true function as trustees. A generous donation from a charitable trust temporarily removed from the Association the element of financial insecurity which had being weighing so heavily upon me, and enabled the provision of a paid secretary, and, later, the appointment of a full-time director. Throughout this period of reorganisation I was, of course, *hors de combat* owing to my illness, though I was kept fully informed of developments. I thus came to see that the Association, which meant so much to me, and which I saw as God's instrument for healing the people, was perfectly well able to function without me, and that there was no need to feel pressurised in this direction. In His own good time God would provide both the resources and the personnel for doing His work on earth – and His timing and understanding of its needs were far better than mine!

There was another unexpected sequel to my cancer. Shortly before I was due to be admitted to hospital for my operation T. came to spend the weekend with us. This I had expected to be the visit of a son to give comfort and strength to a parent about to undergo a difficult and dangerous operation – a conventional expression of filial affection. It turned out to be something far

237

deeper and more fundamental. Though naturally aware of my views about the psychological influences in cancer, T. had always seemed to be somewhat conventional in his thinking, as would befit one who was heavily immersed in the field of commerce. But he had obviously been doing some serious thinking on the subject. 'Do you think, Dad,' he said, 'that what I have done could have had anything to do with you developing cancer?' Of course I had to answer 'Yes'. And so we started to talk. Perhaps for the very first time there was real communication between the two of us. A feeling of harmony developed. I was able to tell him just what his action had meant to me and to understand something of the forces that had driven him to act as he had done. With this expression and understanding came acceptance and forgiveness. I was able to put into practice my own teaching about accepting others for what they are rather than for what we would like them to be, and allow him **his** responsibility in life. The negative forces of anger and resentment were neutralised within me, and, with this neutralisation, the process of true healing could begin. Truly God moves in a mysterious way his wonders to perform.

We have already looked briefly at stress and seen how in the case of Bob it was able to interfere with the smooth functioning of the body to such an extent as actually to produce disease. We have seen it in devastating action in the example of my own cancer just related, and again in the story of H., whose inner feelings of guilt contributed so strongly towards the spread of her cancer and her subsequent death. It has been suggested that stress has to be considered primarily as a state of mind, and that a sharp distinction has to be drawn between that state of mind and the events or problems to which it is a response. It is not so much the stressful circumstances surrounding any particular person which constitute the stress, but the way in which those circumstances are viewed by, and what they mean to, that person. Hans Selye, the doyen of stress researchers, used to speak of what he called 'eu-stress' and 'dis-tress'. 'Eu-stress' was a challenge which the individual was able to handle and which served to stimulate a higher standard of performance. Athletes, orators and artistes know very well how the presence of an audience can enhance their performances. 'Dis-tress', on the other hand, is when the challenge is greater than the individual is able to handle; when the artiste or the orator dries up with stage fright, or the games player freezes and is unable to hole the vital putt or pot the final ball. It is the **meaning** of the challenge to the individual which remains the all important factor in the creation of stress.

Some might say at this point that the way to inner peace rests in the avoidance of challenge: that in withdrawal from the world to the monastery or the yogi's cave can be found the road to God. For some this may indeed be true. The saffron robe and the begging bowl, the freedom from material possessions and worldly responsibility, which these can bring to the seeker, can beckon strongly to those upon the spiritual path. But it is not the way that Jesus taught. For Him, Man's task was to be active in the world, striving to release into a material environment the energies of the Divine. This is what the Incarnation truly meant, when for the first time God was seen revealed in human form. But we cannot do this unless we are at peace within and free from stress.

This means that we have to learn to look at the difficulties and the challenges of life from a different standpoint. We have to realised the *ongoing nature of all Being*; that though temporarily enshrined in matter, our essential Being is no more dependent upon matter than we are dependent for our existence upon the clothes we wear. The stress-producing circumstances which confront us in our daily lives have to be seen as opportunities for growth, for which we should offer thanks rather than recrimina-tion. Once we can make this quantum leap in consciousness we are, as my American friends would say, into a new ball game.

We have to start from the realisation that there is no sanc-tuary in withdrawal. Challenge is necessary for our onward progress. Only when we have met and learned how to handle challenge and find tranquillity amid the turmoil – and this may take many lifetimes to achieve – can we turn our back upon the world and enter upon a life of contemplation. The realisation of this need brings us to the first of the lessons which we have to learn, if we are to find the way to inner peace – the **Lesson of Acceptance**.

Each one of us must learn to accept without grumbling – yes without grumbling! – the various vicissitudes of life, and to understand that ALL things are, at this very moment, actively working together for our good. It is not a matter of believing that they **will** do – that everything will work out all right in the end – but of accepting that **God is in charge**, and that he knows best. Of course, God's ways are not as our ways. They are higher and wiser than the ways of Man, and His loving care for each and every one has to be seen in the context of an ongoing journey of the spirit. The good to which all things are working will not necessarily be of a material nature; nor will it always be immediately apparent. Often and often it can ony be recognised on looking back, in retrospect. Vicky's death seemed to us at the time to be the most cruel and awful thing that could possibly have happened. What had she done, we might have reasoned, to deserve that? Surely no God of love could have allowed such a thing to have happened – let alone have actually planned it. Yet, looking back over the years, as we have done together in this Odyssey, we can see what has flowed from this, and truly count her short life among our greatest blessings.

We must learn to accept that it may be necessary to undergo a particular and painful experience in order that we may learn certain lessons from it. Here again I must refer to my own particular experience related earlier. Except by going down myself into the valley of the shadow of death I could not possibly have experienced the depths of fear and misery which beset the cancer patient. Except by going through the trauma of major surgery and the intensive care unit I could never have known the power of Love and Prayer which carried me through the ordeal. **The whole purpose of life is the learning of lessons and the gaining of experience**. In this no experience is so trivial as to be irrelevant. All experience is important, even if – *and perhaps especially if* – it is traumatic. The patterns of our lives and the challenges which we shall have to face have been largely predetermined and accepted. Each one of us has seen the blueprint for our life in this present incarnation – as Vicky showed us – and has voluntarily accepted this in order that we may learn certain specific spiritual lessons.

Our view here on earth is so limited that we cannot possibly realise at the time the true meaning and importance of each particular happening. We must learn, as Paul and Snowdrop taught me, to be able sincerely to pray in thankfulness for the 'blessings of our sorrows'. So often when things on earth are going smoothly, we forget all about God, simply taking His blessings for granted. Then when things start to 'go wrong', we are all too apt to turn and whine, 'What have I ever done to deserve this? I've always tried to live a good life. It's not fair!' Such a question is like a schoolchild asking the teacher, 'Why have you given me such a hard exercise to do?' In reply, there comes the answer from God, the All-loving and All-wise teacher; 'Because, dear child, you are ready for this at this particular moment'. All the trials and tribulations, the successes and the failures of life, with which we have to contend, are, as it were, the exercises in the text book of life. These have to be done. There is no good in running away from them. That merely results in the lessons not being learned, and, as at school, in having the exercise to do again!

Implicit in the Lesson of Acceptance is that of learning to accept others – for what they are, and not for what we would like them to be! This leads us on to the second important lesson that must be learned so as to change our outlook upon the happenings of life; **The Lesson of Forgiveness.** Jesus taught us to pray that we might be forgiven the wrongs which we had done even as we forgave those who had wronged us. This forgiveness, both of ourselves and of others, is crucial to our inner peace and to our health and healing. Of all the emotional forces helping to create disease within us those of personal guilt and resentment are the most damaging to health. We all need forgiveness, both for our treatment of others and for our neglect of God. But the spiritual law is that of sowing and reaping. 'Whatsoever a man sows, that he shall reap.' Every single thought, or word, or deed has its corresponding effect upon the recipient. It is this effect which is ultimately to be reaped by the doer; not as a matter of reward or punishment awarded by an all powerful judge, but simply as the experience of cause and effect. Each one of us will feel for ourselves precisely what we have caused others to feel, whether it is pain or blessing.

> 'Whosoever shall give to drink unto one of these little ones a cup of cold water only, in the name of a disciple, verily I say unto you, he shall in no wise lose his reward.'
>
> *Matthew x. 42.*

Thus in giving way to thoughts and acts of revenge and retaliation we are merely sowing further seeds of trouble for ourselves, for we shall in our turn experience again what we have caused the other to experience. We have given a push to the swinging pendulum, which will cause it, in due course, to swing back and strike us once again. Rather we must seek to free ourselves from this constant ebb and flow, and bring the pendulum to rest. This can only be done through the operation of compassionate love, even upon those who have wronged and wounded us. It is all there, set down in the teachings of the Master, upon whom we are inclined so glibly to turn our backs today.

> 'Love your enemies, do good to them which hate you, bless them that curse you, and pray for them that despitefully use you.'

*   *   *

> 'As ye would that men should do unto you, do ye also to them likewise.'

*   *   *

> 'Love ye your enemies, and do good, and lend, hoping for nothing again; and your reward shall be great.'

*   *   *

> 'Judge not, and ye shall not be judged; condemn not, and ye shall not be condemned; forgive, and ye shall be forgiven.'

*   *   *

> 'Give and it shall be given unto you.'.

*   *   *

> **'With the same measure that ye mete withal it shall be measured to you again.'**
> *Luke vi. 27–38.*

242

Our thoughts must be those of compassion, as for one who is about to suffer, rather than ones of gloating satisfaction – for those thoughts themselves set up powerful forces which will in the end rebound upon us.

Further, we have to learn to forgive ourselves for our own mistakes and shortcomings. There is nothing to be gained by clinging to the past. The past is past, with all its hurts and pains, its joys and sorrows.

'The Moving Finger writes; and, having writ,
  Moves on: nor all thy Piety nor Wit
  Shall lure it back to cancel half a Line,
  Nor all thy tears wash out a word of it.'

Omar Khayyam ed.1, li.

The past cannot be changed. It is a sobering thought that no word that has been said can be unsaid; no thought unthought; no deed undone; no lost opportunity grasped again. Remorse, sorrow, guilt, all alike are useless, save to stir our determination not to make the same mistake again.

We have, therefore, not only to learn to accept others as they are, but also ourselves as we are – warts and all, as it has been said. When contemplating past mistakes and wrongs committed, we have to accept that **we did that deed** or **said that word**. That really was us, bitterly as we may now regret it in the light of our present knowledge and standards. But we may take comfort from one thing. In due course, as we experience the consequences of what we may have said or done, the slate will be wiped clean once more. It is for us to learn and grow, and to profit from our errors. We may, however, take comfort in the extremity of our need from the knowledge that through the love of the Divine Creator, God, there is Grace abundant to help us on our way, if we will only accept it. As my discarnate communicators so often said: 'We stretch out our hands to you. All we ask is that you should take our hands. But – you must take our hands. You must listen and obey.'

We have several times referred to life on earth as being like a spiritual school. If we accept the concept of reincarnation (see Appendix B), we can perhaps understand that we are not all in the same form at school, even though we are alive together at the same time on earth. Therefore we do not all act in the same

243

way in any particular set of circumstances. Each of us acts in the way that seems to us to be right **at that particular moment**. We do the thing that seems right and natural in the light of our own perceptions at that time. As we learn and grow through our experience of living, those perceptions may well change. Indeed, it is to be hoped that they will! Otherwise we are wasting our time here on earth. But, at the time of acting, we do not feel that we have anything with which to reproach ourselves. We do what seemed to be right. If, of course, we do not; if we turn a deliberate deaf ear to the promptings of that inner voice which speaks to us of what is right and wrong, then our situation is indeed unhappy. But even here, provided the error is accepted as having been within our power to avoid, the Divine law of reaping and sowing allows the eventual cleansing of the slate. So we must learn neither to judge nor to condemn the behaviour of others. They will, in God's good time, reap what they have sown!

There is another aspect to learning the Lessons of Acceptance, and Forgiveness. Next to the law of Sowing and Reaping comes the second great spiritual law: **All Things in Due Season Come**. It is very easy to allow ourselves to become frustrated and angry when our efforts to promote some worthy objective do not meet with the success which they seem to deserve. If something for which we have been working or hoping does not come to pass when we wish, it means either that the time for that particular happening is not yet – or that it is not meant to happen. But we have to remember always that God's time is not as our time. God works upon a totally different time scale to that perceptible to our earthbound minds.

'A thousand ages in Thy sight,
Are like an evening gone;
Short as the watch that ends the night
Before the rising sun.'

I. Watts. Hymns A&M 165.

If we can realise this, and accept the wisdom of the timing of God; if we can walk in His pace, and not drive ourselves into the ground because things are not working out as we think they ought to, then much of the stress and anxiety of action are removed from our lives. We can face delays and failure without any sense of personal guilt or shortcoming.

This lesson has been brought very forcefully home to me as

the result of my own experiences during the past eight years. I had been involved in the Gentle Approach to cancer right from the days when I first heard about it at the Iona Conference on Healing, and after I had seen the benefits which cancer patients could derive from meditation and visual imagery, I decided that it was time that the wraps should be taken off the methods employed and that they should be brought out into the open. I therefore took advantage of a gathering together of members of the Medical and Scientific Network, whom I knew would be sympathetic and understanding, at the first Mystics and Scientists Conference organised by the Wrekin Trust at Winchester, to speak about this and make a plea for its more general adoption. I also started to play a prominent role in the cancer conferences set up by the Health for the New Age Trust. Two years later, together with Dr Alec Forbes and Colonel Marcus McCausland, I helped to set up the Association for New Approaches to Cancer, with the hope that my medical colleagues might begin to embrace these ideas and embody them in their own therapies. I met with very little support and much hostility. Surgeons and oncologists did not want to know, and refused point blank to discuss the new approaches with their patients, or even to inform patients that they existed. Foolishly I took this as personal rejection and felt increasingly frustrated at what I looked upon as failure. I now know that, had this idea really taken off at that time, as I would have liked it to have done, we should not have been able to handle the demand for help. There were simply not enough facilities or sufficient people with the knowledge and training available. It is only now, several years later, that we are beginning to build up the infrastructure necessary to support such a course. Moreover, the climate of opinion is changing slowly. Medical science has started to research the role of the mind in healing, and an increasing number of doctors within the orthodox fold are beginning to recognise the deficiencies in their therapies. As that great soldier/healer, Bruce MacManaway likes to put it, the general staff 'upstairs' can see far further than we can, and their timing is always spot on and perfect!

'I will walk in the pace of my Lord,
And dwell in His house for ever.'
Japanese Paraphrase Psalm 23.

All this really amounts to the third of the great lessons which have to be learned, **The Lesson of Faith**. This means learning to realise that all things are being taken care of, right at this very moment, and taking quite literally the Master's words:

> 'Take no thought, saying 'What shall we eat? or, What shall we drink? or, Wherewithal shall we be clothed?' For your Heavenly Father knoweth that ye have need of all these things. But seek ye first the kingdom of God and His righteousness, and all these things shall be added unto you. Take therefore no thought for the morrow: for the morrow shall take thought for the things of itself. Sufficient unto the day is the evil thereof.'
>
> *Matthew vi, 31–34.*

What this means is that we need to develop a new sense of values for what is really important, seeking first things first and allowing the material to find its own place. (We see this especially exemplified in the holistic approach to healing with its emphasis on healing the inner man, and allowing the healing of the body to flow from that.) We need also to learn to live in the present moment. 'Living in the now', to use Metropolitan Anthony Bloom's lovely phrase, we develop a sense of timelessness, in which every moment – every second, every minute, every hour, every day attains its proper value. Like the Boy Scout's 'Be Prepared' and the military man's 'contingency plans' we make our plans for future events, but we no longer worry about them nor allow them to dominate our lives. We no longer go out to meet trouble halfway, or cross bridges before we come to them, realising instead that all problems bring with them their own solutions, and that so often these solutions arrive from the most unexpected direction. **If a thing is meant to be, it will be. If it is not, it will not, and there is no good in wasting time and energy striving after the unattainable.** God's purposes will be served.

We must at all costs get out of the pernicious habit of saying or thinking, 'What will I do if . . . ?' Thought is a powerful energy – next to love the most powerful energy there is – and when we clothe a fear or an idea in thought, we have given it a form in the world of thought, and created a link between that form and ourselves, which may well serve to draw towards us the very thing that we fear. This is negative thinking, and the complete reversal of faith. We need, instead, to meditate upon and visualise very powerfully the desired objective as if it were already attained, when, in the fullness of God's time, it will come to pass.

'If ye have faith as a grain of mustard seed, ye shall
say to this mountain, Remove hence to yonder place;
and it shall remove.'

Matthew xvii.20.

In doing this we learn to bring our problems to God in meditative prayer. We lay them upon the altar with a prayer for the help which is always present, if we would only believe it, and even as we do so, we breathe a sigh of thankfulness for the help that will assuredly be granted. God knows our real needs far better than we, and too much thinking on our part merely serves to get in His way. Often, as I think of this, there come into my mind the lovely words of Cardinal Newman:

'I do not ask to see the distant scene.
One step enough for me.'

Hymns A&M 266.

We are surrounded at all times, did we but know it, with a multitude of heavenly helpers, who are only a single thought away.

There is one other lesson, which we have to learn in our pursuit of inner peace: **The Lesson of Obedience.** We have to learn to follow willingly the path before us, without asking too many questions, and no matter how inadequate we may feel. God tries no one beyond their strength, and strength is given for every need. But this strength is given in the moment of need, and not necessarily in advance. All of us have the power to rise to meet that need when the occasion demands, and there are within each one of us hidden reserves of strength and fortitude which probably neither we nor anyone else have ever suspected of being there. There is NEVER any need for feelings of inadequacy, for we will always be given the strength to perform God's will – if we will only believe it. Our task is to keep our spiritual eyes and ears keenly alert to discern that will. Always the choice of whether or not to follow that will remains with us. That is the meaning of God's gift of freewill to Man. But, if we choose not to follow that will, then we have to bear the consequences of our choice. For that is the rule, the ever present law of cause and

247

effect. But even here, such is the mercy of God, we are given a second chance. The lesson to be learned, the choice to be made, is presented once again, albeit, perhaps, in another lifetime and another context.

There is a beautiful prayer, attributed to Charles de Foucauld, the great geographer of the Saharan desert, which I often use, and try to make my own:

> *'Father! I abandon myself into your hands. Do with me what you will. Whatever you do, I will thank you. Let only Your Will and Purpose be done in me this day, as it is in all your creatures.*
>
> *'Father! Into your hands I surrender my spirit. I give it to You with the love of my heart. For I do love You, Father! I need to give myself, to surrender myself, with a trust beyond all measure; because You are my Father!'*

If we can make this prayer our own, and pray it regularly and day by day, and Oh! How hard it is to pray, then together with the other of the four lessons, it will take the heat out of our lives.

> 'Then may our ordered lives confess
> The beauty of Thy peace.'

The stress level which we create within ourselves becomes reduced as we accept the overall control of God. The springs of self-healing are set free to reorder first our minds, and then our bodies. We become truly whole; able to carry out God's work in the world.

We started this chapter with the ideas of tranquillity and inner healing uppermost in our minds, and, indeed, no true healing can take place except this is so. But the world is a stressful and often violent place. How can we find this tranquillity? What must we do to seek this inner peace?

> 'There is no peace but where I am, saith the Lord,
>   I alone remain, I do not change.
> As space spreads everywhere and all things
>   move and change within it,
>   But it moves not nor changes,
> So I am the space within the soul, of which
>   the space without
>   Is but the similitude or mental image;

Comest thou to inhabit Me thou hast the
    entrance to all life –
Death shall no longer divide thee from those
    thou lovest.
I am the sun that shines upon all creatures
    from within –
Gazest thou upon Me thou shalt be filled
    with joy eternal.
Be not deceived. Soon this outer world shall
    drop off –
Thou shalt slough it away as a man sloughs
    his mortal body.
Learn even now to spread thy wings in that
    other world,
To swim in the ocean, my child, of Me and my
    love.'

Edward Carpenter.

This inner peace lies at the core of every one of us and can be reached and experienced – if only we know the way! It is the 'Good News' of the gospel which Jesus preached – the Kingdom of Heaven, which lies within. (The correct translation of the Greek phrase ' εντος ὑμων ', used here by St Luke in Luke 17.21, is 'inside you', and not 'among you' as rendered in the New English Bible.) It is of crucial importance to the understanding of Jesus' teaching. Inner stillness! **Be still, and know that I AM God!** There lie Peace and Harmony and Truth; not in the ephemeral delights and fading pleasures of material joys and worldly pleasures, or in the elusive pursuit of power or riches or success, but deep within each human heart. Nor is the way there difficult to find. It requires only persistence and determination, and a willingness to set aside the time and permit the values of the unseen world to take over from those of the material world. Through regular and daily meditation a sense of peace and harmony will come into the lives of all who practise it. Very gradually a sense of the loving reality of a higher power will begin to grow – and this, of course, is the answer to the problem of 'converting the atheist, or non-believer'. It is also the answer to our own doubts and hesitations, as, switching off and turning aside from the material and sensory reality, we allow our consciousness to ascend into the clairvoyant and the spiritual realities, and touch the central core of Truth within.

> 'Truth is within ourselves, it takes no rise
> From outward things, whate'er you may believe
> There is an inner centre in us all
> Where Truth abides in fullness; and around
> Wall upon wall, the gross flesh hems it in
> That perfect, clear perception, which is Truth.
> A baffling and perverting carnal mesh
> Binds all and makes all error, but to know
> Rather consists in finding out a way
> For the imprisoned splendour to escape
> Than in achieving entry for a light
> Supposed to be without.'
>
> *Robert Browning. 'Paracelsus.'*

Through the daily practice of meditation we reach out to and find this consciousness of God, becoming aware of His presence within ourselves and in all around us. We need this sense of His vivid presence; all around us, and through us, and in us; all of the time; every moment of our waking day and every moment of the night. For God is IN all things; and THROUGH all things; and OVER all things; IMMANENT and TRANSCENDENT.

> 'Whither shall I go then from Thy Spirit?
> Or whither shall I go then from Thy Presence?
> If I climb up into Heaven, Thou art there;
> If I go down into hell, thou art there also.
> If I take the wings of the morning and remain in
> the uttermost parts of the sea,
> Even there also shall Thy hand lead me and Thy
> right hand shall hold me.
> If I say 'Peradventure the darkness shall cover me
> Then shall my night be turned into day.
> Yea, the darkness is no darkness with Thee, but
> the night is as clear as the day.
> The darkness and the light to Thee are both alike.'
>
> *Psalm 139, 7–12.*

It is this sense of the vivid reality of God which has been lost today and is the foundation of true healing. It is this which we can recover through the daily practice of meditation. Through it we find a sense of Oneness: of oneness with all created things; with one another; with the world in which we live; with the **living** cosmos, of which this world is an integral, breathing part. It is this which we need to find, and which we can approach more nearly through the daily practice of meditation than by any other means. Through this we can best realise our true potential; God-seekers, and in the end God-children, practising the continuing presence of God within us and about us. So shall we become God-channels, Not just for the healing of disease, important though that is, but for the healing of this strife-torn world. For, with this sense of God, there comes a sense of certainty and security. We know where we are going, and we know that it is good.

APPENDIX A

MEDIUMS AND COMMUNICATORS

'In my end is my beginning.'
(Last words of Mary Queen of Scots.)

Any intelligent consideration of the journey described in the earlier part of this book must involve alike both the genuineness and the propriety of the communications. Are the events what they purport to be? Is there a *post mortem* state in which individuality is maintained – at least for a while? In other words, do we survive the death of the body? If we do survive, is it possible to communicate with those still alive on earth? Finally, if we do survive and communication is possible, is it right and proper to communicate?

Modern scholarship has shown that the traditional and orthodox view that such communication was divinely forbidden, and that the whole area of life after death was, and was intended to be, **occulta**, was due in part to mediaeval superstitions and in part to a failure to understand the real meaning of what was written in the Bible, and was represented as Divine Prohibition.

It reveals that, properly understood, the Great Prohibition is partly concerned with ensuring that the purity of the worship of YAHWEH was not defiled by the Canaanite religious practices, and partly with necromancy and the often obscene rites associated with it, and with the worship of the dead and the exploitation of individuals by fraudulent mediumship. The motivation for such acts consisted usually either in greed, fear, or a lust for power and control, and thus was totally different from the motives prompting man to accept communication from loved ones who have pased through the Gateway of Death. Against such there is no prohibition. This is neither the time nor the place to go into the detailed and often rather obscure realms of Hebrew scholarship and mediaeval customs. Those desirous of

252

making a detailed study of the subject should consult the literature on the subject. Amongst this *Nothing to Hide* by the Revd Leonard Argyle (CFPSS, St Mary Abchurch, London EC1) and the chapter on 'Psychical Research and the Biblical Prohibitions' by the Revd Donald Bretherton in *Life, Death and Psychical Research* (Rider & Co, London 1973) are to be recommended as good starting points for study. The historical background and the mediaeval approaches to the subject are well covered by the article on Witchcraft in *Chambers Encyclopedia*.

Donald Bretherton writes in the *Christian Parapsychologist*: 'The superstitious belief that dead bodies could be revived by ritualistic means has persisted throughout the centuries up to the present day, representing one of the darker sides of human history. It was **this** kind of practice that was so soundly condemned in scripture, because it involved orgiastic rites, pagan deities, sexual perversion, blood sacrifice and even the worship of the dead.

'The growing interest in the occult amongst people of all ages presents real dangers today. Serious investigators and students of the paranormal recognise the dangers of "dabbling" in the hope of producing unusual psychic phenomena, and attempts to rediscover the supposed arts of the ancient necromancers in raising dead bodies still persist amongst those foolish enough to experiment in this way . . . We are learning far more about the human psyche and uncovering much that has for far too long remained either latent or misunderstood and condemned. **Obstinacy, fear and prejudice have so often been the enemies of truth, proving as destructive of spiritual and religious understanding as they have been so frequently in the past of scientific progress.**'

The term 'medium', Donald Bretherton continues, is a loaded word, weighted with preconceived ideas, and most modern mediums or so-called 'spiritists' are sensitives with gifts that enable them to communicate on a level which 'interpenetrates the purely material, mental and spiritual dimensions'. But the Biblical prohibitions cannot be dismissed as unimportant even today. They are a warning against the misuse of psychic gifts, and confirm in their way what my spiritual mentors told me: that it was the motive for enquiring which was the all important thing. In their words, **'The channel must be pure'**. However, prejudice and preconceived ideas must be rooted out if man is to progress, and because ordinary believers and Biblical scholars have persisted in assuming that the prohibitions referred to all forms of mediumship, and failed to consider the environment to which they applied (c.f. here 'Paul's' remarks about the words attributed to him as being relevant to the time in which he lived), the Church has consistently refused to regard what modern sensitives say as being in any way relevant to death and the life to come. There is little likelihood of progress being made so long as the prohibitions of the Old Testament continue to be mis-understood and translated by the terms 'medium', 'spiritist', and 'familiar spirit'.

Those who are too ready in their condemnation of the Odyssey which I have described, and who regard all attempts at communication with our loved ones and those who have our spiritual welfare as their concern, are asked to review their ideas about 'the Great Prohibition' in the light of what I have written above. It is also not without relevance to note that 'discernment of spirits' is amongst the gifts of the spirit outlined by St Paul in 1 Corinthians 12. It is also plain from the words in 1 John 4, 1–3 that communication was not unknown among the early fathers of the Church nor is there any suggestion of prohibition. All that is said is that it is necessary to 'test the spirits to see whether they are of God'. In other words, we should not blindly accept what is said, but should submit it to our critical assessment, since not all spirits are 'of God', i.e. are evolved spirits. As we have already seen, some are very confused, and not all have 'benefited by the experiences through which they have passed'.

Thus we are left at this stage with the second question. Is there survival of death? Does personal consciousness survive the death of the body? If the answer to this is in the negative, then the rest of the question falls to the ground, for obviously there can be no communication unless there is someone there with whom to communicate. If the answer is 'Yes', we must then con-sider whether or not the communications are genuine. Are these messages what they seem to be? Or are they artefacts, explicable upon another basis?

The first part of the question is too big to attempt to answer here. Right back into the mists of antiquity and primitive man there has always been an intuitive belief that part of man went on after death, however vague and shadowy that part might be. It is, and has always been, a fundamental ingredient of every form of religious belief. It is only since the Renaissance, with the spread of the mechanistic ideas of The Age of Reason and, in particular, the scientific revolution of the past 150 years, that such beliefs have been seriously challenged. The original account of the happenings upon which this book is based was compiled as a lecture, illustrated by recorded extracts from the various communications, in an attempt to bring conviction to the newly bereaved on just this very point. Those with open minds, who remain as yet unconvinced on the survival of death, are invited to study the voluminous literature upon the subject, of which one of the best of the more recent books is *Living On* (George Allen and Unwin, 1980) by Paul Beard, for many years President of the College of Psychic Studies, London. Another excellent book, and worthy of detailed study, is *Life, Death and Psychical Research* edited by Canon J. D. Pearce-Higgins and the Revd G. Stanley Whitby (Rider, 1973). With out-and-out materialists, atheists and other compulsive sceptics there can be no arguing. Their minds were made up long ago, and, as Vicky so truly said, 'There are none so blind as those who do not wish to see'.

Let us then agree, for the purposes of this appendix, to assume that a part of man survives death, and remains independent of the death and disintegration of the physical body. It is helpful here to pause and to consider just what the nature of this part might be. It would seem from the evidence accumulated, both experimental and anecdotal, that there is a whole range of perceptions open which lie outside the sensory field. Extrasensory perception, as it is termed, is a fact, although it seems that not all persons are able to experience it. That being so, WHAT is it that perceives? Sensory perception takes place within the brain, and we can now map the precise areas on the surface of the brain where this occurs. It obeys certain strictly defined, physical laws such as the laws of heat, light, and sound, etc: e.g. – energy travels in a straight line; the intensity of energy received falls off in proportion to the square of the distance between the emitter and the receiver; a stimulus cannot be perceived until after it has been emitted; between the act of emission and perception there is a finite time interval; there has to be a point or moment of contact between the emitter and the perceiver. Such are some of the laws governing sensory perception. We are all familiar with them. We know, too, that the receptor organ, the brain, must be functioning if perception is to take place; that it can be distorted by drugs; and if that functioning is inhibited, as for instance by anaesthesia, or insufficient oxygen, conscious perception does not take place.

Yet our consciousness can perceive information which does not appear to be conveyed to it through the senses, and does not obey the laws governing sensory perception. Telepathy has been demonstrated to be a fact, and, whatever may be the source of the energies involved, those energies appear to be of a type with which we are not yet familiar, and to be subject to different and as yet little understood laws. Well documented examples of clairvoyance, precognition, retrocognition and out-of-the-body experiences abound throughout the literature of psychical research. Nor can we conveniently shrug these off as the hallucinations or wishful illusions of the half-baked. The data are too compelling, and the investigating minds too acute and too numerous. In 1935 Professor C. D. Broad wrote:

'For my own part I have no doubt that telepathy among normal human beings happens . . . But we know quite well that most scientists and the bulk of the general public would not admit this for an instant. And we know that this is not because they have looked into the evidence and found it faulty, or have suggested plausible alternative explanations. They would no more think of looking into the evidence for telepathy than a pious Christian thinks of looking into the evidence for Mahometanism or a pious Mahometan of looking into the evidence for Christianity.' (quoted from The Imprisoned Splendour p 145, Raynor Johnson, Hodder & Stoughton 1953.)

If we examine the data carefully, critically, and with minds free from the stultifying influence of preconceived ideas and foregone conclusions, we are inevitably forced to the recognition that these phenomena are supported by as great a weight of evidence, based upon observation and experiment, as supports the basic facts of other sciences. Yet it remains that the majority of scientists continue to be hostile to the subject. This hostility is probably due to the realisation that such data do not fit into the well established laws governing the material world. Two examples of this hostility suffice.

The writer was once taking part in a discussion forum with a well-known scientist shortly after the publication of a book in which he described his researches into 'metal-bending' children and discussed his findings. 'There are three things that I cannot accept,' he said. 'All the rest – telepathy, telekinesis, psychometry, healing etc – I can fit into the model of what I call the extended properties of Man. But precognition, materialisation and dematerialisation, and anti-gravity (levitation) I cannot fit into such a model. Consequently if any of these were to be definitely proven, I would have to go back to square one and rethink the whole of my scientific philosophy and my approach to life. I am not prepared to do that. Therefore I would fight tooth-and-nail to prove that any evidence that seemed to prove these things was false!' Another similar example was related to me by Max Payne, who teaches philosophy at Sheffield. During his undergraduate days at Cambridge he attended a lecture by a distinguished teacher of philosophy at which telepathy was discussed. 'Gentlemen,' remarked the speaker, 'we know that telepathy cannot possibly exist. If it did exist, it would overthrow all the accepted laws of science and the natural world. Those laws have served us very well, and are well proven and established. We cannot afford to have them overthrown. So any evidence that seems to suggest that telepathy exists must be either false or fraudulent. Therefore telepathy does not exist!'

A large part of the problem results from our failure to comprehend the true nature and function of the brain and its relationship to the mind. Materialist concepts attribute the latter to physiological activity of the brain cells. Thus the mind is seen as the consequence of brain activity and as being incapable of existence without it. According to this view the brain is seen as an organ of perception and storage, and both cognition and memory as being dependent upon its functioning. This implies that all the input to cognition has perforce to arrive through sensory channels. However when we start to look at the sensory channels involved, we rapidly realise that the range of data to which they are capable of responding is extremely limited. We can buy a whistle to summon our dog which we are incapable of hearing ourselves, though he can hear it perfectly well (even if he sometimes appears to prefer not to!). The colour film in our camera responds to light which to our eyes is invisible. The X-ray machine in the hospital clinic emits rays which pass straight through our bodies and of which we are totally unaware, but which are able to produce changes in photographic film. In fact, in both the visual and the auditory fields the sense organs respond only to the middle part of the total frequency range. It would seem that the brain, and its extension, the organs of sensory perception, serve more as organs of limitation of perception than of information, and that their true function is that of concentrating attention upon everyday life. We live and move and have our being in such a sea of energies (and every sensory stimulus is a manifestation of energy in one form or another), that unless some such system of filtration existed we should be totally overwhelmed by the mass of information received. Our position would be like that of a highly sensitive radio receiver which had no capacity for tuning in on a particular station and was incapable of excluding unwanted signals from other stations.

This view was propounded with great force and clarity by Henri Bergson. He viewed the brain as being primarily the originator of action. Its perceptive function he considered to be selective, that of shutting out from consciousness the great bulk of impressions which were irrelevant, and permitting awareness only of that part of the whole which was relevant to action. Perception was seen as being primarily in aid of action, and not as a knowledge gathering process. This could be acquired otherwise. The brain, in his views, served to limit perception and to focus the attention of the mind on 'life'.

Bergson's view of the process of thinking differed entirely from the conventional one which postulates a specific brain state corresponding to each mental state. Apart from its sensory functions, which, as we have seen, he considered to be merely selective and limiting, the functions of the brain according to this view are simply to express in action what the mind is thinking. Thus the act of speech, involving muscular movements controlling the breathing, the larynx, the tongue and the lips and so on, requires brain cell activity. An expert neurophysiologist, observing the activity of the brain cells, might be able to deduce these, but he would have no knowledge of the ideas and information contained in the sounds so produced. Such interpretation is psychic. Thus the brain simply expresses in action the mental life of the individual, so enabling him/her to continue existence in a material environment. Bergson says: 'Though consciousness is not a function of the brain, at any rate the brain keeps our consciousness fixed upon the world in which we live: it is the organ of attention to life . . . To orientate our thought towards action, to induce it to prepare the act which circumstances require, that is the task for which our brain was made.' The brain is, as it were, the executive of the mind, which originates the idea of action and then programmes the brain to initiate the necessary physical response to the idea previously conceived in the mind. The brain is also the receptor station for information transmitted to it by the senses, which is then relayed on to the mind where it takes the form of an idea or of knowledge.

It is because we are so dominated by the overpowering evidence of the senses, with all their focused attention upon the day-to-day business of living, that we so readily identify knowledge with brain activity. Yet if knowledge can be acquired or transmitted from one mind to another without having recourse to sensory perception, which must be relayed through the brain, we are at once, as our American cousins would say, in a totally different ball game. It is this capacity to acquire and transmit information at an extrasensory, or, as I would prefer to term it, a supersensory level, that is the hallmark of the medium. If one mind is able to transmit and acquire information either to/from another mind or from the physical environment, and the laws which operate in the physical environment appear to be irrelevant to that exchange or transmission of information, it becomes a powerful argument for the existence of the mind in another dimension of being, which is independent of the physical body. Such an existence is the *sine-qua-non* of survival of death, so it is hardly surprising that those concerned with attempts to prove survival have paid intense attention to the phenomena of extrasensory perception.

However I am not concerned in this chapter with attempts to prove survival, or indeed with consideration of the essential nature of what, if anything, survives. I personally am firmly convinced that the personality of each one of us, of which the mind is an integral part, does survive death in recognisable form. This belief was initially intuitive, but following the experiences already related, it soon moved from the intuitive to the experiential. Those needing to study further the evidence upon which my beliefs are based are invited to study the books listed in the bibliography at the end of the book. My concern here is with mediumship and with trying to understand as far as possible the ways in which the medium acquires his/her information.

Before we can begin to do this, it is necessary first to consider in more detail the fundamental make up of Man. The current uncertainty over the roles of brain and mind in the human creature, which has been outlined above, has existed since classical times. Although the historical roots of psychology are commonly thought to arise in the philosophies of the ancient Greeks, these were themselves considerably influenced by even earlier cultures, and especially by those of ancient Egypt.

Prior to Socrates, Empedocles expounded a materialistic view of the mind, in which all thought and perception were considered to depend upon bodily function. Pythagoras, however, taught a mystical view, including the independent existence of the soul, and even extending to the transmigration of souls, and it is to him that we are indebted for the profound observation: 'There are no miracles: there is only ignorance.' Socrates introduced the concept of the soul as the 'psyche', being the seat of intelligence and character. Plato dealt explicitly with the question of consciousness, and, in the *Phaedrus*, introduced the picture of the soul as the charioteer, driving two horses, one representing bodily passions, and the other the higher emotions. Aristotle, on the other hand, wrote the first treatise on consciousness, and expounded a biological and materialistic approach to psychology, which became elaborated still further by the Stoics, of whom the humanists are the present day counterparts.

The last of the great philosophers of antiquity was Plotinus, the founder of Neo-Platonism, who taught that the soul is immaterial and immortal, and that consciousness is the image of God, and present at all levels of reality. Thus throughout history there have been two diametrically opposed approaches towards the problem of consciousness, the biological and material, and the mystical and spiritual. This conflict still rages today and lies at the very heart of the controversy over healing and survival.

As usual in this controversy, we come back to the ideas of Descartes, both as originally propounded and as developed by his successors. Descartes made a sharp division between mind (or soul), which he considered indestructible, and body, which was mortal and destructible. He further suggested that there should be different methods adopted for their study: the mind should be studied by introspection, and the body by the methods of natural science. However, in later years psychologists adopted both methods, the structuralists studying the mind through introspection, and trying to analyse consciousness by breaking it down into component parts, in accordance with Newtonian teaching, and the behaviourists concentrating entirely on the study of behaviour as a series of responses to external stimuli – these being the 'component parts' of Newtonian thinking – and ignoring altogether the existence of abstract mind. Both of these had adopted into their procedure the practices of classical Newtonian mechanics.

According to Descartes mind and body belonged to two separate and fundamentally independent levels of existence. Each could be investigated without reference to the other. The body was ruled by mechanical laws, but the soul (mind) was free and immortal. The soul embraced the area of consciousness, and interacted with the body through the medium of the pineal gland. Emotions were a combination of six elementary 'passions', and must be considered in a mechanical way; but perception and knowing were a property of the soul and could occur independently of the brain. Ideas were not to be thought of as being derived from the senses, but were the product of innate knowing.

As I write these words I am continually struck by how closely the ideas of Descartes, so deeply derided by so many in 'The New Age' today, approximate to the truth as I see it. It is no big leap from the concept outlined above to the views of Bergson, and to modern ideas of left and right brain function. The weakness in Descartes' thinking was his failure to understand how spirit, mind and body all inter-related and interacted with each other.

261

Unfortunately the purity of Descartes' ideas soon became lost. Subsequent philosophers discarded his concept of innate knowing, and considered instead that there was nothing in the mind that had not been implanted there by the senses. Locke, especially, considered the mind to be an empty slate upon which ideas were written by the senses. Thus sensations came to be considered as the building blocks of the mind, which were combined through association into larger and more complicated patterns. Later the concept of association of ideas became combined with that of the neurological reflex to produce a totally neurologico-physiological model of all mental activity. The growing understanding of neuro-anatomy, and the ability to demonstrate the localisation of motor and sensory functions in the brain, lent further force to this concept and led many to associate precise areas in the brain with particular functions of the mind. Despite the breakdown of this approach when applied to such functions as learning and memory, many neuro-scientists have continued to research along these lines. Further food for the mechanistic view was provided by the school of reflexology, and especially by Pavlov's discovery of the conditioned reflexes, and this gave many to hope that human behaviour would ultimately be understood in terms of conditioned reflexes. It is easy to understand the magnitude of this shot-in-the-arm to the mechanistic school of thinking.

This digression into the history of psychology has been necessary in order that we may understand the depth of the gulf which separates the scientific and mechanistic view of Man from our own. Telepathy, as we have said, has now to be accepted as an established mode of transmission of information between one mind and another, and this is substantiated by a great weight of experimental evidence. However the normal laws of distance, place and time no longer seem to apply. For instance, it is by no means necessary for both parties to be in the same place for the successful transmission of information between the two. The distance between sender and percipient appears to have no bearing upon the strength and accuracy of the information received. Neither is it invariably necessary for the transmission of information to precede its reception. (Precognition, despite the anguished protests of conventional scientists, would appear to be a fact.) Edgar Mitchell, the astronaut, relates a fascinating account of an experiment with numbers, in which, owing to an unexpected change in the timetable of the mission, he received the message some eight hours before it was actually transmitted!

In the classical 'card guessing' experiments of G. N. M. Tyrell and others certain subjects were found whose guesses, though wide of the mark in relation to the card selected at that moment, were found to relate accurately to the card which was to turn up one or two tries ahead, or, in one percipient, had already taken place. Thus, in these people the extra-sensory faculty was apparently not only one of clairvoyance of contemporary events, but extended to future, and, in one case, to past events. This aspect of extra-sensory perception was investigated at great length by Whateley Carrington. He conducted experiments in clairvoyance with drawings over many years and with a very large number of percipients in different parts of the country. His method was to select an object by using mathematical tables opened at random and opening a dictionary at the page indicated. He would then make a drawing of the first concrete object on the page and pin this up in his study from 7.00 pm to 9.30 am. This was repeated on ten successive nights. Each percipient was provided with ten forms and asked to guess the object drawn and make a drawing of it. The comparison of the drawing with the original was made by a third party and precautions were taken to ensure that too much rigour or laxity in such comparisons whould eventually cancel each other out. A run of ten such trials constituted an experiment. Eleven experiments were conducted in all, in some of which some 250 percipients took part. Carrington found that the nearer to the actual day of display of the 'target' the higher was the proportion of correct guesses, reaching a maximum on the day of display and declining as the day of the guess moved forwards or backwards. There was thus a higher proportion of correct guesses at 48 hours before or after the target was displayed than when the interval was a week before or after. This proportion was greater when the interval was 24 hours and even greater on the actual day of display.

The implications of this for us are the extra-sensory perceptions seem to take place at a level which lies beyond that of the sequential, cause-and-effect, time-tied relationship, with which we are familiar. This becomes even more obvious when we start

263

to look at information acquired spontaneously, as opposed to experimental findings. Numerous examples are to be found in the literature of the Society for Psychical Research and in a number of books devoted to the subject. Of theses those by H. F. Saltmarsh (*Foreknowledge*; G. Bell & Sons 1938) and Mrs Alfred Lyttelton (*Some Cases of Prediction*; G. Bell & Sons 1937) are worthy of study, as is J. W. Dunne's famous book, *An Experiment with Time*. The subject is also discussed at some length in *The Gate of Healing* pp 79–86. (Neville Spearman 1983). Dunne, who was a careful and systematic observer of his dreams, noted many examples in these of precognition. To explain these he developed the philosophy of 'Serialism' and adopted the view of experience which may be briefly termed 'The Eternal Now'. Space precludes a detailed discussion of Dunne's famous theory and the conclusions at which he arrived, and which, in any case, are not acceptable to most thinkers today. For a detailed criticism the views of Professor C. D. Broad, to be found in *Proc Aristotelian Soc Supp* Vol XVI, pp 177–245, should be consulted.

The problem which we have to consider, briefly, is this. An event, E, happens at a particular point in time. At some earlier point in time there is precognitive knowledge, PK, of that event. How are they causally related? It would be difficult to argue that PK is the cause of E. We are therefore left with two alternatives: either that E is the cause of PK, as when an observer obtains knowledge, OK, of an observed event; or that both E and PK are the effects of a common cause preceding both. There are many examples of PK which cannot be fitted into such a hypothesis. For instance, what is the common cause of the dream described below and the subsequent event fulfilling it?

'Mrs C related to her husband and family at breakfast that she had had a most unpleasant dream of being followed by a monkey. After breakfast she took the unusual course of going out for a walk with her children to try to throw off the depressive atmosphere of her dream. While walking in the streets of London, she was to her horror followed by a monkey which she described as the very monkey of her dream.' (*Proc SPR*, Vol 48, p 306, 1938. Quoted from *The Imprisoned Splendour* p 165–166.)

Similarly a common cause preceding both PK and E is no explanation of experimental results such as those obtained by Tyrell, and in the drawing tests of Whateley Carrington.

We are thus left with the alternative explanation that E, though lying in the future, is in some way a cause of PK. Our immediate response to this is to reject the idea, because we are conditioned – in the material plane – to consider that causes must always precede effects. However, cognition, whether retrocognition or precognition, does not lie within the material plane. (It is this which disturbs the material scientist so greatly when he comes to consider precognition! He does not like to admit to himself that there are planes beyond the material.) Cognition is a psychical event, not a material event, and as we have seen, different laws apply at this level.

So let us start by affirming that there is for each individual a deep transcendental self, which lies beyond the body/mind complex. Time, I would suggest, is a phenomenon of the material world, the world of Self and Not-self. The transcendental self exists beyond the material world; in a world in which it is no longer set apart from, but, on the contrary, **is actually a part of all-around-it**, as all-around-it is a part of the self. In that transcendental world there is no separation into self and not-self, into observer and observed, or into present, past and future, for all of them are 'Now'. The transcendental self is thus able to know both the future and the past, as well as the content of another mind because they are all a part of it and contained within its own knowing.

It is important to realise here that this view does not deny the concept of freewill and the right-to-choose of the superficial self of the mind/body complex. This is not an argument in favour of a rigidly applied theory of predestination. The transcendental self knows the future because it knows how the superficial self will choose. The future which the transcendental self knows is the-future-which-results-from-the-exercise-of-this-freedom. It is not a future created by some power external to ourselves. It is a future very largely created by this transcendental self, which **deliberately leaves a very limited but important area of choice to the superficial self**. The knowledge of the future which the transcendental self possesses, and which it sometimes throws up as a precognition into the consciousness of the superficial self, is based on its knowledge of how the latter will use its limited freedom of choice. It is the so-called future event which conditions the knowing of the transcendental self; not the present knowing of the latter which conditions the event. To ask whether the future can be altered has no meaning. The future, which 'will be' for the superficial self, and becomes for it in due course 'the past', exists 'now and always' for the transcendental self or spirit. (Rayner Johnson: *The Imprisoned Splendour*, p 167.) A convenient analogy might be a cinematograph film. Each event in the story is already present in the film, although we, the observer, view the film through a slit which shows only one frame at a time. The transcendental self is like the director of the film, in whose mind every event within the film is already present, although individual players within the film are permitted freedom of interpretation of their roles and how each scene is played.

The medium, I contend, is a person who is able to contact at will the transcendental level of his/her being. At that level not only is there no separation into past, present and future, as at the material level of existence, but there is also no separation into discrete individuals, and into subjects and objects, observers and observed. There is a blurring of the hard demarcation lines of the sensory world, and a gentle merging of one creature with another, so that so far from 'reading the mind' of another, the medium is dipping the silver cup of consciousness into the pool of his/her own cognition, and bringing its waters to the surface.

It may be objected at this stage that this is no explanation of the events recounted in the preceding chapters of this book. I contend that it is. I am not concerned at this point, as I have said many times, to 'prove' survival. My concern here is whether, if survival is true, communication with the survivors is possible. In any case, if there is no survival, then satisfactory explanations will have to be found for the events of the previous chapters, including how such a person as Mrs D could produce philosophy and teaching of the level of wisdom experienced, which was clearly beyond her own conscious knowledge or understanding. To those persons who, after reading this book, attempt to point the finger at myself as the unconscious source of the wisdom produced, I can only say that *at that stage in my development* such gems of wisdom and spirituality were far beyond my ken.

We have seen from the literature and from the evidence that transmission of information does not necessarily depend upon physical factors; that minds can communicate direct; and that such communication lies outside the space/time continuum. We have suggested also that cognition, i.e. knowing, is a psychic state, and not dependent upon the functioning of the cells of the brain. Granted then that minds survive death, and that transmission of information can take place directly between mind and mind, and probably does so at a transcendent level beyond the time/space continuum, it is no great jump in the argument to postulate that there can be exchange and transmission of information between a discarnate mind and an incarnate mind. The requirement for this is that the minds of both parties should be able to meet upon the same level. Each one, of course, must know how to reach that level. Initially it generally happens that the seeker, who is almost always totally inexperienced in such matters, has to have recourse to a third party – a medium – who is able to relay the thoughts and words of each to the other party. Even in this instance, as we have seen, a common level is not so easily reached, so that not only the medium but also the discarnate requires practice and training in finding the way there. In this the medium generally has the assistance of one or more discarnates who assist the newcomers on the discarnate side. They also help to protect the medium from the attention of undesirables and mischief makers.

After a while, and especially if the right form of spiritual disciplines are followed, the sitter may learn to find his/her own way to the meeting point, and the aid of the medium becomes no longer necessary. This in fact is what has happened in my own case. Vicky and her band of helpers and co-workers now communicate direct, dropping their thoughts and ideas into the deep places of my mind, from whence they have to be clothed with thoughts and actions. On a very few occasions, perhaps when she wants to be very certain that I have got the message accurately, she will descend to the use of words herself, and I will hear her words spoken directly on the inner ear. Thus on the very morning of my retirement from my family practice in the NHS I heard her speak the following words: 'Now your real work is just about to begin. All that has gone before has been a preparation for these years that are to come.'

In mediumship the fundamental act is the transmission of knowledge in thought form from the mind of the discarnate to the mind of the medium. The form in which this knowledge is then conveyed to the sitter depends upon the medium. The medium may describe what she is being told, and convey back in thought form the queries of the sitter to the discarnate. In some cases when the sitter is him/herself able to shift the level of consciousness the discarnate may so programme the mind of the sitter as to write down what they wish to say as 'automatic writing'. Automatic writing, of course, does not *necessarily* originate from the discarnate. It can, and frequently does, come from the subconscious mind of the sitter. All examples of it need to be very carefully and critically assessed.

In deep trance mediums, such as Mrs D, however, the process seems to be short-circuited. Instead of the mind of the discarnate impressing the mind of the medium, which thereupon programmes the brain into specific physiological actions eventuating in speech or writing, the intermediate stage, that of the mind of the medium, is omitted, and the brain of the medium (which remains in control of the body, of course) is programmed directly by the mind of the discarnate. There is thus complete control of the body of the medium, which responds by alteration in appearance as well as by speech. Habit characteristics such as mannerisms, traits of speech, accents, and even foreign languages previously spoken by the discarnate and retained in the mind of the discarnate are common features of such sittings. For such control to be possible, a very profound shift in consciousness is necessary on the part of the medium, as well as the ability on the part of the discarnate to 'step into the empty space' through a similar shift in consciousness downwards from the transcendental to the sensory level. Such a shift in consciousness requires every bit as much training and practice on the part of the discarnates as does the shift to the transcendental level by the medium. Mediumship of a physical nature, such as direct voice, materialisation, apports etc, belongs to another system of energies, and is not a part of the process described above. So far I have had no experience of this, and it has played no part in my odyssey. It therefore falls outside the scope of this book.

Having established (I hope to the satisfaction of the reader!) the possibility of communication from the discarnate world, it remains to be considered whether the communications are genuine. Are the communications truly what they purport to be, or is there another explanation? In any case, who are these people? Are they real people at all?

The common explanation advanced by the sceptic for this sort of thing is that the 'information' given by the medium has been acquired from the sitter, either through conversation and observation – especially observation of 'body language' – or by a process of telepathy from the mind and memories of the sitter. Personalities appearing and speaking through the medium are generally considered to be secondary personalities of the medium. Those who put forward such explanations are wont to quote such classical cases as those of Sally Beauchamp, (*Proc SPR*, Vol 19, p 140) Doris Fischer (*Ibid*, Vol 31, p 30) and *The Three Faces of Eve* (Secker & Warburg). As we have seen, trance mediums have a control, sometimes more than one, and it these who are considered to be secondary personalities, split off parts of the medium's personality, able only to come to the surface when the normal personality is quiescent. These 'controls', however, whatever they may be, operate in a completely orderly fashion. They do not intrude or burst into the normal life of the medium, except for some very urgent reason. In the cases quoted above, and in cases of pathological multiple personalities, the irruption is subject to no such control and is completely involuntary. Such irruption is often fraught with confusion and distress for the victims, through repeated and unpredictable intrusions. This is never seen in the case of the trance medium. Where the 'guide' wishes to control the medium unexpectedly for some good reason, the medium is usually given a clairaudient or clairvoyant warning beforehand. In any case there is welcome and co-operation between the conscious personality of the medium and the controls, all of whom work in harmony together. 'In multiple personality cases', says Canon John Pearce-Higgins, 'there is most certainly "war in heaven", with the personalities not only fighting the conscious persona of the patient, but also among themselves.' (*Life, Death and Psychical Research*: p 62, Rider 1973).

T. K. Oesterreich (*Possession – Demoniacal and Other*: Kegan Paul, 1930) speaks of such mediumistic activity as impersonation, since the medium suddenly seems to become 'another person'. Another suggestion has been that trance mediumship is related to dramatic ability and literary and artistic creativity. A parallel is drawn with the good actor, who 'becomes' another person – Hamlet or Ophelia – for the time being, and with the way in which many authors, including Charles Dickens, have told of how their characters seem to possess them and produce their own independent activities. To those who have experienced the mediumship of Mrs D none of this seems to apply. To attribute the deep wisdom set forth by Tania, Snowdrop and Paul in the preceding chapters to this humble, unlettered Yorkshire woman raises yet another, and to my mind, even more difficult question. If this is indeed of herself, speaking from some deep level of herself, from where did she acquire such knowledge? It is totally out of character with her background. It is equally out of character to credit her with any deep-seated dramatic talent. Consider for a moment the range of 'personalities' apart from the 'guides' and 'controls' who spoke through her. Eric's father, Roger, Vicky, and the lost soul, Cath's brother. And I have been privileged to be present upon another occasion when Eric and I took a recently bereaved friend of his to visit Mrs D and his wife 'came through' with convincing certainty. Each personality was totally distinct and consistent throughout the whole two years of the journey. Never was there a moment of confusion or inconsistency. Moreover, it is necessary to consider also the logical and purposeful sequence of events, from the moment of its inception with the glass and the letters on the dining-room table of Eric's friends to the climax of Paul's appearance in the sitting-room of Mrs D's quiet north London house. Paying due weight to all these considerations, and to the powerful significance of my own intuitive perceptions, one must, I think, accept the story at its face value, and the communicators for whom they proclaim themselves to be.

APPENDIX B

REINCARNATION

I hold that when a person dies
  His soul returns again to earth;
Arrayed in some new flesh-disguise,
  Another mother gives him birth.
With sturdier limbs and brighter brain
  The old soul takes the road again.

John Masefield.

Of all the experiences which Eric and I underwent on our spiritual journey none was more disturbing to me than the revelation that Vicky had lived before. What it did was to start me reading about the subject. I found to my astonishment that although probably originating with the ancient sages of India, and finding a fundamental place in both Hinduism and Bhuddism, reincarnation was taught among the classical Greeks by Empedocles, Pythagoras and Plato. Certain passages in the gospels, or so it appeared, seemed to be strongly suggestive of a current belief in it at the time of Jesus. Hints of it appeared in the teaching of Philo of Alexandria and in several of the early Christian fathers. I found to my surprise that it was not until the fifth ecumenical council at Constantinople in AD 553 that it had been officially declared a heresy. Despite this, the concept of reincarnation had been supported by many eminent thinkers in later times, including Bruno Giordano, Swedenborg, Goethe, Hume, Ibsen and Maeterlinck to name but a few. The late Dean Inge had confessed, 'I find the doctrine both credible and attractive'. Many passages occur among the poets of the nineteenth century suggesting their belief in it.

Thus Browning writes in a poem to Evelyn Hope:
  I claim you still, for my own love's sake!
    Delayed it may be for more lives yet,

271

Through worlds I shall traverse, not a few;
    Much is to learn and much to forget
Ere the time be come for taking you.

D.G. Rosetti writes in *Sudden Light*:
    I have been here before,
        But when or how I cannot tell:
    I know the grass beyond the door,
        The sweet keen smell,
    The sighing sound, the lights around the shore.

    You have been mine before –
        How long ago I may not know:
    But just when at that swallow's soar
        Your neck turned so,
    Some veil did fall – I knew it all of yore.

Whereas in the time of my boyhood any westerner declaring a belief in reincarnation would undoubtedly have been considered as distinctly 'odd', and a likely candidate for the lunatic asylum, today there has been a remarkable rise in interest in the subject. Sylvia Cranston in the preface to her book on reincarnation (*Reincarnation*: Sylvia Cranston and Carey Williams, Julian Press, New York, 1985) states that in the United States the 1981 Gallup Poll on religion revealed that 38 million Americans – 23 per cent of the population – admitted to a belief in reincarnation. Of these 21–26 per cent were Protestants, and 25 per cent Catholics. Over one hundred books on the subject are listed in the *Subject Guide to Books in Print*. While most of these deal with the subject on a fairly superficial level, it is intensely significant that in a Christian western country so many people have abandoned the previous once-for-all philosophy in which they and I were brought up.

At the present time Death has replaced Sex as the great taboo. As outlined in my opening chapters, it is the subject we least like to contemplate. For so many it represents extinction of the individual and waste of all the lessons learned, the experience gained. Faced with the swelling tide of materialism the teachings of the Church no longer suffice. Nor, indeed, does the picture of Heaven and Eternal Bliss outlined in those traditional teachings appeal very greatly to sophisticated modern man. Lloyd George once confessed:

'When I was a boy, the thought of heaven used to frighten me more than the thought of hell. I pictured heaven as a place where there would be perpetual Sundays with perpetual services, from which there would be no escape, as the Almighty, with cohorts of angels, would always be on the lookout for those who did not attend. It was a horrible nightmare. The conventional heaven with its angels perpetually singing, nearly drove me mad in my youth, and made me an atheist for ten years. My opinion is that we shall be reincarnated.' (*Lord Riddell's Intimate Diary of the Peace Conference and After:* Victor Gollancz, London, 1933, pp 122–23. Quoted from *Reincarnation:* Sylvia Cranston and Carey Williams, Julian Press, p ix.)

As I write, the great problem facing western society is the use of drugs. The input of marijuana, cocaine and heroin into the western democracies has become a positive tidal wave and threatens the very fabric of society. Teenagers and schoolchildren are becoming addicted to drugs at an early age. Alcoholism is rife, even amongst the young, and the suicide rate for young people is climbing year by year. Why? Why, in the midst of affluence and material prosperity beyond the dreams of our forefathers are we seeing such a concentration upon the possession of goods and the pursuit of pleasure? Why, on the other hand, are we seeing so many of our young people preferring to 'drop out' from educational courses, and from conventional employment? What has gone wrong with the society in which we live? Why is so much emphasis placed upon escaping from society?

I would submit that the prime reason for all of these troubles is that **life has lost its meaning** for the majority of people. The industrial revolution created great wealth in society. At first this benefited only the industrialists and the property owners. The poor continued to be poor, work was long and hard and life was grim and ugly. Homes were cramped and uncomfortable. Sickness and loss of employment were an ever present threat. To the great mass of the working population the most desirable things were the possession of goods, and the recreations, the leisure and security, which made the lives of the rich seem so colourful and so worthwhile. Even as recently as during my childhood life was for many just a struggle for mere survival. Times were hard and dangerous, and all the effort of life was directed towards remaining alive and supporting the family. There was no time for anything else.

Gradually the introduction of a fairer society has made it possible for the ordinary man to achieve a more comfortable and satisfying way of living. Labour saving gadgets, washing machines, refrigerators and freezers, television, radio, motor cars, cheap travel to faraway places have revolutionised the lives of many people. The result has been that, for very many, material objects have become like gods to be striven for, worshipped, thanked and appreciated as the providers of 'the good life'. But a new, young generation is growing up; one which has never known the struggles of their parents, or experienced a world without the colour television, the microwave, the video, the holidays on the Costa del Sol. To many of them, unaware of the bleakness of the lives of their parents and grandparents, the fruits of modern civilisation have little meaning, seeming to be like Dead Sea apples, without taste or flavour. They have little sympathy with the rat race of modern life, or the urge for the acquisition of material possessions. In consequence they seek a more satisfying and more meaningful way of life. Some find this in leaving the rat race; in retiring to a cottage life, doing their own things, fulfilling themselves in the craft of their hands. Others, perhaps lacking in the necessary skills or imagination to embark on such a course, seek relief in drug-begotten fantasy and euphoria. Others, lacking either of these two outlets, sink into depression and melancholy.

There are many signs that the era of materialism which led to the emptying of the churches over the past two generations is coming to an end. The youth of today is on the march, no longer satisfied with the fetishes and shibboleths of their fathers. A new generation is searching for spiritual enlightenment, unsatisfied by the old time religion or simple faith. It is seeking a deeper and more profound understanding of the universe and the mystery of life. Symptomatic of this hunger are the rapid multiplication of books and library sections dealing with occult and mystical subjects, and the almost mushroom growth of societies concerned with arcane and esoteric practices.

Up until the Renaissance and the dawn of the so-called Age of Reason the teachings of Christianity satisfied the spiritual hunger of the western world. In the Protestant world these were based on the authority of the Bible as 'The Word of God', and for fundamentalist Christians this meant, and for that matter still means, equating the Bible to a handbook of science, Ptolemy said, and the Church accepted and taught, that the sun revolved round the earth, but Copernicus invented instruments which showed that it was the earth which revolved around the sun. Aristotle, whose psychology and science were fully embraced by the Church, wrote that if two objects of different weights were dropped, the heavier would reach the ground first, but Galileo showed by a simple experiment from the top of the Leaning Tower of Pisa that if two objects of similar size but differing weights were dropped, they would reach the ground simultaneously. Many passages in the Bible suggested that the earth was flat, but explorers like Magellan and Columbus showed that this was incorrect by circumnavigating the earth. Thus there began the erosion of the Bible and the authority of the Church as the repository of truth. The subsequent discoveries of Darwin, the theory of evolution, the evidence from fossils and geology all combined to throw doubt upon the Bible and to disturb the neat picture of the world which Man had constructed and the Church had taught. Spirit? Who had ever seen a spirit? Soul? No one had found a soul sitting on top of the pineal gland, where it ought to have been found, according to Descartes. Immortal life? What evidence have we of that? Heaven? God? We have been to the moon and explored the mysteries of space, but none has seen God. (It is reported that when Yuri Gagarin, the first Soviet astronaut, returned to earth, he was questioned by Khruhschev about his experience. 'Did you see God up there?' Khruhschev is reported to have asked. 'No,' replied Gagarin. 'You have nothing to worry about! I saw no God.') 'God is dead' cries the philosopher of today. 'What we describe as God is no more than the mental projection of one who needs a father-substitute.' 'The universe is a gigantic clock which is slowly running down – a geo-physical machine. Man is no more than a little machine, the product of chance atomic intercourse and evolutionary forces.

Life is the product of the interaction of molecules and atoms, and suffering is the inescapable lot of Man as he struggles to survive in a hostile world. It has no meaning beyond that. Death is the dissolution of the chemical elements of which Man is composed, and the cessation of being.' Such is the bleak picture of materialist philosophy.

In place of the authority of the Bible, the Church, the Great Teacher, we have substituted that of the evidence of our senses and their extension by the instruments which science has constructed. But during the past half century the instruments have rebelled, and shown us that these five senses, even when expanded by our brave new instruments, give us but an imperfect picture of the world around us. This is very far from being the solid place of which our senses convey such a convincing impression. We are, in truth, adrift in a mighty sea of energy, and these 'solid' bodies, with which we identify 'ourselves', are themselves no more than concentrations of energy. Nor indeed, as we have seen in the previous chapter, are our senses the only means of acquiring knowledge, or are we ourselves limited to the concentrations of energy which we call our bodies. There is a part of each one of us which is independent of our bodies and which we call our mind, and this exists on a number of different levels.

It is this search for meaning in life which I believe has fuelled the present day interest in reincarnation. If death is not the end; if there is indeed a part which travels on and in due course returns to earth, what is the meaning of this? Why does it do so? Many, looking back on their lives today, would be tempted to say, as I have heard it said, 'Good riddance! I want no more of that. The worst thing that I can conceive of is to have to return to earth and live another life. I would far sooner be dead!' Why should the spirit have to return again to the earth it left?

To answer this we have to evoke two principles: the principle of continuing evolution, and the Law of Karma. We are already familiar – or should be! – with the evolution of the species, the gradual journey upwards over many millions of years from the primitive unicellular organisms which swam in the primaeval seas, through the fish, the amphibian, the mammalian kingdoms to the higher animals and anthropoids, and finally, to the summit of creation, *Homo sapiens* himself. Step by step the

276

world has seen life evolve ever higher and more complex forms. First the simple cells of the Protozoa; today the complex, intelligent, sensitive rational human being, a creature so advanced as to be capable of 'self' consciousness. Alone amongst living creatures Man is aware of himself, conscious that he is an individual, able to say 'I am', 'I want', 'I will'.

If we now look at the evolutionary scale, we can see that there is an infinite variety of graduations as we progress upwards. There are many forms in the vegetable kingdom between the slime mould and the oak; there are many different levels of being between the amoeba and the elephant. All manifest differing levels of evolution, yet all manifest the common thread of life. Similarly there is an infinite variety in Man, from the Australian aborigine or the Amazonian pygmies to the grandeur of Beethoven, Einstein, Leonardo da Vinci, Jesus. All are at different stages of evolution. As we look out at the world and our fellow men we see enormous differences in ability, in intellect, in physical, mental and spiritual development. The greatest myth that was ever perpetrated is that of the 'Equality of Man'. Quite plainly in material and intellectual terms all men are NOT equal. There is an immense gulf between the peasants of Ethiopia or Bangladesh and the sophisticates of western civilisation. All men are of equal VALUE – Yes! Every soul is a spark of the divine creative fire, which is God, and hence is beloved by Him, but plainly at a more superficial level not all are equal.

Why is this? Why is there such a tremendous disparity in the conditions in which souls are born into this world? Even at our own material level we see this variety. Some have sound and healthy bodies, with good brains, and are surrounded with every circumstance to help and encourage their onward development. Others seem to be handicapped from the beginning, with unhealthy bodies, defective brains and intelligence, or are born to live amid an environment of squalor and depravity. For some there is the traditional silver spoon in the mouth, with opportunity knocking at the door; for others there is just a piteous and overwhelming weight of suffering.

Are these things just chance? Or are they planned by God? We believe that God is just and good, all-wise and all-loving. how then can we accept, if each soul born into the world is a fresh and new creation of God, that there is such a vast disparity in their circumstances? There is no doubt that the conditions into which some souls are born are such as would seem to preclude their development. For some the environment is one of security and affection, encouragement, culture and aesthetic interest; for others it is squalor, depravity, indifference or neglect by parents; or an environment of fear, vice and brutality likely to crush and brutalise the developing personality before it can resist it. How can we believe that this is the work of a just and loving God? Can we possibly conceive that God is capable of doing something that any ordinary decent person would do everything possible to avoid? We have the words of Jesus before us, 'If ye then, being evil, know how to give good gifts to your children, how much more shall your Father which is in heaven give good things to them that ask him?'

The common answer which is given by the Church simply avoids the question. It runs something like this: 'Yes, of course there are inequalities, but these have to be considered in the light of a future state in which justice will be done. Life is a handicap race in which all must just try to do their best, remembering that to whom much is given, from him will much be expected. Those with great gifts, the Einsteins, the Shakespeares, the Beethovens must make the best use of their gifts. The handicapped, the suffering and the crushed must just do their best, remembering that God is just and merciful and expects no more from any person than is commensurate with their gifts, and that in the end all will have been made worthwhile.'

I have always found this very hard to swallow, and I believe that it is one of strongest arguments of the atheists and the humanists. 'There is no God!', they cry. 'All is the work of random chance. All men are equal and all men are good and kind and gentle. It is only the chance of circumstances that make them seem otherwise.' **This is the philosophy of humanism.** 'There are no evil or dishonest men; criminals are created by the injustice of society, which gives much to some and little or nothing to others; men steal out of necessity to provide for themselves and their families, who otherwise would starve; violence and aggression come because men are insecure and afraid; they fear hunger, unemployment, poverty, sickness and homelessness; they fear for themselves and their families. Let us create a Welfare State which will take care of all these things, and then

278

everyone will be friendly and loving and neighbourly. Vandalism, hooliganism and other such anti-social behaviour is the result of a lack of education. Universal education is the answer to falling standards of behaviour.'

Much has been done in the last thirty years to bring about the conditions for which humanism is asking, but it is plainly no answer to the problems besetting the human race. Violence and dishonesty are by no means confined to the underprivileged, and the realisation of the humanist dream has coincided with moral decay and political enslavement. Stiffer and harsher punishments for crime are no answer to the problems, for while the return of hanging and the birch might do something to deter people from embarking on crime, they would do nothing to reform the criminal tendencies in people, or to make saints of evil men. Only a new vision, a renewal of spirituality can bring this about, since as long as mankind sees nothing beyond the present life – and that itself as the mere lawless product of random chance – each individual will reach out to grab for himself, regardless of others, all that he desires to make life more pleasant and easy and fulfilling. 'You only live once,' the saying goes, 'therefore eat, drink and be merry, for tomorrow you die.'

Such is the atheist and humanist argument, and such is the state to which it has reduced us. But, I contend, it is based upon a false premise. 'You only live once.' But do we only live once? What evidence is there for this tremendous assumption? Many millions of people throughout the world believe otherwise. It seems that it is only the west, the christianised minority, who believe otherwise, and even they did not always do so. If we abandon the idea that each soul brought into the world is a fresh and new creation of God, and accept the idea of pre-existence, we can take our stand on the law of cause and effect, and say that all these grossly unequal conditions may well be the result of prior causes, not in any way apparent in our present life. We could say that we are the product of our past, and that present circumstances arise as the result of forces generated by us in prior states of existence. This was the view of Origen, one of the ablest of the early Christian theologians who lived from AD 186–253.

Origen was born at Alexandria, son of Leonides, a Christian convert martyred in AD 203. He was entrusted by Bishop

Demetrius, with the task of completing the Christian apolo-getica relinquished by Clement of Alexandria, whose most dis-tinguished pupil he was. Clement's theology, which contained many of the germs of later mysticism, drew freely on non-Christian sources, especially Plato, the Stoics and Philo. He took the view, in the face of the prevalent semi-pagan gnosticism, that the only true gnostics were to be found among the true believers. Origen carried on this work, but the relationships into which he was forced by his work led him to self-castration, which was later used to disqualify him for the priesthood. He had a tremendous reputation at the start of the third century, though Bishop Demetrius viewed him with considerable suspi-cion and eventually, in AD 230, had him deposed from the priesthood.

His theology was developed by analogies: nothing can be asserted about God himself save the constant and eternal passion of love; but a disciplined soul, aided by the Holy Spirit, can discern analogies within the sensible universe by which to ascend to knowledge of God; and such analogical illumination of the human intellect is epitomised in the gospel of the incarna-tion of the Logos. Thus Origen's doctrine of salvation is by education: every soul needs redemption from prenatal apostasy (original sin); the powers to whom has been given control of nature are rebel angels, who will be converted by being defeated by God in their opposition to the conversion of souls; evil is negative and will disappear with the redemption of the wills of the creatures, and the world process will end with the salvation of all, including Satan. Origen saw the Son of God as a 'creature', i.e. as being dependent on the Father's will, the divine life essentially and timelessly in the Father truly giving and the Son truly receiving: the Father eternally begets the Son so that the Son's being flows eternally from the Father as the rays flow from the Sun. The Holy Ghost was seen by Origen as being a third in an eternal partnership. While divine purpose is one, the process of its fulfilment is threefold, as creation, redemption and sanctification are proper respectively to the three persons, yet belonging to the Trinity.

Origen's most famous work today is his *De Principiis, (On First Principles)*, an ambitious work attempting an all-embracing Christian philosophy, which was written between AD 215 and

230. In this great work he stated, as quoted earlier: 'Every soul comes into this world strengthened by the victories or weakened by the defeats of its previous life. Its place in this world as a vessel appointed to honour or dishonour is determined by its previous merits or demerits. Its work in this world determines its place in the world which is to follow this.' Thus Origen clearly held that souls pre-existed. Conditions of life on earth were the consequences of their past experience, and their future state would be determined by the way in which they lived their present lives. Their purpose in coming into this world was to be purged from their prenatal fall, and they bore within them the faded outlines of suprasensual truth, which it is the work of the Logos to retrace, through that sense which allegorism finds in scripture. He saw himself as an instrument of the Logos in interpreting all knowledge by the light of scripture. Thus Origen's view is that redemption comes through education, which is itself acquired through experience.

Origen died at Tyre in AD 253, his death being hastened by imprisonment and torture during the Decian persecution. He was an original thinker and prolific writer. His thinking was far ahead of his time and he was in constant trouble with the ecclesiastical establishment, though he had an immense following outside the Church of the day. After his death Theophilus, Bishop of Alexandria, condemned his memory in AD 399, chiefly because the Egyptian monks would not support the contention that God is bodiless. Pope Anastasius repeated the condemnation at Rome in AD 400. In the middle of the sixth century a movement among Palestinian monks of 'questionable' speculations, whose inspiration might be traced to Origen, led Justinian, a very authoritarian ruler of the Byzantine empire, to call the 5th ecumenical conference at Constantinople in AD 553 as much for political as for theological reasons. At this council, which was not attended by the Pope, the teachings of Origen were finally anathematised and condemned as heresy and the circulation and study of his writings prohibited. Writing of this Council Canon Pearce-Higgins states in his preface to *Testimony of Light* (C. W. Daniel, 1977): 'It is far from clear that the Church ever officially rejected such belief, however little the mediaeval mind was able to contain it. The Council of Constantinople in AD 553, at which it seems that a *corrupt* (my italics) of Origen's teaching was anathematised, is held by many historians to have been imperfectly constituted – the Pope himself refused to be present – and even Roman Catholics contest its validity as a General Council.' The Church has never retreated from this stance, so that in the eyes of the traditional Christian reincarnation remains a heresy.

It is strange that in the West we have come to accept the Law of Cause and Effect in the scientific realm but are so reluctant to admit that it can apply at other levels. Yet this is part ot the ethical teaching of every great religion. 'Whatsoever a man sows, that shall he also reap.' (Galatians: vi, 7–8, Matthew: ii, 16–18.) In the East this is called the Law of Karma. Whatsoever a man sows, whether by thought or word or deed, the fruits of it will be reaped by him personally, sometime and somewhere. An inexorable law of justice runs through all creation on all its levels. It is not a case of rewards and punishments, but simply one of inevitable consequence, which applies alike to good and evil things. Allied to this is the fact that none of us exist in a state of isolation. Each single one of us is part of a complicated web of relationships and interactions. We are interlinked with persons both in this world and in others, and are affected by their thoughts and actions as we in turn affect them. We reap effects which others have sown, and we in turn sow seeds which others will reap. (This is plainly to be seen at the present time in the affairs of Northern Ireland and the Middle East.) However, in the end justice is present in all things.

The Christian Church attempts to evade this law by its teaching of the Atonement: that Christ, by his death upon the Cross, took upon himself the consequences of the sins of all the world, and, if I read St Paul's words aright, that confession of the authority of Christ and determination to amend, neutralises the karmic law and protects the individual from the consequences of his actions. I would contend that this is a misinterpretation of the events of the Cross. When we do wrong – or when our children do wrong – the effect is to erect a barrier between the wrong doer and the one who is wronged. The Cross demolished this barrier. It meant that the way of reconciliation is always open, the outstretched hand is always there. In my view it emphatically does NOT mean that we shall avoid reaping what we have sown or evade the karmic law.

This karmic viewpoint is entirely logical and avoids the unacceptable belief that a loving, just and righteous God places one newly created soul in a position of advantage over another. What we experience now, is what we have created for ourselves in the past. Those who expressed cruelty and caused suffering to others will have to experience the precise measure of the pain they caused. Those who gave love and care, will receive that same measure of love. This law was clearly expressed by Jesus in his teaching.

'Judge not, and ye shall not be judged: condemn not, and ye shall not be condemned: forgive, and ye shall be forgiven: give, and it shall be given unto you; good measure, pressed down, and shaken together, and running over, shall men give into your bosom. For with the same measure that ye mete withal it shall be measured to you again.'

(Luke, vi, 37–38)

The pre-existence of the human soul is also supported by the vast differences in spiritual development which we see around us. There is such a tremendous gulf between the best and the worst of us – between the saint or sage on one hand and the degenerate or the habitual criminal on the other – that it is not possible to account for it in terms of failure and achievement in one life span of seventy years or so. It seems to represent a variation just as great as that which we find in the evolutionary ladder between the protozoa and the primates, and suggests the likelihood that the two differing states are the result of much struggle and many experiences of living.

Consider also the vast chasms of variation in intellectual and artistic achievement. On the one hand there are intellects such as Einstein, Plato, Galileo, Michaelangelo or Beethoven; on the other the primitive tribesmen of Borneo or the Amazonian jungles. One simply cannot accept that the difference is simply that of one life-time of effort. My personal belief is that the process of creation is a continuing one, and that new souls are constantly coming into being, starting each at the bottom of the evolutionary ladder of the soul. This reasoning can also apply to the appearance of youthful prodigies: Mozart or Chopin composing works of great musical maturity or playing an instrument with outstanding skill at an early age, when the teaching environment would seem to be quite inadequate; mathematical prodigies reaching university standards while still only just emerged from the kindergarten; linguistic prodigies, like Sir William Hamilton, who started to learn Hebrew at the age of three, and by the age of thirteen could speak thirteen foreign languages; persons who have spoken in trance in ancient languages long since disused, or written during sleep in archaic dialects of foreign languages. (cf *The Cathars and Reincarnation:* Dr Arthur Guirdham, C. W. Daniel.) All of these phenomena call for explanation. By recognising pre-existence we may reasonably attribute such outstanding gifts to a form of memory of the appropriate skills acquired during a previous lifetime.

Differences between individual members of a family can also provide food for thought. Some are undoubtedly due to genetic variations and to variations in the experiences of the individual during the formative years. Yet these are unable to account for all the variations in mental, moral and artistic characteristics which may present. I know a family with three children. All are extremely able and mature for their years. But about the youngest there is something different (just as there was about Vicky); something exceptional in her nature, her capacity to be at ease and her capacity for loving. All have been treated alike by parents who are at once highly intelligent and aware. Yet this child is different. This is quite inexplicable on biological or behavioural grounds. One knows of other families amongst whose children there is one obvious 'odd one out', the black sheep of the family. Occasionally this may be the result of environmental influences – but not always. If we assume that the soul has a past behind it, and chose the particular family into which it was to incarnate as providing the necessary environment for its present incarnation, these matters can readily be understood. For example, both Mozart and Johann Sebastian Bach were born into musical families. These would have been chosen by the incarnating soul as being the most readily able to provide a suitable environment for the development of their gift and the provision of the particular type of experience required by the soul.

Personal relationships form another area for speculation. Love at first sight – the instantaneous recognition of an old and well tried comrade on the path? Deep friendships and antipathies where no rhyme or reason seems to exist, where a relationship is felt immediately on meeting, may well represent the continuation of a situation hanging on from previous lives. Some instances of marriage, especially where the couple are plainly unsuited and subsequently part, may be the continuation of a relationship begun but left unresolved in a previous life.

A final and cogent argument is advanced by Plato in the *Phaedo*. If the soul is only supposed to come into existence at birth, it would appear unlikely that it will persist after death. But if the soul is immortal (as Plato believed), an infinite future should imply an infinite past, since the soul is truly without beginning and without end. If we can accept this reasoning, then there can be no objection on logical grounds to the concept of reincarnation. What the soul has done once, it can surely do again. This does not mean, of course, that I, Ian Pearce, have lived on earth before as Ian Pearce in physical form. What it means is that Ian Pearce is the particular and temporary expression of an immortal spirit which has had quite separate and different experiences. The situation is rather like that of an actor. During the course of his lifetime he plays many roles, in many places and periods, in many costumes and disguises. From the experience of each of these roles and characters he takes a little into himself, but he himself remains the same basic individual through all these experiences upon the stage. Moreover he selects the roles that he is going to play according to his own requirements at the time. So it is, I believe, with the human spirit. It clothes itself with many different personalities in different epochs according to the requirements of its evolution and experience, but the spirit within is still the same. Its different lives remain like beads strung out upon a string.

It is not to be supposed that reincarnation necessarily implies automatic and immediate rebirth, though one eastern school of thought would appear to think that it does. It is more commonly believed amongst western reincarnationists that after the death of the physical body the soul has a life upon the 'Astral' plane for some considerable period, perhaps for hundreds of years of earth time. During this period it undergoes other experiences and learns further lessons, before discarding the astral body and moving on to another level, thought by some to be the mental level, but still retaining a body or form. Finally, when the higher self has absorbed all that it can, there comes the moment of realisation that more experience on earth is necessary for further progress, and the process is reversed, culminating in rebirth. Others say that it is 'desire' for earthly experiences – the Sanskrit word is **Trishna**, which means thirst for sentient experience – which draws the soul to earth again. Hence the dominant feature of Eastern teaching is the cultivation of detachment and the elimination of material desires, so as to escape from the Wheel of Rebirth, and its incessant round of births and deaths.

Though much research has taken place, and is still going on, this is not a subject which lends itself to objective proof. A formidable body of evidence in its favour has been accumulated, but it still remains a hypothesis. It is not my intention to attempt to summarise this evidence here, nor to prove its truth to the reader. I do not seek to convert you, dear reader, to my views. If you want to know more, the reading list at the end of the book will start you off. All I ask is that if you do not accept my views at the moment, you should pigeon-hole them within your mind, and from time to time act as if they might be true.

It is impossible to divorce the consideration of reincarnation from that of karma. Basically this is the operation of the law of cause and effect, of sowing and reaping, to which reference has already been made. To many, however, the concept of karma is associated with that of a hard and irrevocable 'Fate', a sense that all things have already been predetermined, and that there is no freewill left to Man. Are our lives, in actual fact, already determined in every single detail, so that all that we do throughout life is to play out an already written scenario?

> The Moving Finger writes, and having writ
> Moves on: nor all thy Piety nor Wit
> Shall lure it back to cancel half a Line,
> Nor all thy Tears wash out a Word of it.

Was old Omar Khayyam right when he wrote those words? Because, if he was, it makes a mockery of Life as a spiritually educational experience.

To answer this very valid objection, let me quote from Professor Huston Smith's study, *The Religions of Man*. Writing of karma in relation to rebirth he said:

> 'Science has alerted the Western world to the

importance of causal relationships in the physical world. Every physical event has its cause, and every cause will have its determinate effects. India extends this concept of universal causation to include Man's moral and spiritual life as well. To some extent the West has also. 'As a man sows, so shall he reap'; or again, 'Sow a thought and reap an act, sow an act and reap a habit, sow a habit and reap a character, sow a character and reap a destiny' – these are ways the West has put the point. The difference is that India tightens up and extends its concept of moral law to see it as absolutely binding and brooking no exceptions. The present condition of an individual's interior life – how happy he is, how confused or serene, how much he can see – is an exact product of what he has wanted and got in the past; and equally, his present thought and decisions are determining his future states. Each act he directs upon the world has its equal and opposite reaction on himself. Each thought and deed delivers an unseen chisel blow toward the sculpturing of his destiny.

'This idea of karma, and the complete moral universe it implies, commits the Hindu who understands it to complete personal responsibility. Most persons are unwilling to admit this. They prefer, as the psychologists would say, to project – to locate the source of their difficulties outside themselves. This, say the Hindus, is simply immature.

'Because karma implies a lawful world, it has often been interpreted as fatalism. Karma decrees that every decision must have its determinate consequences, but the decisions themselves are, in the last analysis, freely arrived at. Or, to approach the matter from another direction, the consequences of a person's past decisions condition his present lot, as a card player finds himself dealt a particular hand, but is left free to play that hand in a number of ways. This means that the career of a soul as it threads its way through innumerable human bodies is guided by its choices.'

(Huston Smith: *The Religions of Man*. New York: Harper & Row, 1958, pp 35–37. Quoted from *Reincarnation*, Sylvia Cranston and Carey Williams: New York: Julian Press, 1985, p 21.)

To assume, however, that difficulties in the present life, such as persistent physical disability or sickness, are necessarily the inherited consequences of past decisions, and therefore to be born uncomplainingly without making any effort to overcome them is to over-simplify the question. *While this may be, and very frequently is, the case, it can also happen that the soul has made a deliberate choice for such an existence, in order to satisfy the need for a particular type of experience either for itself or for another. It will be recalled that Vicky, speaking of the time when she was 'in suspension', that is to say between incarnations, revealed that she **knew** that this was only to be a short experience, but that she undertook this because she had to learn something, and I had to learn something. In the same way, Christians may be able to understand that some great souls voluntarily enter into a life of suffering in order that they may share, even if only to a very limited degree, the sufferings of Jesus on earth.

*Comment: this is a problem which troubles many healers, which may be briefly stated thus: If a sickness is karmic in origin, is it right to attempt to heal the sickness? If healing is attained, are they not then condemning the soul to a further period of karmic suffering? In answer to this, and it is a very real problem for many, I can only say that healing is something more than just the cure of a physical condition, and that if healing does take place, it too will have been subject to the law of karma, and it may be that contact with the healer is an important part of the learning process for that soul, In any case, the task of the healer is to offer healing, and not to be deflected into making judgements.

To traditional Christians the idea of reincarnation appears, as it did to me at first, as a dangerous and pagan heresy. I believe this view to be incorrect. It was certainly acceptable during the first four centuries of the Christian era, and there are passages in the gospels which would appear to suggest that Jesus was both familiar with the concept and accepted it. Certainly at no point in the gospels is he recorded as having condemned the idea. The following instances are put forward for consideration by the reader before coming to a conclusion on this point.

> 'As he went on his way, Jesus saw a man blind from his birth. His disciples put the question, Rabbi, who sinned, this man or his parents? Why was he born blind?' 'It is not that this man or his parents sinned' Jesus answered; 'he was born blind that God's power might be displayed in curing him. While daylight lasts we must carry on the work of him who sent me; night comes, when no one can work. While I am in the world I am the light of the world.'
>
> *(John ix, 1–5)*

The question put by the disciples indicates that they could see only two reasons for the man's blindness; either that he had lived before, or that his parents had sinned. It is plain from this that the idea of pre-existence and rebirth was prevalent among the Jews at the time, and it may be that it was so well known that Jesus did not consider it necessary to teach it.

Another well known instance is recorded in Matthew xi, 2–15. It was commonly accepted among the Jews that the prophecy in Malachi iv, 5 meant that the coming of the Messiah would be preceded by the return to earth of Elijah. (Elijah was traditionally believed not to have died, but to have been carried up to heaven in a fiery chariot with horses of fire. II Kings: ii, 11.) Since the disciples had identified Jesus as the Messiah, they were naturally curious to know what had become of Elijah, who was suposed to have preceded Jesus. Jesus made the astonishing reply to their question:

> 'This is he of whom it is written, "Behold! I send my messenger before thy face, who shall prepare thy way before thee." Verily I say unto you among them that are born of women there hath not risen a greater than John the Baptist . . . and, if ye will receive it, this is Elijah who was to come. He that hath ears to hear, let him hear.'
>
> *(Matthew xi, 11, 14–15.)*

The Reverend Thomas Strong writes in *Mystical Christianity*: (Regency Press, London, 1978 pp 37–38):

'Jesus took his three most spiritually evolved disciples, Peter, James and John, up on to a mountain. There the three frightened disciples experienced an extraordinary phenomenon. Jesus began to glow as though lit by a brilliant inner light. He was transfigured so that his material body was changed and etherialised. Jesus was seen to talk with materialisations of Moses and Elijah.

'The three disciples were extremely disturbed because they knew that Elijah should have been reborn as a forerunner of the Messiah. If Jesus had been talking to Elijah, how could he, Jesus, be the Christ? The troubled friends ask Jesus to explain the situation. The reply is interesting for it indicates that belief in Re-Incarnation was accepted by the disciples, and Christ's reply confirms that he also believed in it. Jesus did not say that the prophecies of Elijah's re-birth were nonsense, or dismiss them as old wives' tales. No, he clearly and distinctly confirmed the doctrine of rebirth by giving his disciples the facts. "I say unto you that Elijah is come already and they knew him not, but did unto him whatsoever they listed." Then understood the disciples that he spake to them of John the Baptist. Jesus said to them "Tell the Vision to no man" – a clear indication that behind the public teaching of Jesus there was an esoteric doctrine current within the inner circle. The three disciples accepted the explanation as simple and obvious.

'On another occasion, Jesus challenged the disciples, asking them whom the multitudes said he was, and was told that it was said that Jesus was one of the prophets returned to earth. Jesus again did not scorn the idea, but asked them "Who do you say that I am?" This led to St Peter's declaration that he was the Christ (a unique incarnation).'

In all of this there is no suggestion that the idea of reincarnation was in any way unusual. It seems to be taken as the accepted thing. The only point of interest was the previous identity of the individual reborn. A point of criticism sometimes raised against this view is that when asked directly by the priests from Jerusalem whether he was Elijah, John replied that he was not. However, this is quite a usual phenomenon. Only a very few have the gift of far memory and spontaneous recall of previous lives. We should not expect John the Baptist to have remembered his previous incarnation.

The common traditional Christian explanation of these verses is that Elijah never died in the first place, but was translated into heaven. Thus his subsequent return was not re-birth at all, but merely a return visit in his old body. This view is that put forward by Tertullian writing in the second century. However, in the case of John the Baptist we are specifically told that he was conceived and born in the normal way, and was in fact a cousin of Jesus. In Luke i, 13–17 we are told that an angel made this prophecy to Zacharias when he was standing in the temple: '. . . thy wife, Elizabeth shall bear thee a son, and thou shalt call his name John . . . and he shall go before him in the spirit and power of Elijah . . .' Some have said that this means that John was over-shadowed by Elijah, and was not a reincarnation at all. But Jesus was quite explicit on this point. 'This is Elijah . . . He who has ears to hear, let him hear.'

Many Christians opposed to the idea of reincarnation will quote a verse from the Epistle to the Hebrews (ix, 27) which appears categorically to rule out the possibility of rebirth: 'It is appointed unto men once to die, but after this (the) judgement.' The word in brackets, though present in the King James translation has since been found to be an interpolation, and the New English Bible translates the passage: '. . . it is the lot of men to die once, and after death comes judgement . . .' Professor Geddes MacGregor, when asked about this verse in Hebrews, once replied:

'I do not think that is a great difficulty really. Of course, there is judgement; there is judgement all the time, and the notion that there is a special judgement for the world – the whole of this planet – all that is perfectly comprehensible, and perfectly compatible with the notion of reincarnation. It is appointed for

291

me, that is the present me, once to die. I do not die any more than once in my present incarnation, and I am also judged. The law of karma or however you like to put it, symbolises the concept of judgement. We are all being judged if there is any moral law at all; we are being judged all the time, but there is a special judgement when I die.' (*Reincarnation*: Cranston & Williams, p 207).

My friend, the late Thomas Strong, Anglican priest and author of *Mystical Christianity* (Regency Press: 1978), when questioned about the statement in Hebrews by Sylvia Cranston, replied:
'I have frequently had Hebrews ix, 27–28 put to me, and it appears as a kind of ace card (disallowing reincarnation.) I have examined the text in Greek and it appears to me that the passage is ambiguous . . .

'Hebrews was written specifically for Jewish converts to convince them that the Temple ritual sacrifices were no longer relevant to the Jewish Christian. The author had no eschatological intention to put reincarnation out of court. He was subject to the common, but erroneous idea of his time (x, 36–37) that Christ's return was near at hand. Questions of rebirth, etc simply would not have occurred to him.' (Quoted from *Reincarnation*: Cranston & Williams, Julian Press: p 207).

Jesus spent very little time teaching about life beyond the grave, and apart from telling us that there are 'many mansions' in the Father's House, his teaching is directed towards telling us how to live our lives on earth. However it is pretty plain from what is said in the New Testament that both Heaven and Hell are very real. However a good deal can be learned about that future state from psychic investigation, and from the numerous books and papers that have been written on the subject. I can particularly commend Thomas Strong's *Mystical Christianity* for a concise summary of the *post mortem* state and Dr Raynor Johnson's *The Imprisoned Splendour* for a concise summary of the evidence. Other books worthy of study are to be found in the bibliography at the end of this book. It would appear from all the evidence available that Judgement is a very real experience and is undergone by all shortly after death. Psychic communications suggest that this takes the form of a review of the past earth life in which the soul compares the actual achievements with the intentions with which it entered into incarnation. It also experiences itself precisely what it has caused others to experience. The soul, by this way of thinking, judges itself. This *post mortem* review experience is paralleled by the experiences related by some of those who have passed through near-death experiences. Following this review, which is invariably a most painful and humbling procedure, it would seem, according to some accounts, that the soul has the help of its guide or guardian angel in coming to terms with the experience, before it moves on to the next stage of existence. For myself, my own position is clear. Though when the concept was first presented to me, with the realisation of Vicky's previous life, it aroused considerable repugnance. I am now convinced as far as one reasonably can be, that the hypothesis is true and valid.

BIBLIOGRAPHY

Argyle, Rev Leonard. *Nothing to Hide*. CFPSS.

Beard, Paul. *Living On*. Allen and Unwin, 1980.

Burr, H. Saxton. *Blueprint for Immortality*. C. W. Daniel, 1972.

Borgia, Anthony. *Life in the World Unseen*. Psychic Press, 1954.

Capra, Fritjof. *The Tao of Physics*. Fontana, 1982.

Capra, Fritjof. *The Turning Point*. Wildwood House, 1983.

Carlson, R. (ed). *The Frontiers of Science and Medicine*. Wildwood House, 1975.

Cerminara, Gina. *Many Mansions*. C. W. Daniel, 1975.

Cerminara, Gina. *The World Within*. C. W. Daniel, 1973.

Cranston, Sylvia and Williams, Carey. *Reincarnation*. Julian Press, NY, 1985.

Crookall, Robert. *The Supreme Adventure*. James Clark, 1961.

Crookall, Robert. *What Happens When You Die*. Collin Smythe, 1978.

Dunne, James. *An Experiment with Time*.

Dossey, Larry, MD *Space Time and Medicine*. Routledge & Kegan Paul, 1982.

Grant, Joan and Kelsey, Denis. *Many Lifetimes*. Victor Gollancz, 1974.

Greaves, Helen. *Testimony of Light*. C. W. Daniel, 1977.

Greaves, Helen. *Wheel of Eternity*. C. W. Daniel.

Guirdham, Arthur. *The Cathars and Reincarnation*. C. W. Daniel, 1970.

Guirdham, Arthur. *We Are One Another*. C. W. Daniel, 1974.

Jackson, Rev A. W. *The Celtic Church Speaks Today*. CFPSS, 1968.

Johnson, Raynor. *The Imprisoned Splendour*. Hodder & Stoughton, 1953.

Kubler-Ross, E. *On Death and Dying*. Tavistock Publications, 1970.

Kubler-Ross, E. *Death The Final Stage of Growth*. Prentice Hall, 1975.

LeShan, Lawrence. *The Clairvoyant Reality*. Thorsons, 1980.

Lorimer, David. *Survival?* Routledge, 1984.

Lyall, Edward. *Second Time Round.* C. W. Daniel, 1974.

Moody, Raymond. *Life After Life.* Bantam, 1976.

Oesterreich, T. K. *Possession Demoniacal and Other.* Kegan Paul, 1930.

Ostrander & Schroeder. *Psychic Discoveries Behind the Iron Curtain.* (Abacus) 1970, Sphere Books, UK.

Pearce, Ian. *The Gate of Healing.* C. W. Daniel, 1983.

Pearce-Higgins, Canon J. D. (Ed). *Life, Death and Psychical Research.* Rider & Co, 1973.

Playfair, Guy L. *If This Be Magic.* Jonathan Cape, 1985.

Saltmarsh, H. F. *Foreknowledge.* G. Bell & Sons, 1938.

Sherwood, Jane. *The Country Beyond.* C. W. Daniel.

Sherwood, Jane. *Postmortem Journal.* C. W. Daniel.

Smith, Huston. *The Religious Man.* Harper & Row, 1958.

Strong, Rev Thomas. *Mystical Christianity.* Regency Press, 1978.

Weatherhead, L. D. *After Death.* Epworth Press.

Weatherhead, L. D. *Life Begins at Death.* Denholme House Press, 1977.

Weatherhead, L. D. *Psychology, Religion and Healing.* Hodder & Stoughton, 1953.